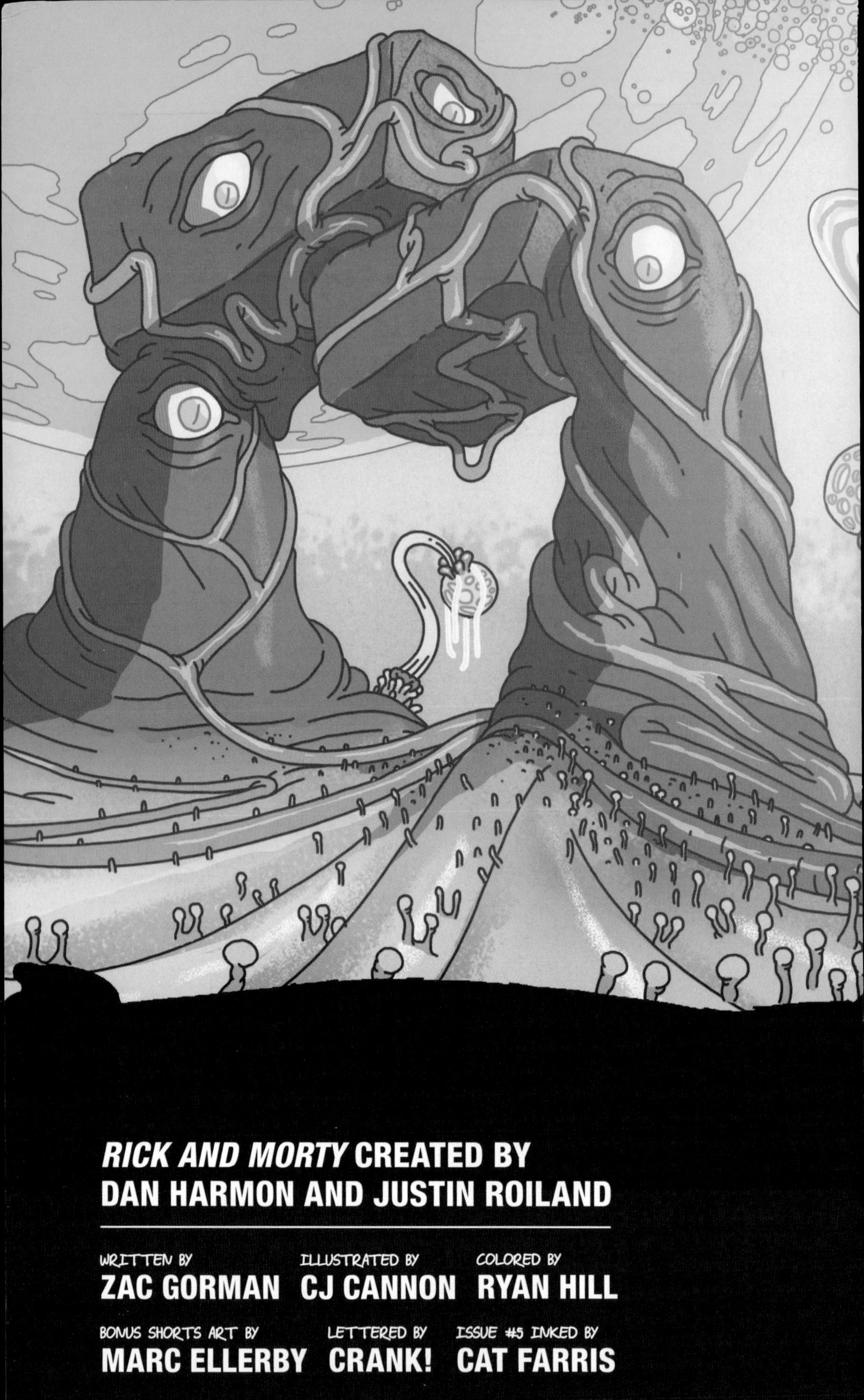

RICK AND MORTY **CREATED BY**
DAN HARMON AND JUSTIN ROILAND

WRITTEN BY
ZAC GORMAN

ILLUSTRATED BY
CJ CANNON

COLORED BY
RYAN HILL

BONUS SHORTS ART BY
MARC ELLERBY

LETTERED BY
CRANK!

ISSUE #5 INKED BY
CAT FARRIS

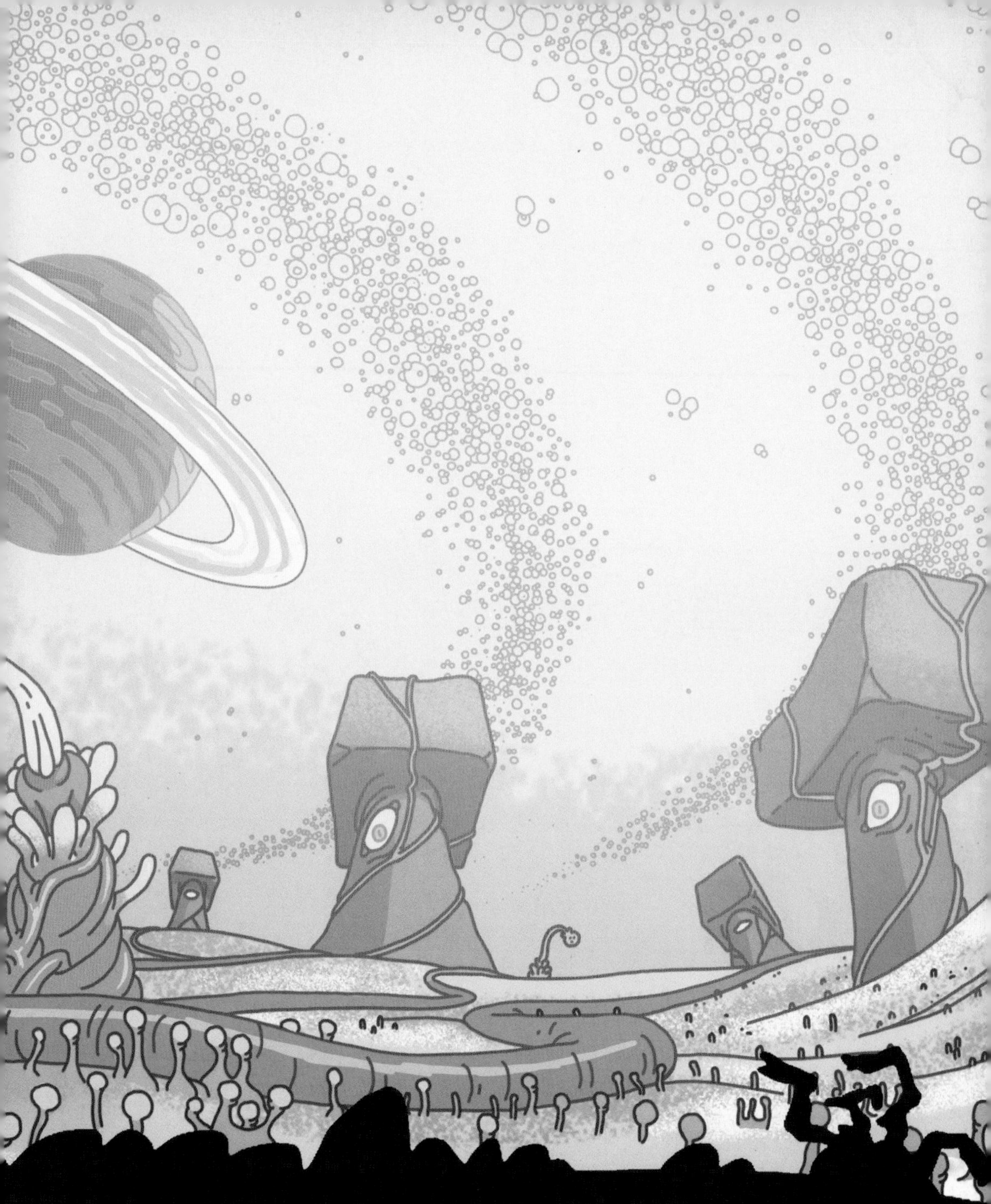

TITAN
COMICS
[adult swim]

[adult swim]

RICK AND MORTY: VOLUME ONE, AUGUST 2016. PUBLISHED BY TITAN COMICS, A DIVISION OF TITAN PUBLISHING GROUP LTD., 144 SOUTHWARK ST., LONDON, SE1 0UP. CONTAINS MATERIAL ORIGINALLY PUBLISHED IN SINGLE COMIC FORM AS RICK AND MORTY NO 1-5. © CARTOON NETWORK (S16) ALL RIGHTS RESERVED. RICK AND MORTY, CARTOON NETWORK, THE LOGOS, AND ALL RELATED CHARACTERS AND ELEMENTS ARE TRADEMARKS OF AND © CARTOON NETWORK. ALL CHARACTERS, EVENTS AND INSTITUTIONS DEPICTED HEREIN ARE FICTIONAL. ANY SIMILARITY BETWEEN ANY OF THE NAMES, CHARACTERS, PERSONS, EVENTS AND/OR INSTITUTIONS IN THIS PUBLICATION TO ACTUAL NAMES, CHARACTERS, AND PERSONS, WHETHER LIVING OR DEAD AND/OR INSTITUTIONS ARE UNINTENDED AND PURELY COINCIDENTAL.

A CIP CATALOGUE RECORD FOR THIS TITLE IS AVAILABLE FROM THE BRITISH LIBRARY.

PRINTED IN SPAIN.

10 9 8 7 6 5 4 3 2 1

ISBN: 9781785859793
WWW.TITAN-COMICS.COM

SPECIAL THANKS TO JUSTIN ROILAND, DAN HARMON, MARISA MARIONAKIS, BRANDON LIVELY, MIKE MENDEL, AND TAMARA HENDERSON.

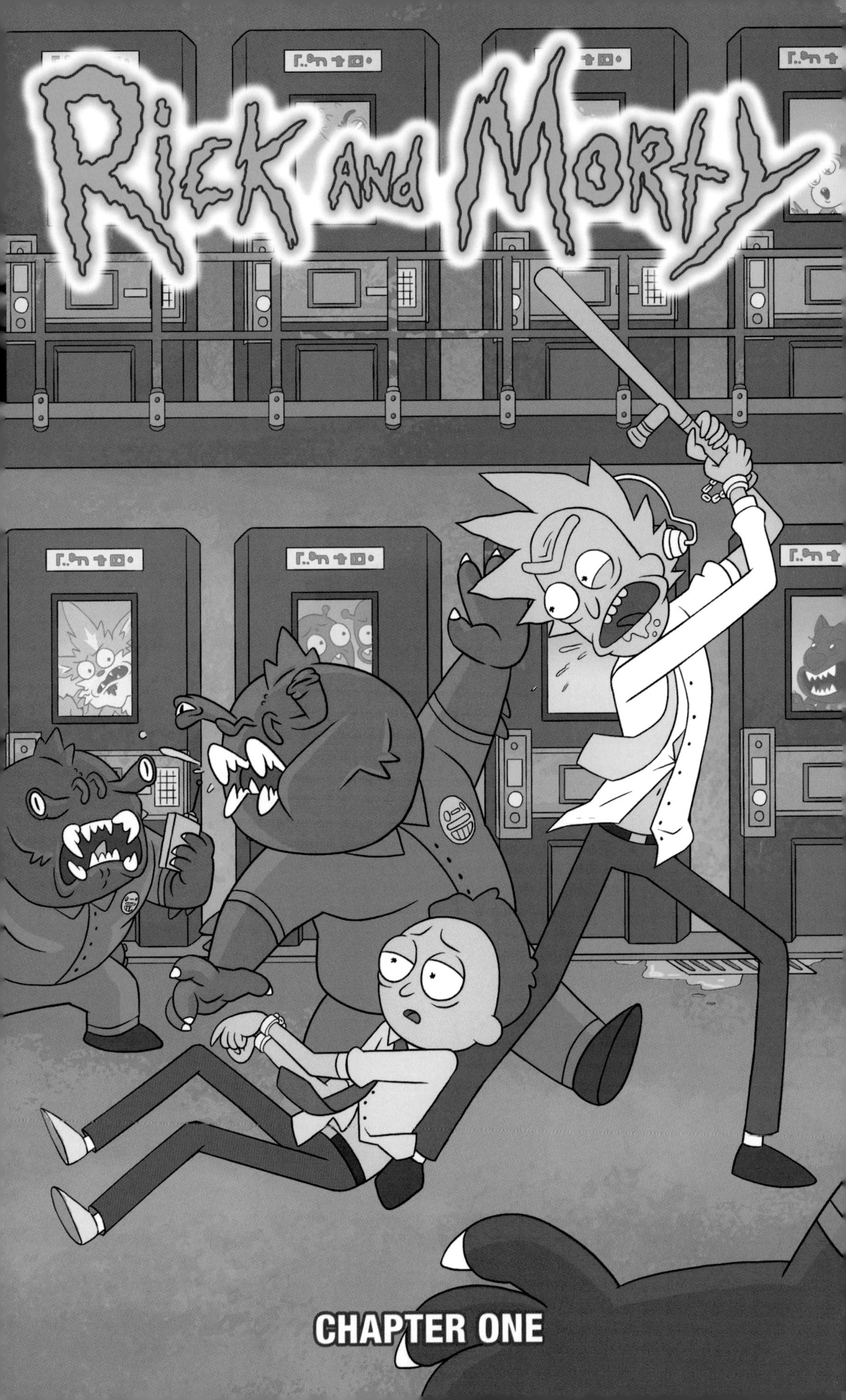
Rick and Morty
CHAPTER ONE

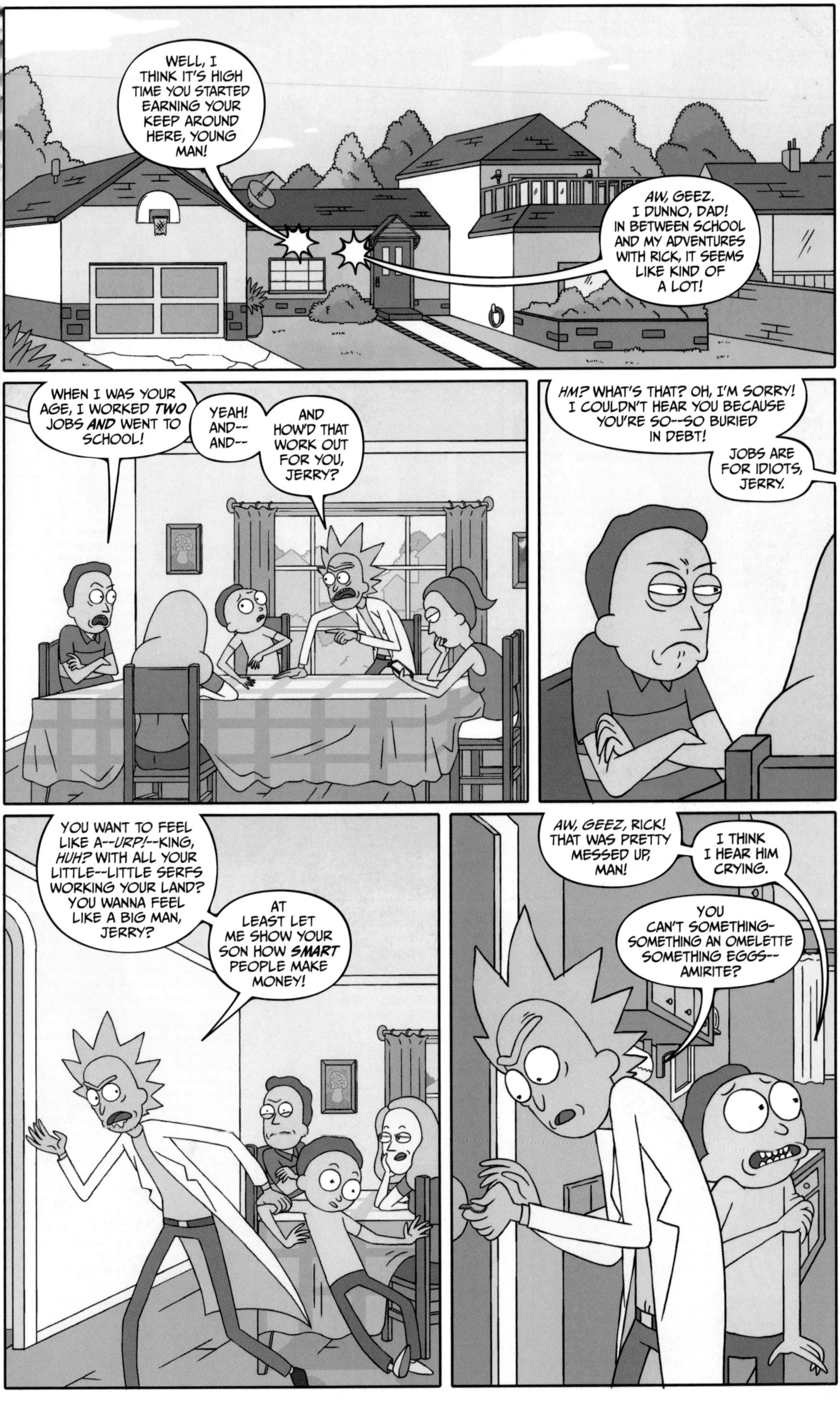
WELL, I THINK IT'S HIGH TIME YOU STARTED EARNING YOUR KEEP AROUND HERE, YOUNG MAN!
AW, GEEZ. I DUNNO, DAD! IN BETWEEN SCHOOL AND MY ADVENTURES WITH RICK, IT SEEMS LIKE KIND OF A LOT!
WHEN I WAS YOUR AGE, I WORKED TWO JOBS AND WENT TO SCHOOL!
YEAH! AND-- AND--
AND HOW'D THAT WORK OUT FOR YOU, JERRY?
HM? WHAT'S THAT? OH, I'M SORRY! I COULDN'T HEAR YOU BECAUSE YOU'RE SO--SO BURIED IN DEBT!
JOBS ARE FOR IDIOTS, JERRY.
YOU WANT TO FEEL LIKE A--URP!--KING, HUH? WITH ALL YOUR LITTLE--LITTLE SERFS WORKING YOUR LAND? YOU WANNA FEEL LIKE A BIG MAN, JERRY?
AT LEAST LET ME SHOW YOUR SON HOW SMART PEOPLE MAKE MONEY!
AW, GEEZ, RICK! THAT WAS PRETTY MESSED UP, MAN!
I THINK I HEAR HIM CRYING.
YOU CAN'T SOMETHING-SOMETHING AN OMELETTE SOMETHING EGGS--AMIRITE?

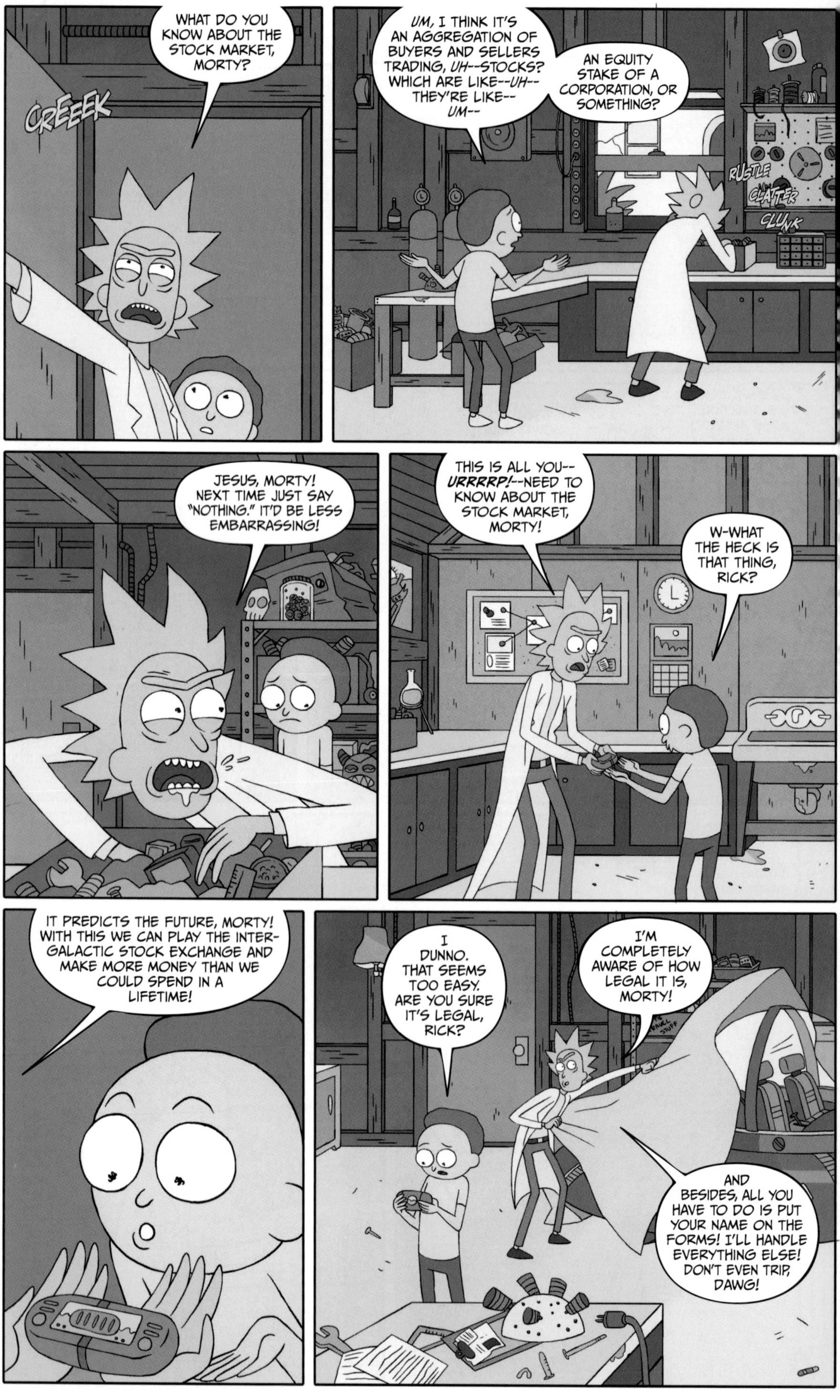
WHAT DO YOU KNOW ABOUT THE STOCK MARKET, MORTY?
CREEEK
UM, I THINK IT'S AN AGGREGATION OF BUYERS AND SELLERS TRADING, UH--STOCKS? WHICH ARE LIKE--UH-- THEY'RE LIKE-- UM--
AN EQUITY STAKE OF A CORPORATION, OR SOMETHING?
RUSTLE
CLATTER
CLUNK
JESUS, MORTY! NEXT TIME JUST SAY "NOTHING." IT'D BE LESS EMBARRASSING!
THIS IS ALL YOU-- URRRRP!--NEED TO KNOW ABOUT THE STOCK MARKET, MORTY!
W-WHAT THE HECK IS THAT THING, RICK?
IT PREDICTS THE FUTURE, MORTY! WITH THIS WE CAN PLAY THE INTER-GALACTIC STOCK EXCHANGE AND MAKE MORE MONEY THAN WE COULD SPEND IN A LIFETIME!
I DUNNO. THAT SEEMS TOO EASY. ARE YOU SURE IT'S LEGAL, RICK?
I'M COMPLETELY AWARE OF HOW LEGAL IT IS, MORTY!
AND BESIDES, ALL YOU HAVE TO DO IS PUT YOUR NAME ON THE FORMS! I'LL HANDLE EVERYTHING ELSE! DON'T EVEN TRIP, DAWG!

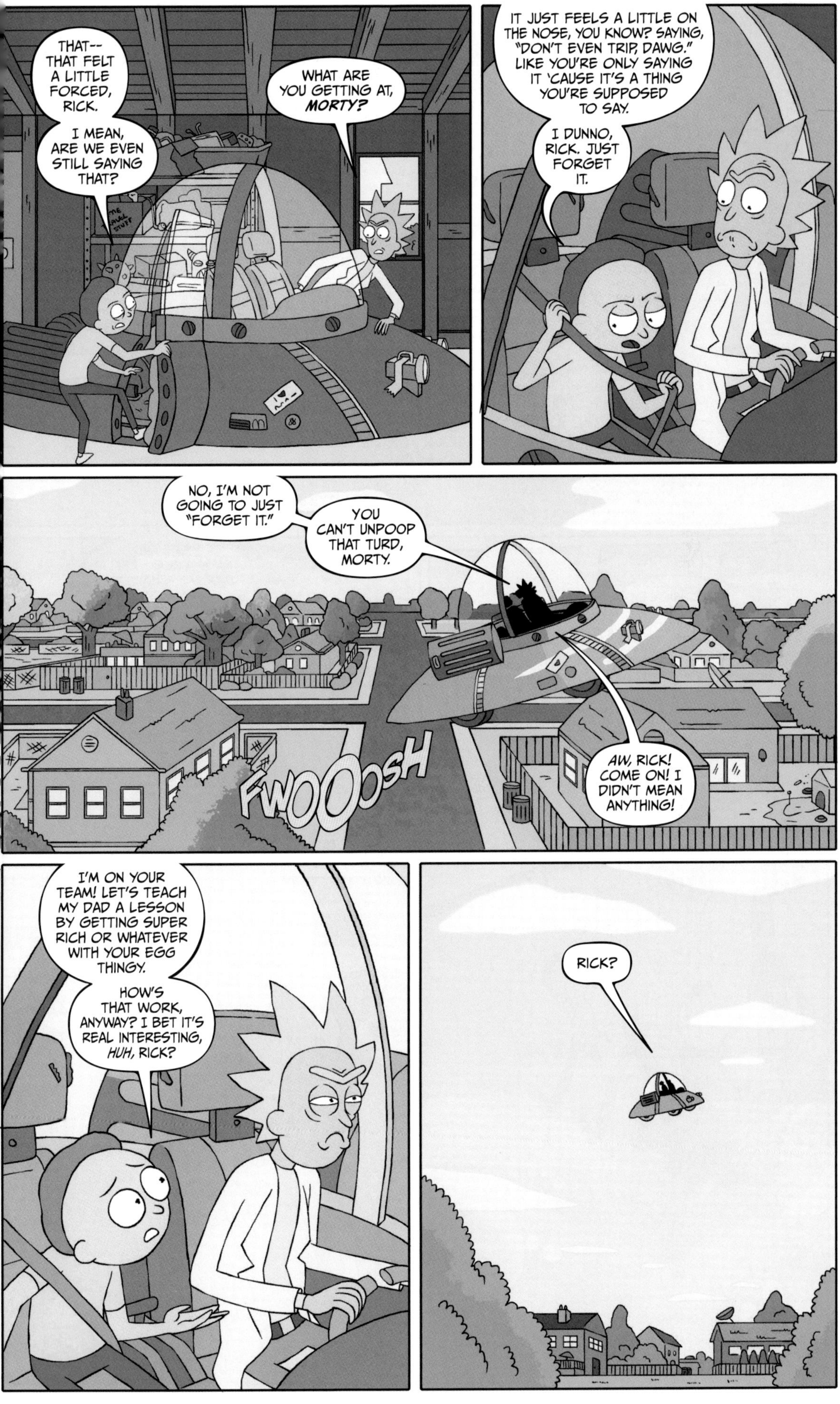
THAT-- THAT FELT A LITTLE FORCED, RICK.
I MEAN, ARE WE EVEN STILL SAYING THAT?
WHAT ARE YOU GETTING AT, *MORTY?*
IT JUST FEELS A LITTLE ON THE NOSE, YOU KNOW? SAYING, "DON'T EVEN TRIP, DAWG." LIKE YOU'RE ONLY SAYING IT 'CAUSE IT'S A THING YOU'RE SUPPOSED TO SAY.
I DUNNO, RICK. JUST FORGET IT.
NO, I'M NOT GOING TO JUST "FORGET IT."
YOU CAN'T UNPOOP THAT TURD, MORTY.
FWOOOSH
AW, RICK! COME ON! I DIDN'T MEAN ANYTHING!
I'M ON YOUR TEAM! LET'S TEACH MY DAD A LESSON BY GETTING SUPER RICH OR WHATEVER WITH YOUR EGG THINGY.
HOW'S THAT WORK, ANYWAY? I BET IT'S REAL INTERESTING, *HUH,* RICK?
RICK?

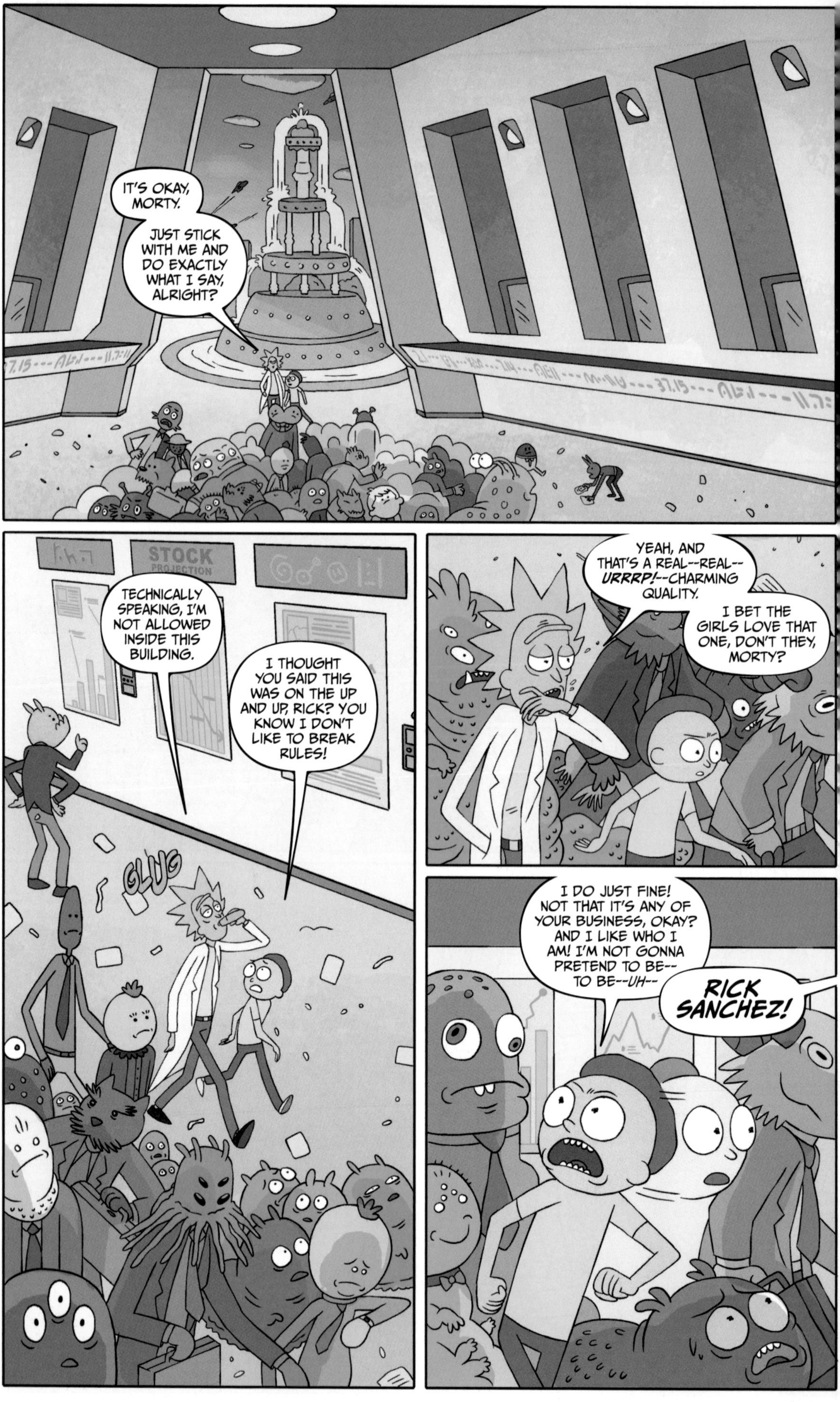
IT'S OKAY, MORTY.
JUST STICK WITH ME AND DO EXACTLY WHAT I SAY, ALRIGHT?
STOCK PROJECTION
TECHNICALLY SPEAKING, I'M NOT ALLOWED INSIDE THIS BUILDING.
I THOUGHT YOU SAID THIS WAS ON THE UP AND UP, RICK? YOU KNOW I DON'T LIKE TO BREAK RULES!
GLUG
YEAH, AND THAT'S A REAL--REAL--URRRP!--CHARMING QUALITY.
I BET THE GIRLS LOVE THAT ONE, DON'T THEY, MORTY?
I DO JUST FINE! NOT THAT IT'S ANY OF YOUR BUSINESS, OKAY? AND I LIKE WHO I AM! I'M NOT GONNA PRETEND TO BE--TO BE--UH--
RICK SANCHEZ!

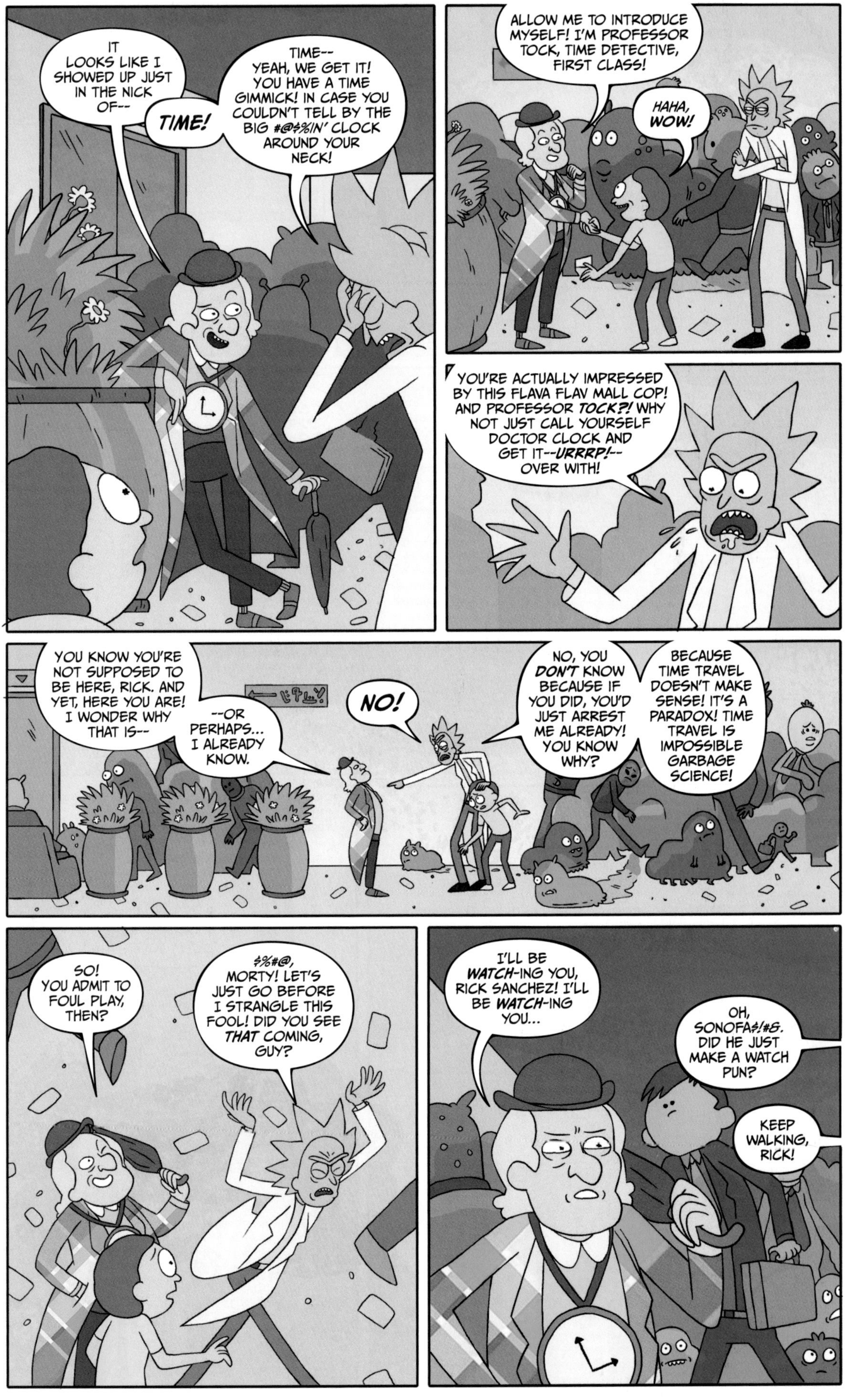

IT LOOKS LIKE I SHOWED UP JUST IN THE NICK OF--
TIME!
TIME-- YEAH, WE GET IT! YOU HAVE A TIME GIMMICK! IN CASE YOU COULDN'T TELL BY THE BIG #@$%IN' CLOCK AROUND YOUR NECK!
ALLOW ME TO INTRODUCE MYSELF! I'M PROFESSOR TOCK, TIME DETECTIVE, FIRST CLASS!
HAHA, WOW!
YOU'RE ACTUALLY IMPRESSED BY THIS FLAVA FLAV MALL COP! AND PROFESSOR TOCK?! WHY NOT JUST CALL YOURSELF DOCTOR CLOCK AND GET IT--URRRP!--OVER WITH!
YOU KNOW YOU'RE NOT SUPPOSED TO BE HERE, RICK. AND YET, HERE YOU ARE! I WONDER WHY THAT IS--
--OR PERHAPS... I ALREADY KNOW.
NO!
NO, YOU DON'T KNOW BECAUSE IF YOU DID, YOU'D JUST ARREST ME ALREADY! YOU KNOW WHY?
BECAUSE TIME TRAVEL DOESN'T MAKE SENSE! IT'S A PARADOX! TIME TRAVEL IS IMPOSSIBLE GARBAGE SCIENCE!
SO! YOU ADMIT TO FOUL PLAY, THEN?
$%#@, MORTY! LET'S JUST GO BEFORE I STRANGLE THIS FOOL! DID YOU SEE THAT COMING, GUY?
I'LL BE WATCH-ING YOU, RICK SANCHEZ! I'LL BE WATCH-ING YOU...
OH, SONOFA$!#G. DID HE JUST MAKE A WATCH PUN?
KEEP WALKING, RICK!

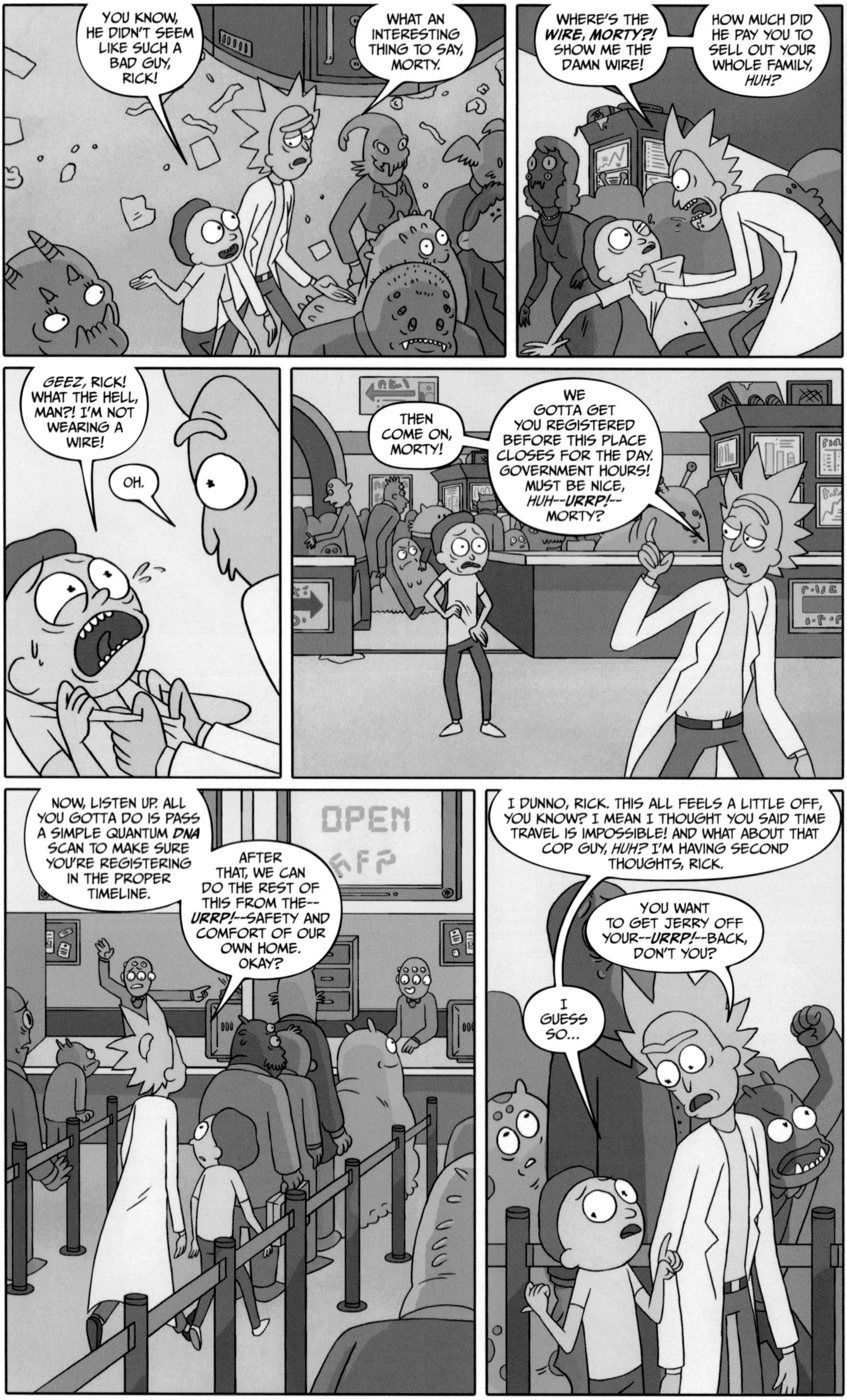
YOU KNOW, HE DIDN'T SEEM LIKE SUCH A BAD GUY, RICK!
WHAT AN INTERESTING THING TO SAY, MORTY.
WHERE'S THE *WIRE, MORTY?!* SHOW ME THE DAMN WIRE!
HOW MUCH DID HE PAY YOU TO SELL OUT YOUR WHOLE FAMILY, *HUH?*
GEEZ, RICK! WHAT THE HELL, MAN?! I'M NOT WEARING A WIRE!
OH.
THEN COME ON, MORTY!
WE GOTTA GET YOU REGISTERED BEFORE THIS PLACE CLOSES FOR THE DAY. GOVERNMENT HOURS! MUST BE NICE, *HUH--URRP!--* MORTY?
NOW, LISTEN UP. ALL YOU GOTTA DO IS PASS A SIMPLE QUANTUM *DNA* SCAN TO MAKE SURE YOU'RE REGISTERING IN THE PROPER TIMELINE.
AFTER THAT, WE CAN DO THE REST OF THIS FROM THE-- *URRP!*--SAFETY AND COMFORT OF OUR OWN HOME. OKAY?
OPEN
I DUNNO, RICK. THIS ALL FEELS A LITTLE OFF, YOU KNOW? I MEAN I THOUGHT YOU SAID TIME TRAVEL IS IMPOSSIBLE! AND WHAT ABOUT THAT COP GUY, *HUH?* I'M HAVING SECOND THOUGHTS, RICK.
YOU WANT TO GET JERRY OFF YOUR--*URRP!*--BACK, DON'T YOU?
I GUESS SO...

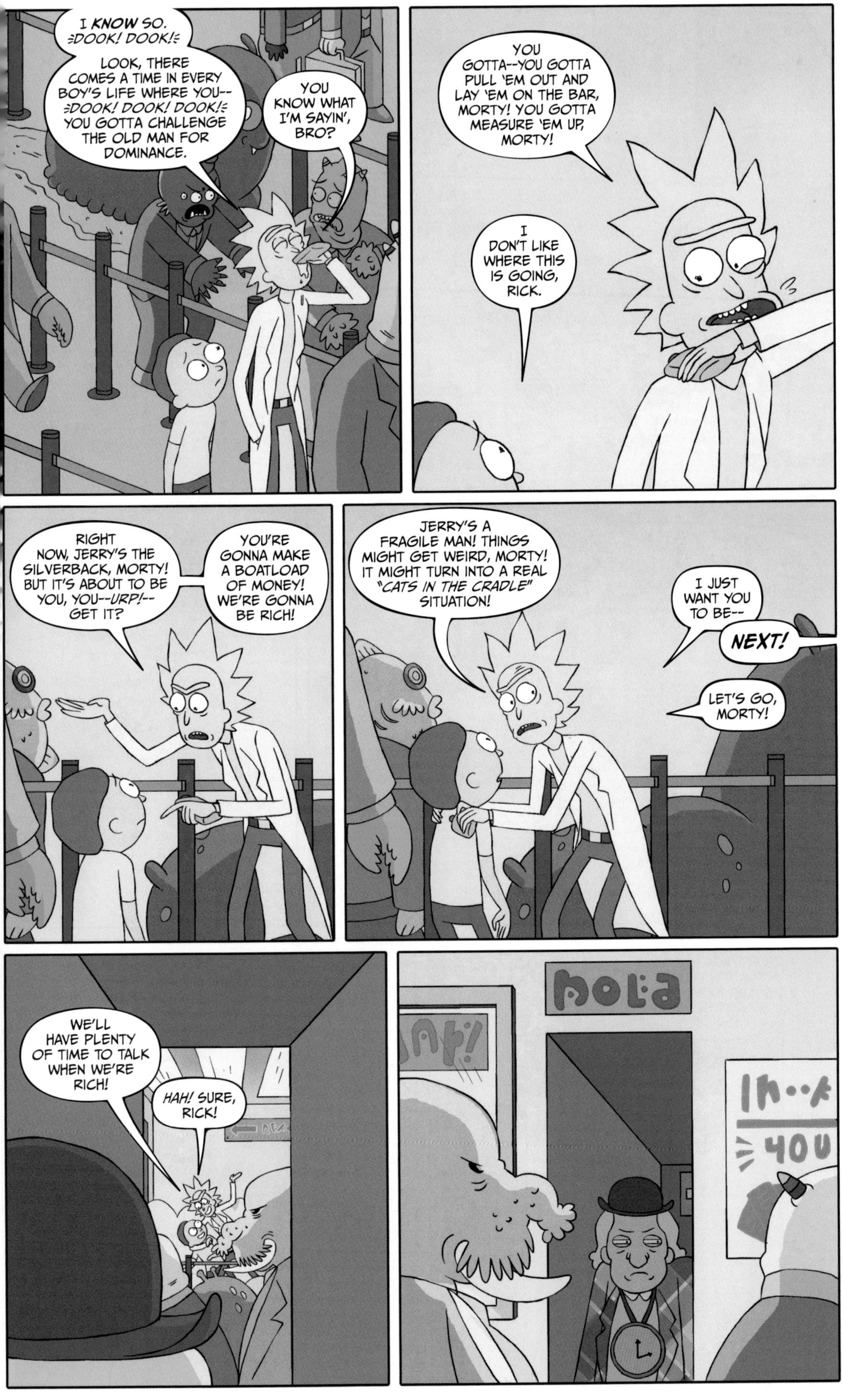
I KNOW SO. ≡DOOK! DOOK!≡
LOOK, THERE COMES A TIME IN EVERY BOY'S LIFE WHERE YOU-- ≡DOOK! DOOK! DOOK!≡ YOU GOTTA CHALLENGE THE OLD MAN FOR DOMINANCE.
YOU KNOW WHAT I'M SAYIN', BRO?
YOU GOTTA--YOU GOTTA PULL 'EM OUT AND LAY 'EM ON THE BAR, MORTY! YOU GOTTA MEASURE 'EM UP, MORTY!
I DON'T LIKE WHERE THIS IS GOING, RICK.
RIGHT NOW, JERRY'S THE SILVERBACK, MORTY! BUT IT'S ABOUT TO BE YOU, YOU--URP!-- GET IT?
YOU'RE GONNA MAKE A BOATLOAD OF MONEY! WE'RE GONNA BE RICH!
JERRY'S A FRAGILE MAN! THINGS MIGHT GET WEIRD, MORTY! IT MIGHT TURN INTO A REAL "CATS IN THE CRADLE" SITUATION!
I JUST WANT YOU TO BE--
NEXT!
LET'S GO, MORTY!
WE'LL HAVE PLENTY OF TIME TO TALK WHEN WE'RE RICH!
HAH! SURE, RICK!

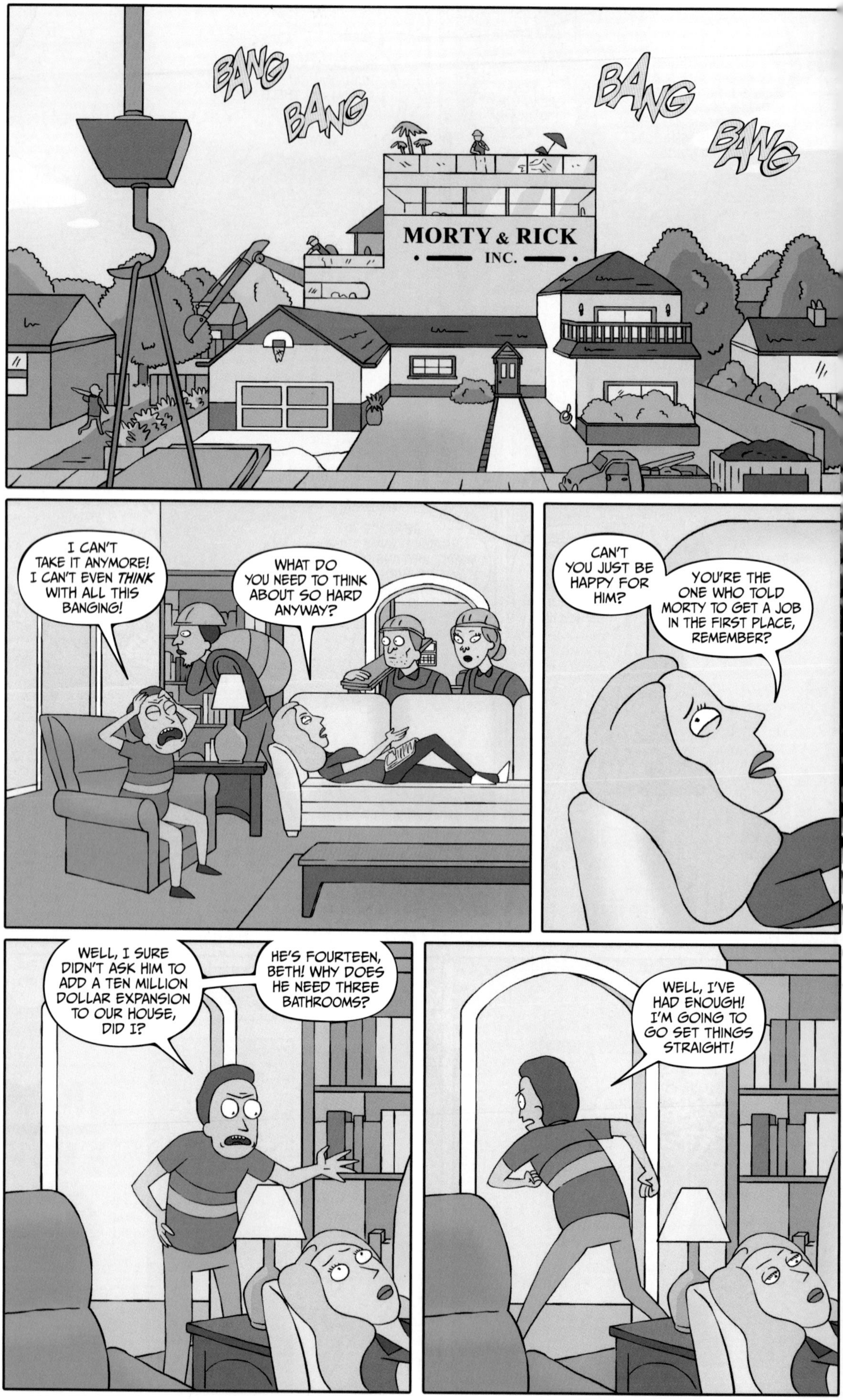
BANG
BANG
BANG
BANG
MORTY & RICK INC.
I CAN'T TAKE IT ANYMORE! I CAN'T EVEN *THINK* WITH ALL THIS BANGING!
WHAT DO YOU NEED TO THINK ABOUT SO HARD ANYWAY?
CAN'T YOU JUST BE HAPPY FOR HIM?
YOU'RE THE ONE WHO TOLD MORTY TO GET A JOB IN THE FIRST PLACE, REMEMBER?
WELL, I SURE DIDN'T ASK HIM TO ADD A TEN MILLION DOLLAR EXPANSION TO OUR HOUSE, DID I?
HE'S FOURTEEN, BETH! WHY DOES HE NEED THREE BATHROOMS?
WELL, I'VE HAD ENOUGH! I'M GOING TO GO SET THINGS STRAIGHT!

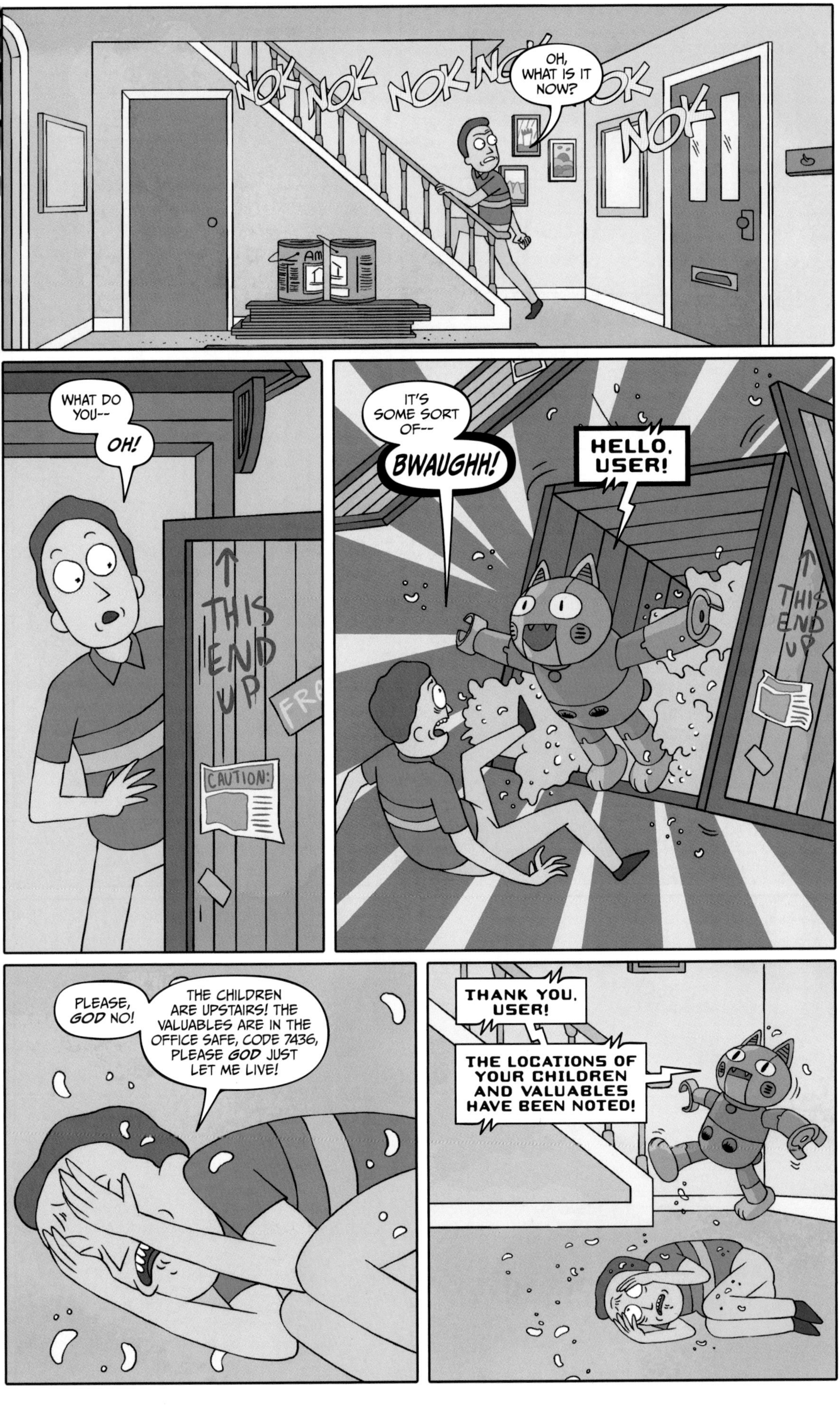
NOK NOK NOK NOK NOK NOK NOK
OH, WHAT IS IT NOW?
WHAT DO YOU-- OH!
THIS END UP
CAUTION:
IT'S SOME SORT OF-- BWAUGHH!
HELLO, USER!
THIS END UP
PLEASE, GOD NO!
THE CHILDREN ARE UPSTAIRS! THE VALUABLES ARE IN THE OFFICE SAFE, CODE 7436, PLEASE GOD JUST LET ME LIVE!
THANK YOU, USER!
THE LOCATIONS OF YOUR CHILDREN AND VALUABLES HAVE BEEN NOTED!

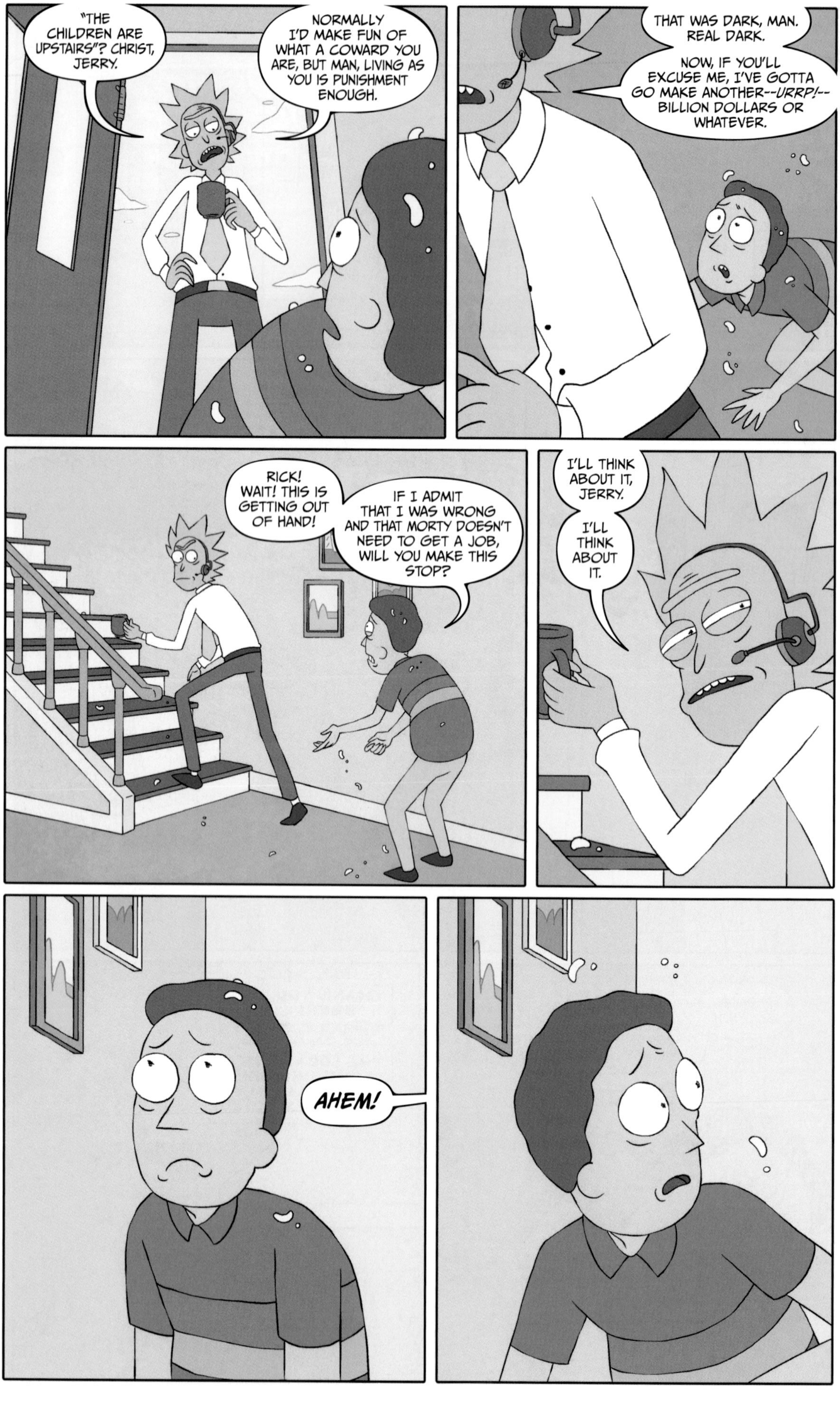
"THE CHILDREN ARE UPSTAIRS"? CHRIST, JERRY.
NORMALLY I'D MAKE FUN OF WHAT A COWARD YOU ARE, BUT MAN, LIVING AS YOU IS PUNISHMENT ENOUGH.
THAT WAS DARK, MAN. REAL DARK.
NOW, IF YOU'LL EXCUSE ME, I'VE GOTTA GO MAKE ANOTHER--*URRP!*--BILLION DOLLARS OR WHATEVER.
RICK! WAIT! THIS IS GETTING OUT OF HAND!
IF I ADMIT THAT I WAS WRONG AND THAT MORTY DOESN'T NEED TO GET A JOB, WILL YOU MAKE THIS STOP?
I'LL THINK ABOUT IT, JERRY.
I'LL THINK ABOUT IT.
AHEM!

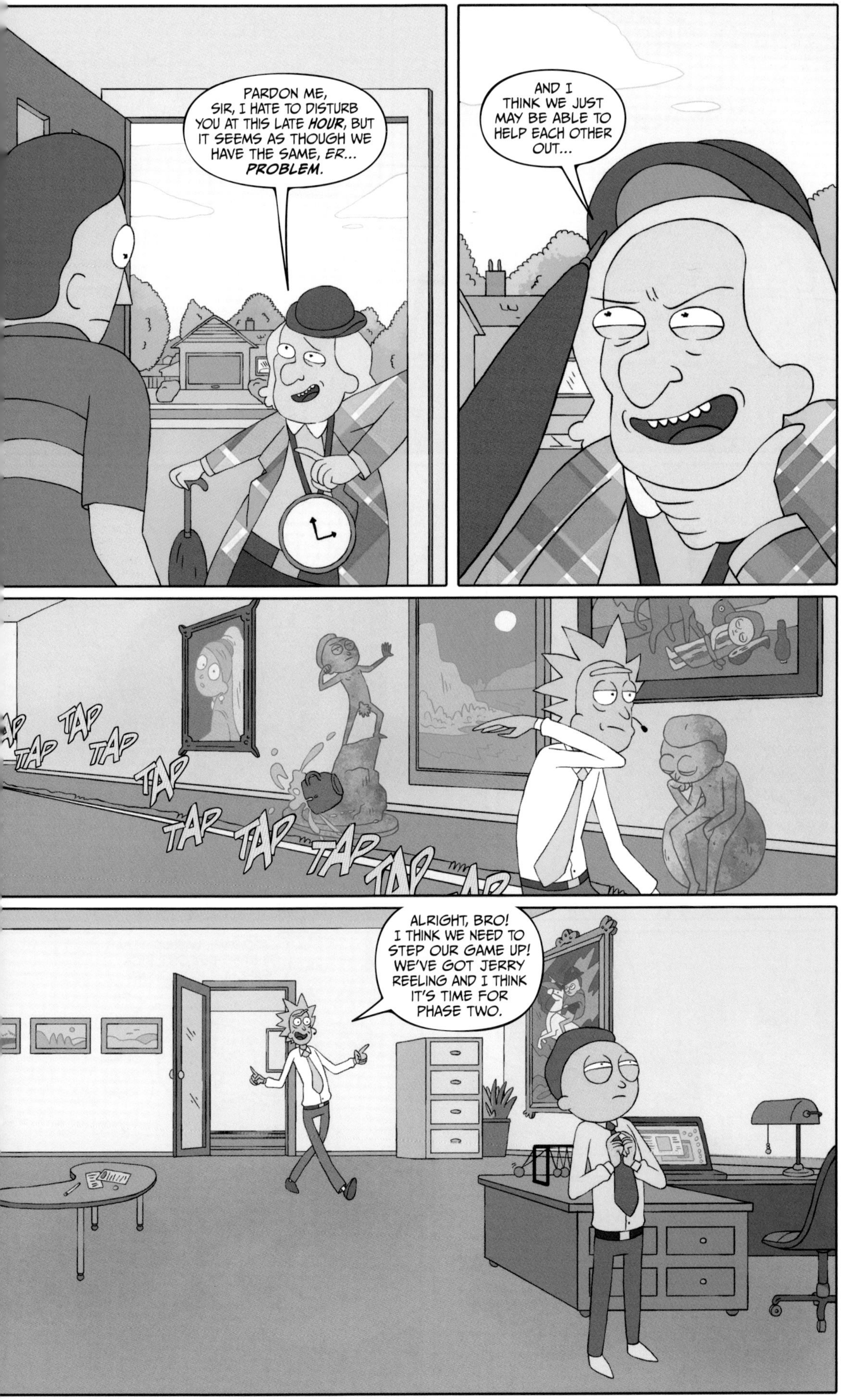
PARDON ME, SIR, I HATE TO DISTURB YOU AT THIS LATE *HOUR*, BUT IT SEEMS AS THOUGH WE HAVE THE SAME, *ER...* ***PROBLEM.***
AND I THINK WE JUST MAY BE ABLE TO HELP EACH OTHER OUT...
TAP TAP TAP TAP TAP TAP TAP TAP TAP
ALRIGHT, BRO! I THINK WE NEED TO STEP OUR GAME UP! WE'VE GOT JERRY REELING AND I THINK IT'S TIME FOR PHASE TWO.

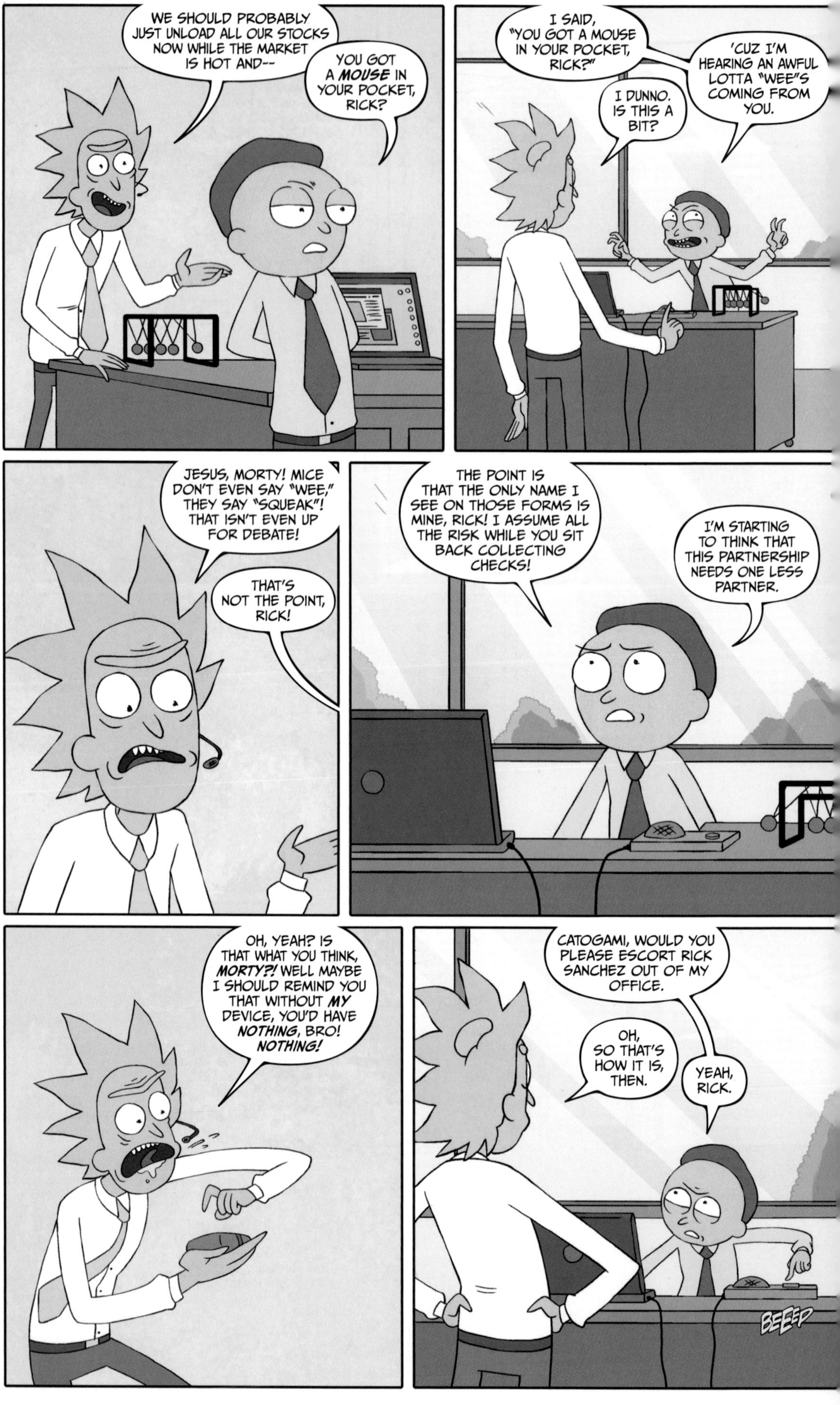
WE SHOULD PROBABLY JUST UNLOAD ALL OUR STOCKS NOW WHILE THE MARKET IS HOT AND--
YOU GOT A *MOUSE* IN YOUR POCKET, RICK?
I SAID, "YOU GOT A MOUSE IN YOUR POCKET, RICK?"
'CUZ I'M HEARING AN AWFUL LOTTA "WEE"S COMING FROM YOU.
I DUNNO. IS THIS A BIT?
JESUS, MORTY! MICE DON'T EVEN SAY "WEE," THEY SAY "SQUEAK"! THAT ISN'T EVEN UP FOR DEBATE!
THAT'S NOT THE POINT, RICK!
THE POINT IS THAT THE ONLY NAME I SEE ON THOSE FORMS IS MINE, RICK! I ASSUME ALL THE RISK WHILE YOU SIT BACK COLLECTING CHECKS!
I'M STARTING TO THINK THAT THIS PARTNERSHIP NEEDS ONE LESS PARTNER.
OH, YEAH? IS THAT WHAT YOU THINK, *MORTY?!* WELL MAYBE I SHOULD REMIND YOU THAT WITHOUT *MY* DEVICE, YOU'D HAVE *NOTHING*, BRO! *NOTHING!*
CATOGAMI, WOULD YOU PLEASE ESCORT RICK SANCHEZ OUT OF MY OFFICE.
OH, SO THAT'S HOW IT IS, THEN.
YEAH, RICK.
BEEEP

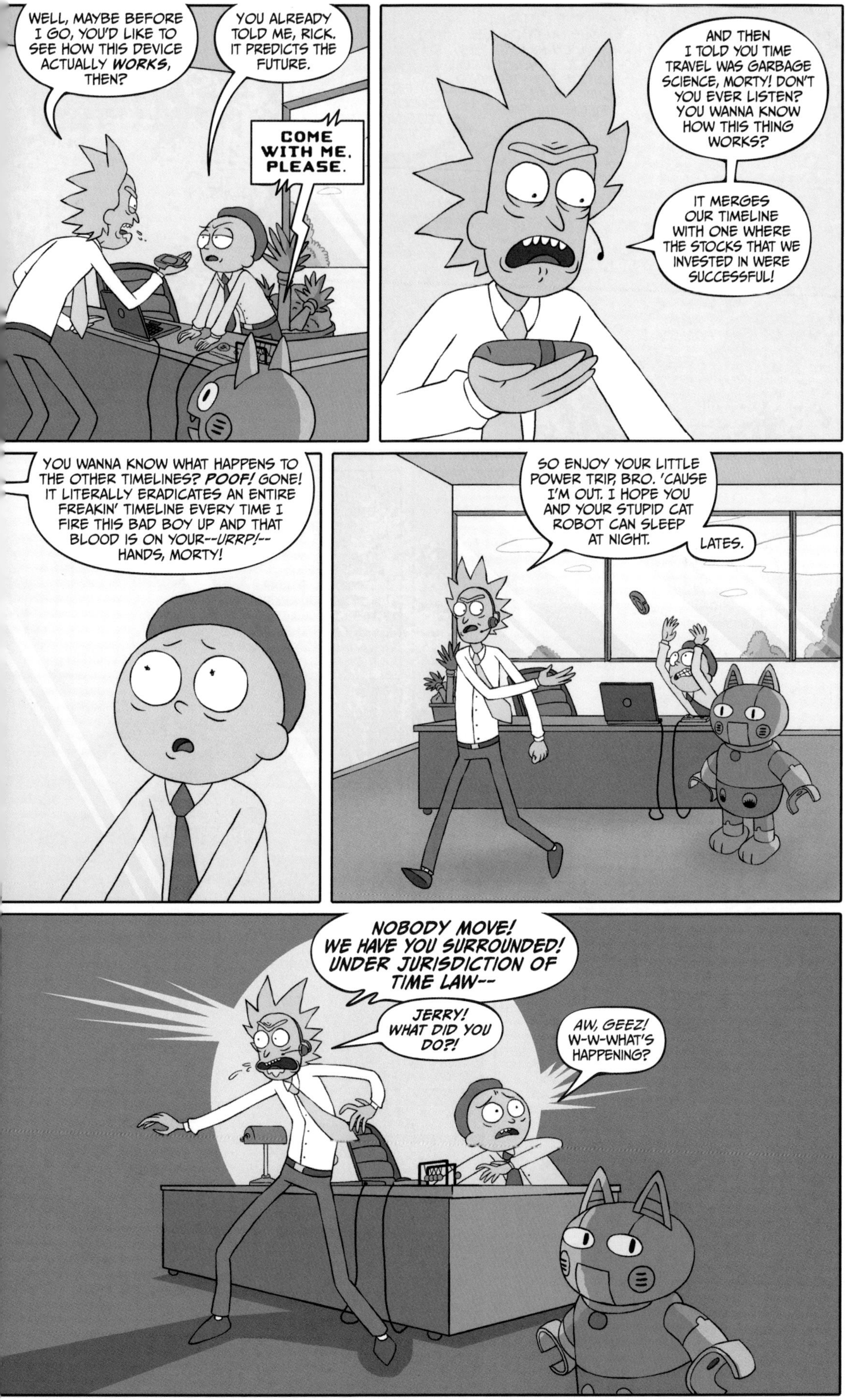
WELL, MAYBE BEFORE I GO, YOU'D LIKE TO SEE HOW THIS DEVICE ACTUALLY WORKS, THEN?
YOU ALREADY TOLD ME, RICK. IT PREDICTS THE FUTURE.
COME WITH ME. PLEASE.
AND THEN I TOLD YOU TIME TRAVEL WAS GARBAGE SCIENCE, MORTY! DON'T YOU EVER LISTEN? YOU WANNA KNOW HOW THIS THING WORKS?
IT MERGES OUR TIMELINE WITH ONE WHERE THE STOCKS THAT WE INVESTED IN WERE SUCCESSFUL!
YOU WANNA KNOW WHAT HAPPENS TO THE OTHER TIMELINES? POOF! GONE! IT LITERALLY ERADICATES AN ENTIRE FREAKIN' TIMELINE EVERY TIME I FIRE THIS BAD BOY UP AND THAT BLOOD IS ON YOUR--URRP!-- HANDS, MORTY!
SO ENJOY YOUR LITTLE POWER TRIP, BRO. 'CAUSE I'M OUT. I HOPE YOU AND YOUR STUPID CAT ROBOT CAN SLEEP AT NIGHT.
LATES.
NOBODY MOVE! WE HAVE YOU SURROUNDED! UNDER JURISDICTION OF TIME LAW--
JERRY! WHAT DID YOU DO?!
AW, GEEZ! W-W-WHAT'S HAPPENING?

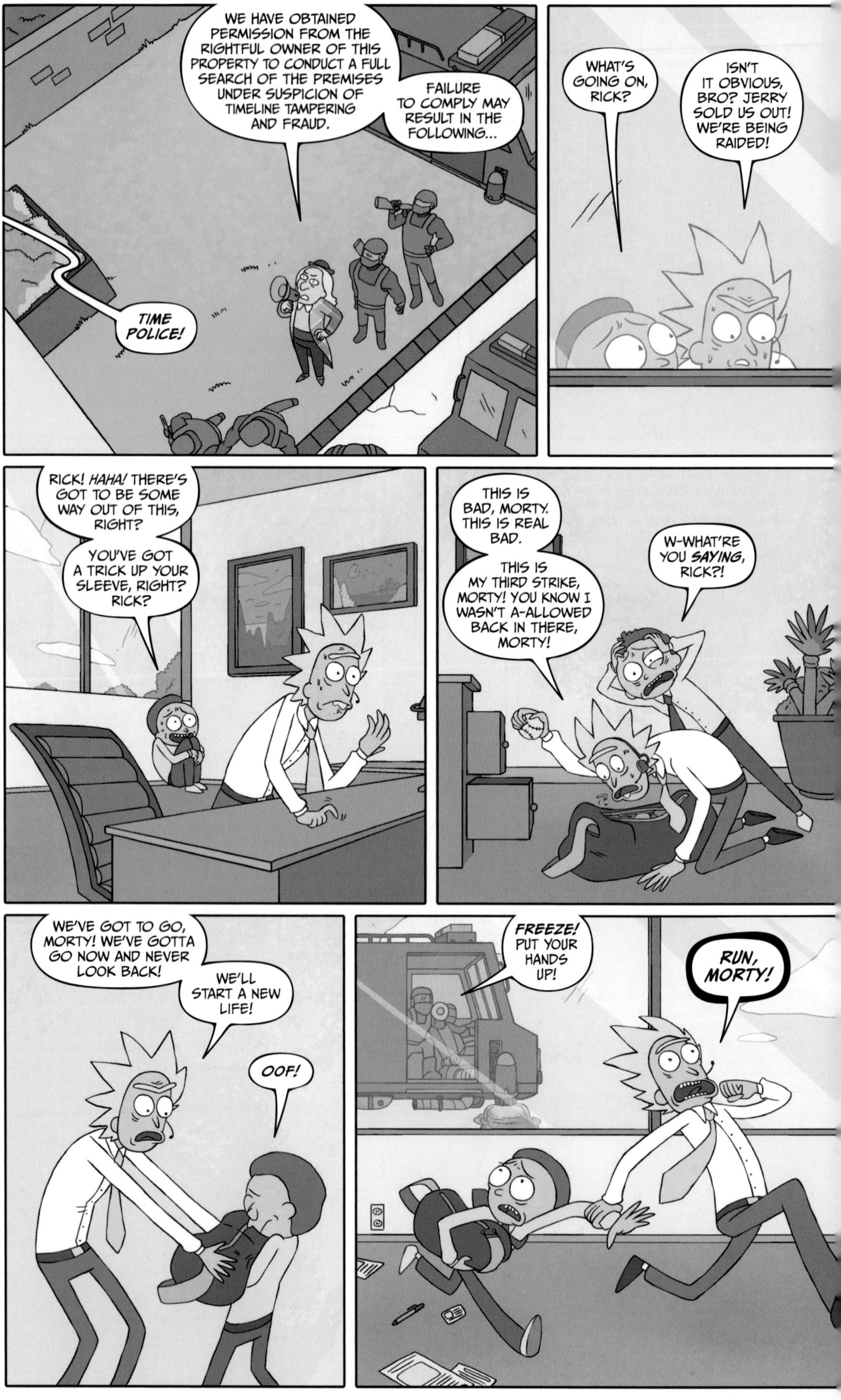
WE HAVE OBTAINED PERMISSION FROM THE RIGHTFUL OWNER OF THIS PROPERTY TO CONDUCT A FULL SEARCH OF THE PREMISES UNDER SUSPICION OF TIMELINE TAMPERING AND FRAUD.
FAILURE TO COMPLY MAY RESULT IN THE FOLLOWING...
TIME POLICE!
WHAT'S GOING ON, RICK?
ISN'T IT OBVIOUS, BRO? JERRY SOLD US OUT! WE'RE BEING RAIDED!
RICK! HAHA! THERE'S GOT TO BE SOME WAY OUT OF THIS, RIGHT?
YOU'VE GOT A TRICK UP YOUR SLEEVE, RIGHT? RICK?
THIS IS BAD, MORTY. THIS IS REAL BAD.
THIS IS MY THIRD STRIKE, MORTY! YOU KNOW I WASN'T A-ALLOWED BACK IN THERE, MORTY!
W-WHAT'RE YOU SAYING, RICK?!
WE'VE GOT TO GO, MORTY! WE'VE GOTTA GO NOW AND NEVER LOOK BACK!
WE'LL START A NEW LIFE!
OOF!
FREEZE! PUT YOUR HANDS UP!
RUN, MORTY!

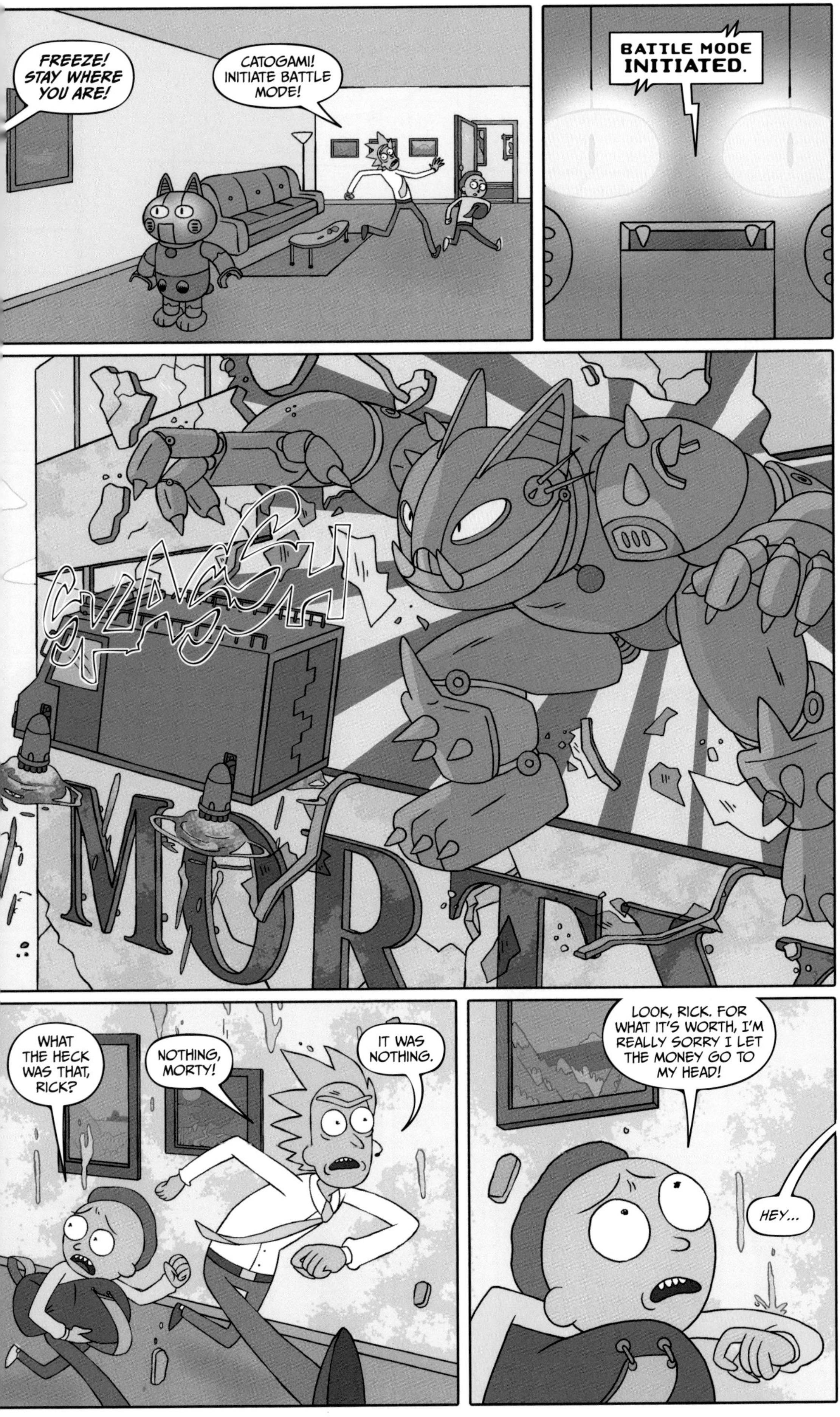

FREEZE! STAY WHERE YOU ARE!
CATOGAMI! INITIATE BATTLE MODE!
BATTLE MODE INITIATED.
SMASH
MORT
WHAT THE HECK WAS THAT, RICK?
NOTHING, MORTY!
IT WAS NOTHING.
LOOK, RICK. FOR WHAT IT'S WORTH, I'M REALLY SORRY I LET THE MONEY GO TO MY HEAD!
HEY...

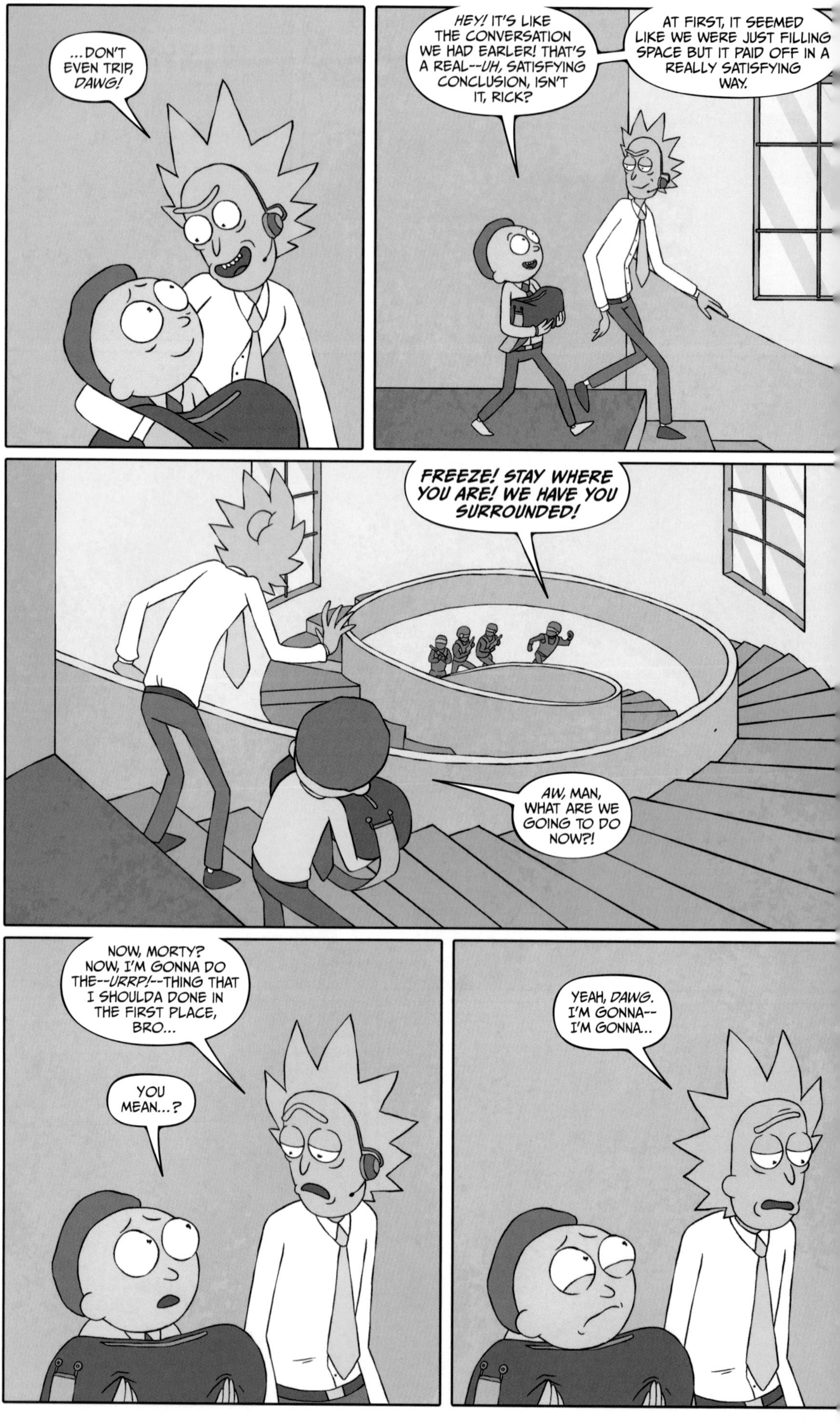
...DON'T EVEN TRIP, *DAWG!*
HEY! IT'S LIKE THE CONVERSATION WE HAD EARLER! THAT'S A REAL--*UH,* SATISFYING CONCLUSION, ISN'T IT, RICK?
AT FIRST, IT SEEMED LIKE WE WERE JUST FILLING SPACE BUT IT PAID OFF IN A REALLY SATISFYING WAY.
FREEZE! STAY WHERE YOU ARE! WE HAVE YOU SURROUNDED!
AW, MAN, WHAT ARE WE GOING TO DO NOW?!
NOW, MORTY? NOW, I'M GONNA DO THE--*URRP!*--THING THAT I SHOULDA DONE IN THE FIRST PLACE, BRO...
YOU MEAN...?
YEAH, *DAWG.* I'M GONNA-- I'M GONNA..

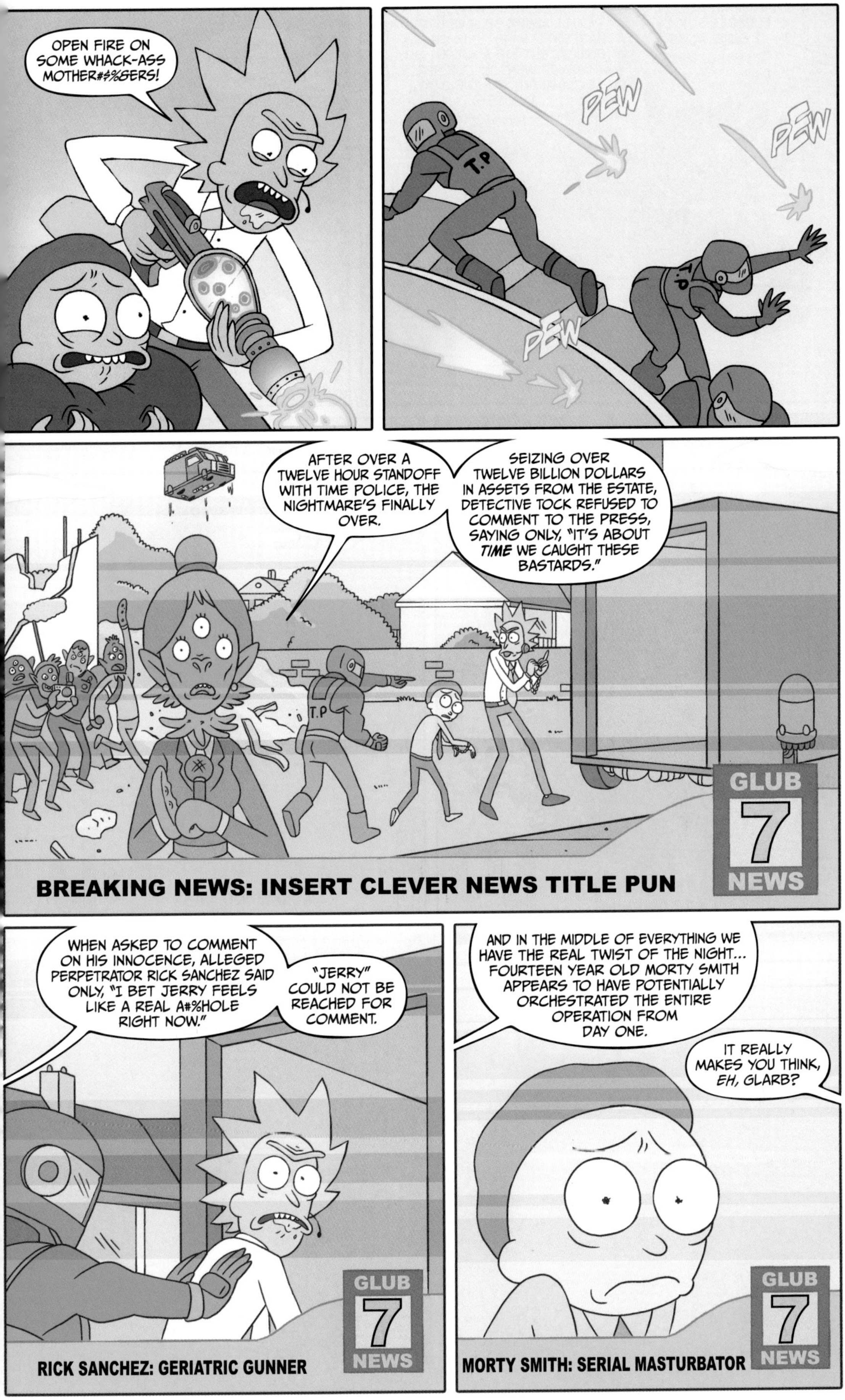
OPEN FIRE ON SOME WHACK-ASS MOTHER#$%GERS!
PEW
PEW
PEW
AFTER OVER A TWELVE HOUR STANDOFF WITH TIME POLICE, THE NIGHTMARE'S FINALLY OVER.
SEIZING OVER TWELVE BILLION DOLLARS IN ASSETS FROM THE ESTATE, DETECTIVE TOCK REFUSED TO COMMENT TO THE PRESS, SAYING ONLY, "IT'S ABOUT *TIME* WE CAUGHT THESE BASTARDS."
T.P
GLUB 7 NEWS
BREAKING NEWS: INSERT CLEVER NEWS TITLE PUN
WHEN ASKED TO COMMENT ON HIS INNOCENCE, ALLEGED PERPETRATOR RICK SANCHEZ SAID ONLY, "I BET JERRY FEELS LIKE A REAL A#%HOLE RIGHT NOW."
"JERRY" COULD NOT BE REACHED FOR COMMENT.
GLUB 7 NEWS
RICK SANCHEZ: GERIATRIC GUNNER
AND IN THE MIDDLE OF EVERYTHING WE HAVE THE REAL TWIST OF THE NIGHT... FOURTEEN YEAR OLD MORTY SMITH APPEARS TO HAVE POTENTIALLY ORCHESTRATED THE ENTIRE OPERATION FROM DAY ONE.
IT REALLY MAKES YOU THINK, *EH*, GLARB?
GLUB 7 NEWS
MORTY SMITH: SERIAL MASTURBATOR

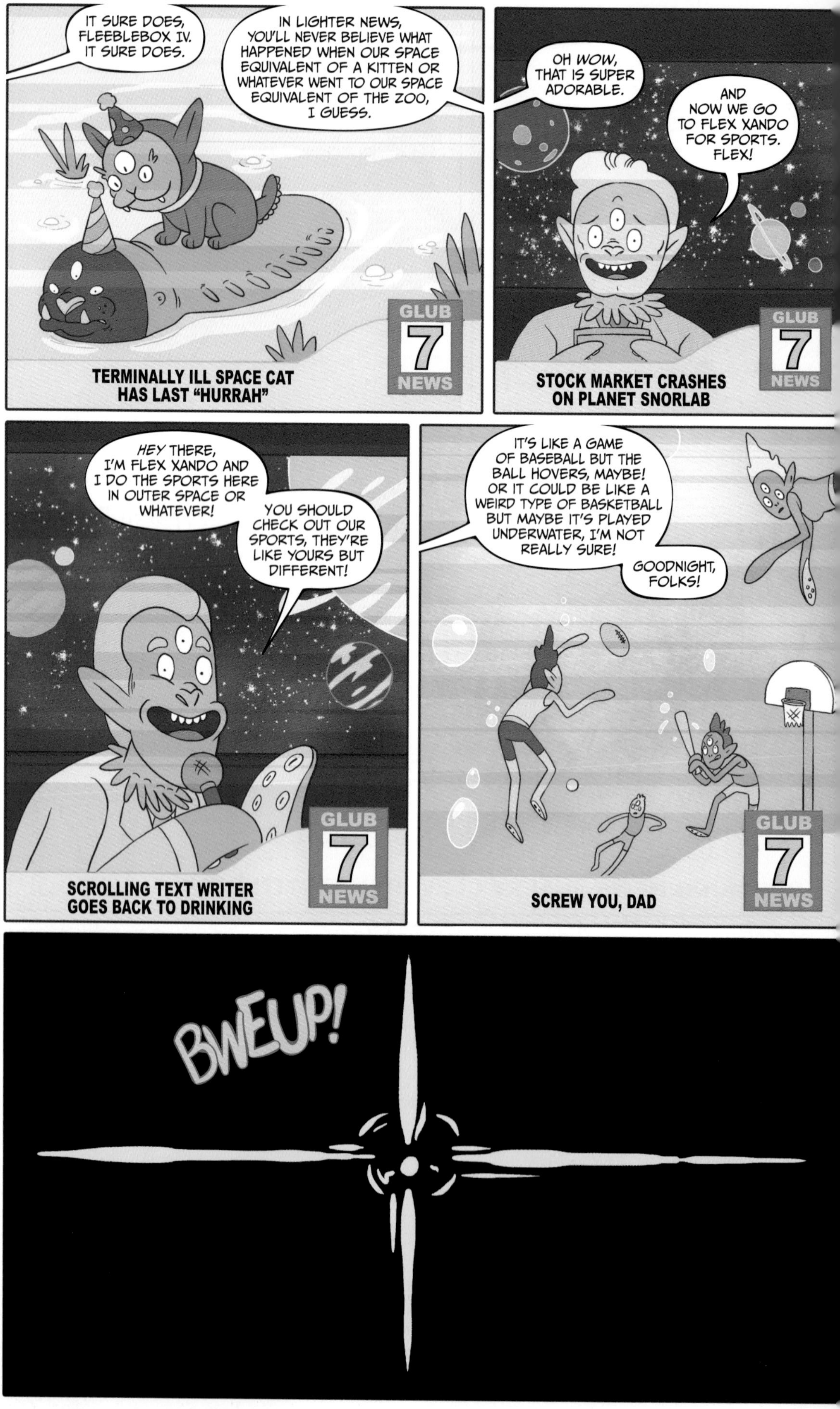
IT SURE DOES, FLEEBLEBOX IV. IT SURE DOES.
IN LIGHTER NEWS, YOU'LL NEVER BELIEVE WHAT HAPPENED WHEN OUR SPACE EQUIVALENT OF A KITTEN OR WHATEVER WENT TO OUR SPACE EQUIVALENT OF THE ZOO, I GUESS.
TERMINALLY ILL SPACE CAT HAS LAST "HURRAH"
GLUB 7 NEWS
OH WOW, THAT IS SUPER ADORABLE.
AND NOW WE GO TO FLEX XANDO FOR SPORTS. FLEX!
STOCK MARKET CRASHES ON PLANET SNORLAB
GLUB 7 NEWS
HEY THERE, I'M FLEX XANDO AND I DO THE SPORTS HERE IN OUTER SPACE OR WHATEVER!
YOU SHOULD CHECK OUT OUR SPORTS, THEY'RE LIKE YOURS BUT DIFFERENT!
SCROLLING TEXT WRITER GOES BACK TO DRINKING
GLUB 7 NEWS
IT'S LIKE A GAME OF BASEBALL BUT THE BALL HOVERS, MAYBE! OR IT COULD BE LIKE A WEIRD TYPE OF BASKETBALL BUT MAYBE IT'S PLAYED UNDERWATER, I'M NOT REALLY SURE!
GOODNIGHT, FOLKS!
SCREW YOU, DAD
GLUB 7 NEWS
BWEUP!

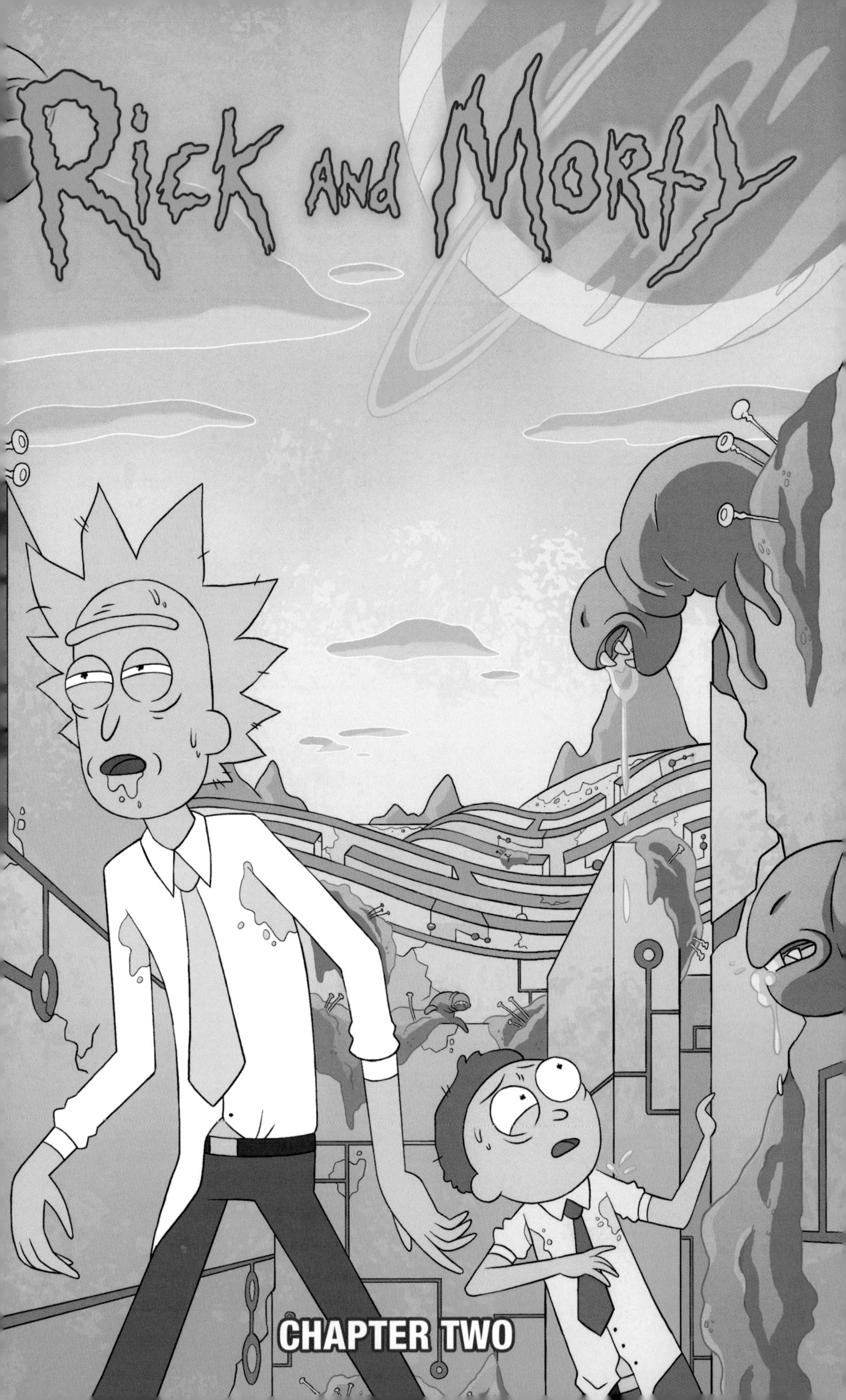
Rick and Morty
CHAPTER TWO

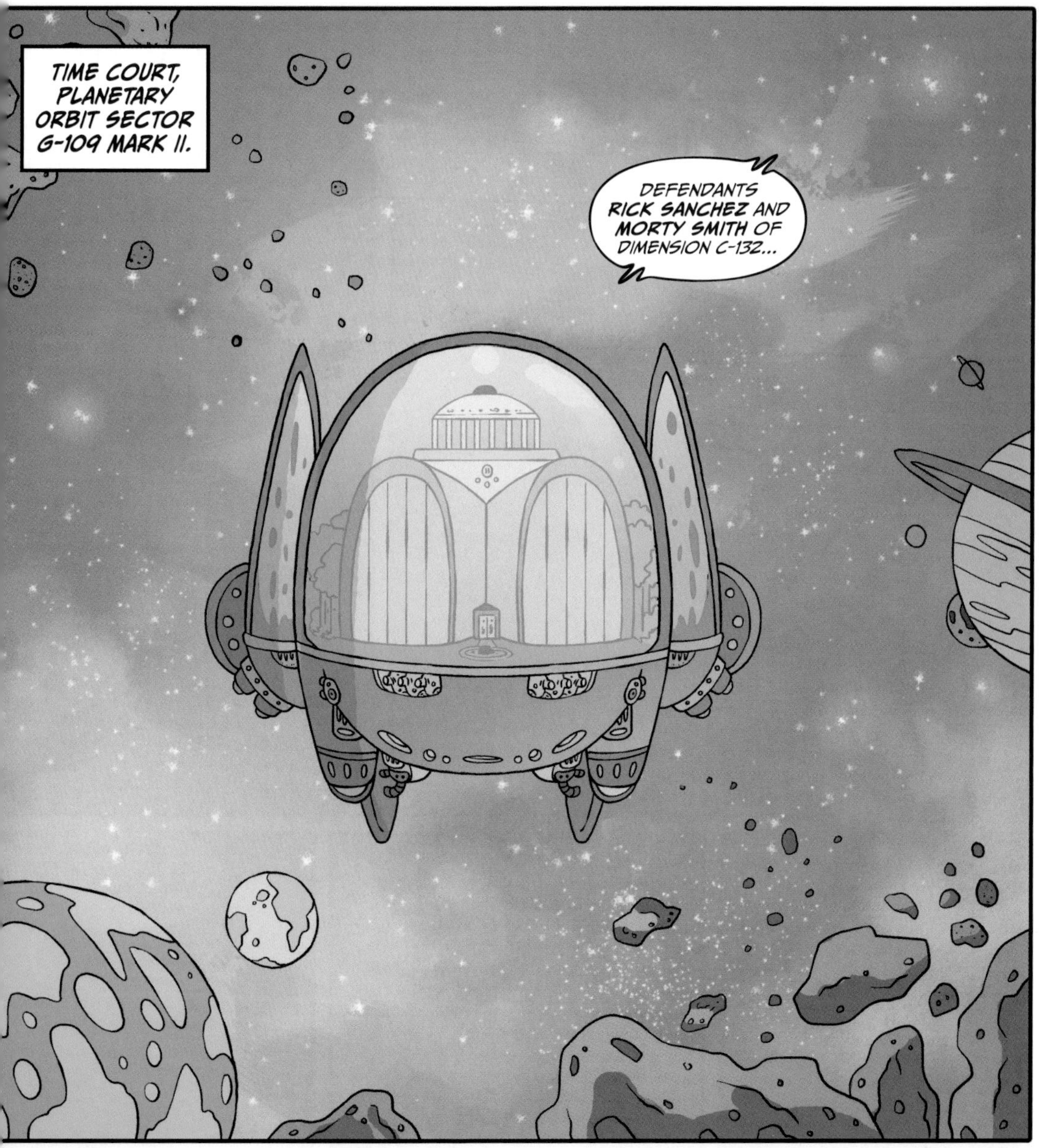
TIME COURT, PLANETARY ORBIT SECTOR G-109 MARK II.
DEFENDANTS RICK SANCHEZ AND MORTY SMITH OF DIMENSION C-132...

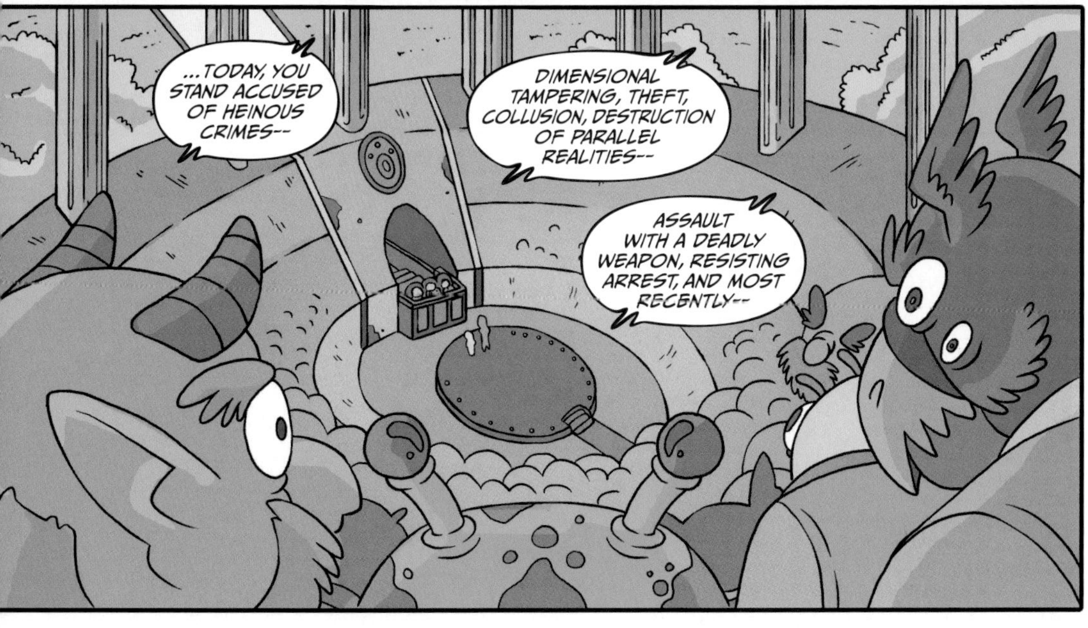
...TODAY, YOU STAND ACCUSED OF HEINOUS CRIMES--
DIMENSIONAL TAMPERING, THEFT, COLLUSION, DESTRUCTION OF PARALLEL REALITIES--
ASSAULT WITH A DEADLY WEAPON, RESISTING ARREST, AND MOST RECENTLY--

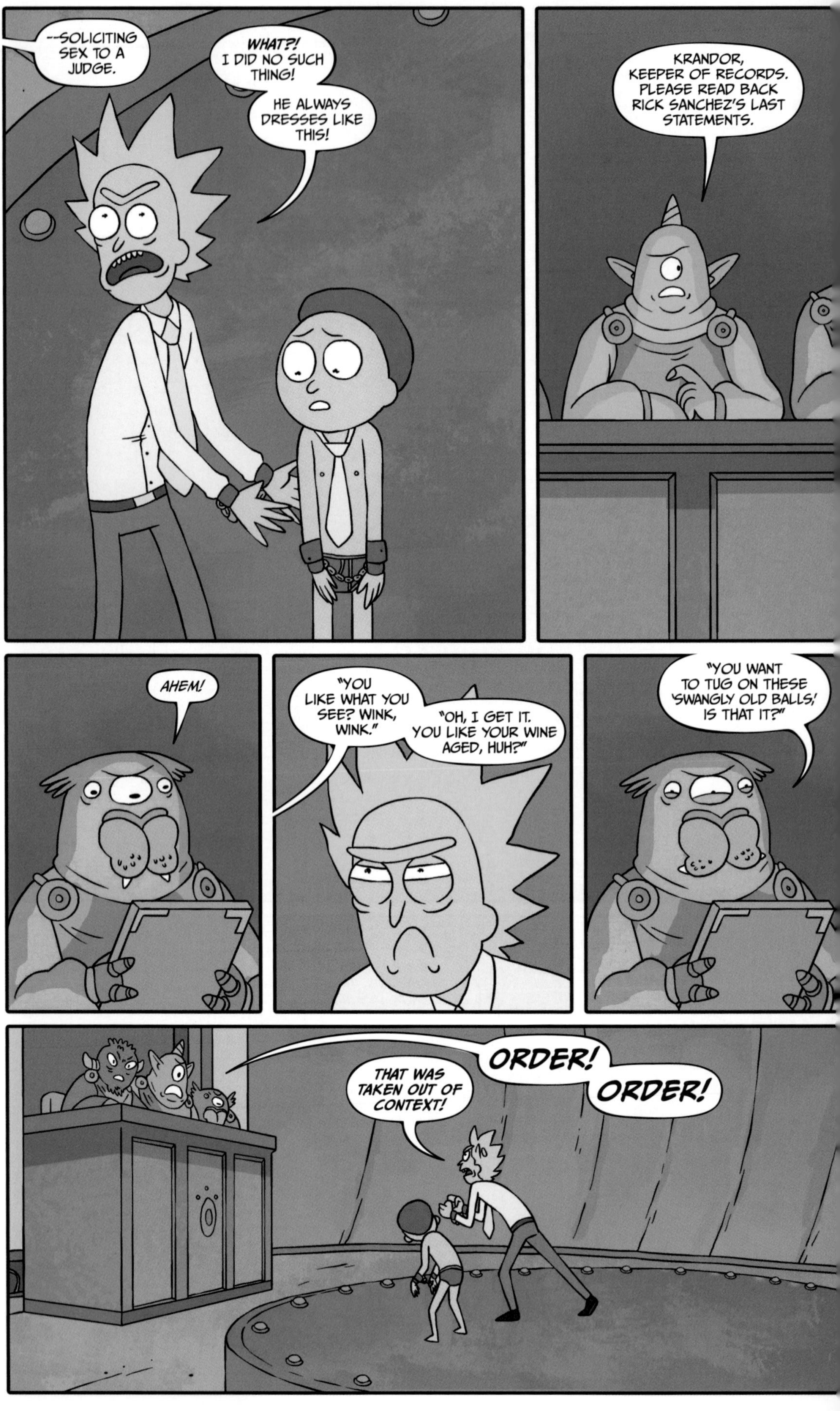
--SOLICITING SEX TO A JUDGE.
WHAT?! I DID NO SUCH THING!
HE ALWAYS DRESSES LIKE THIS!
KRANDOR, KEEPER OF RECORDS. PLEASE READ BACK RICK SANCHEZ'S LAST STATEMENTS.
AHEM!
"YOU LIKE WHAT YOU SEE? WINK, WINK."
"OH, I GET IT. YOU LIKE YOUR WINE AGED, HUH?"
"YOU WANT TO TUG ON THESE 'SWANGLY OLD BALLS,' IS THAT IT?"
ORDER!
ORDER!
THAT WAS TAKEN OUT OF CONTEXT!

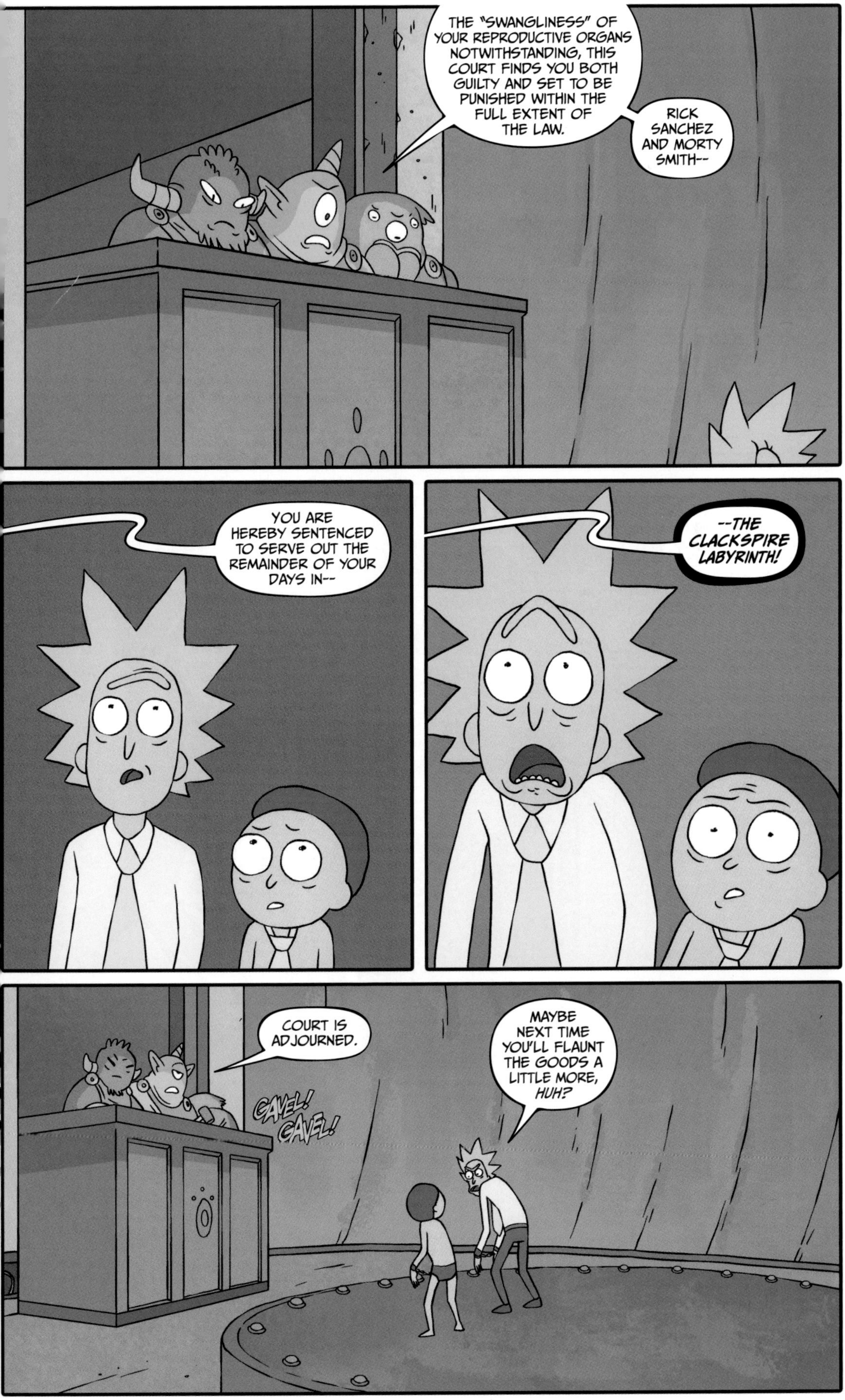
THE "SWANGLINESS" OF YOUR REPRODUCTIVE ORGANS NOTWITHSTANDING, THIS COURT FINDS YOU BOTH GUILTY AND SET TO BE PUNISHED WITHIN THE FULL EXTENT OF THE LAW.
RICK SANCHEZ AND MORTY SMITH--
YOU ARE HEREBY SENTENCED TO SERVE OUT THE REMAINDER OF YOUR DAYS IN--
--THE CLACKSPIRE LABYRINTH!
COURT IS ADJOURNED.
GAVEL! GAVEL!
MAYBE NEXT TIME YOU'LL FLAUNT THE GOODS A LITTLE MORE, HUH?

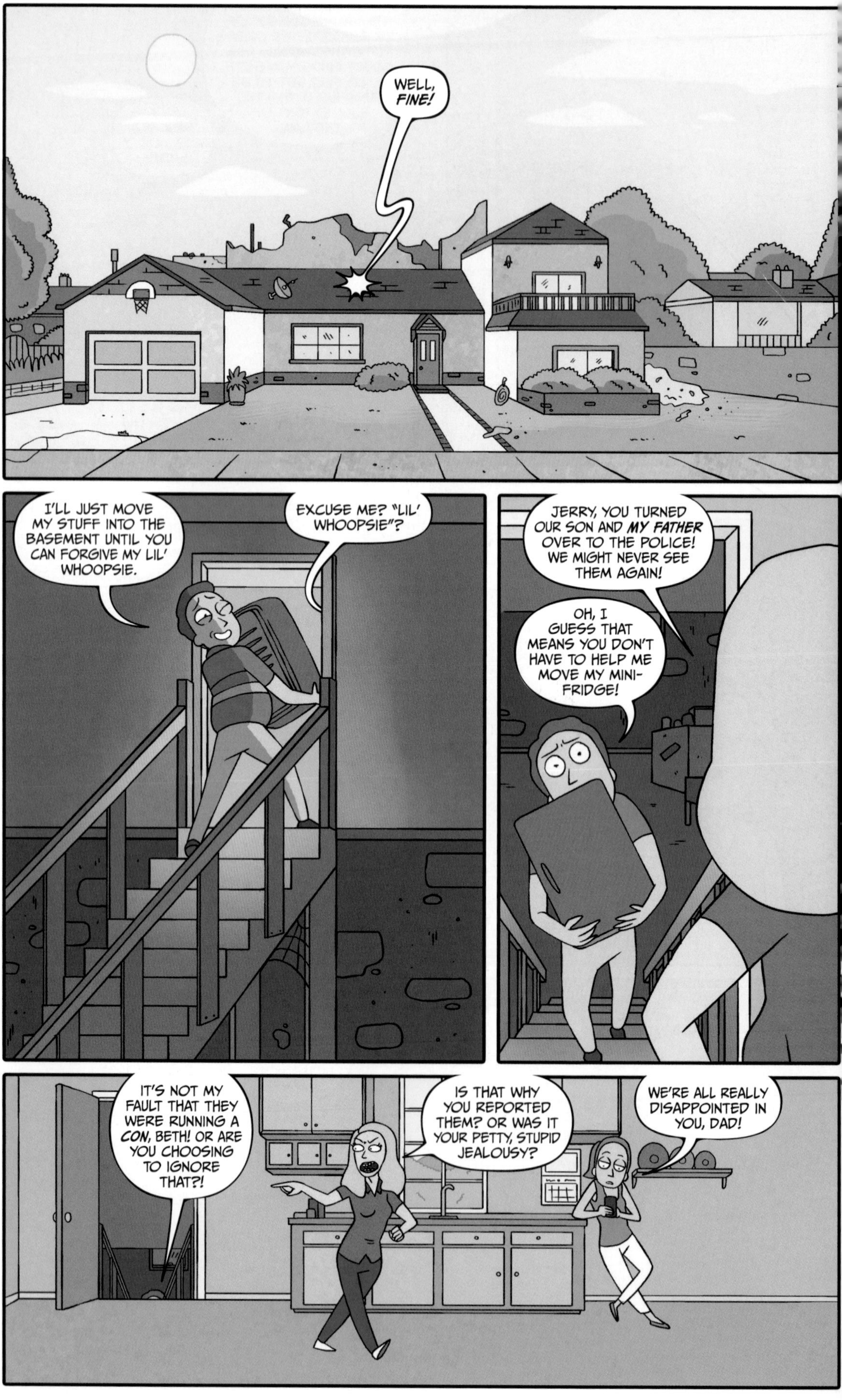
WELL, *FINE!*
I'LL JUST MOVE MY STUFF INTO THE BASEMENT UNTIL YOU CAN FORGIVE MY LIL' WHOOPSIE.
EXCUSE ME? "LIL' WHOOPSIE"?
JERRY, YOU TURNED OUR SON AND *MY FATHER* OVER TO THE POLICE! WE MIGHT NEVER SEE THEM AGAIN!
OH, I GUESS THAT MEANS YOU DON'T HAVE TO HELP ME MOVE MY MINI-FRIDGE!
IT'S NOT MY FAULT THAT THEY WERE RUNNING A *CON*, BETH! OR ARE YOU CHOOSING TO IGNORE THAT?!
IS THAT WHY YOU REPORTED THEM? OR WAS IT YOUR PETTY, STUPID JEALOUSY?
WE'RE ALL REALLY DISAPPOINTED IN YOU, DAD!

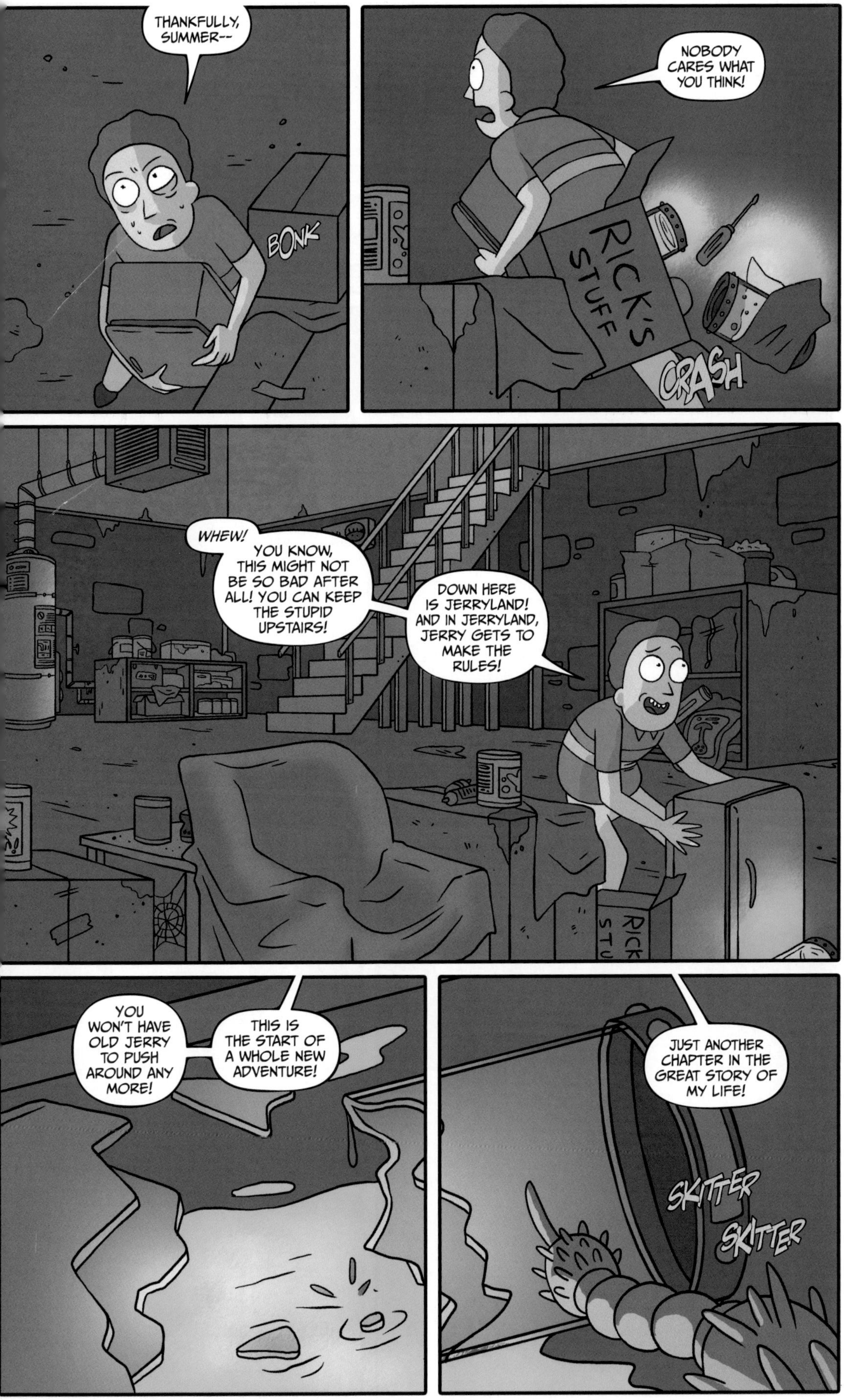
THANKFULLY, SUMMER--
BONK
NOBODY CARES WHAT YOU THINK!
RICK'S STUFF
CRASH
WHEW!
YOU KNOW, THIS MIGHT NOT BE SO BAD AFTER ALL! YOU CAN KEEP THE STUPID UPSTAIRS!
DOWN HERE IS JERRYLAND! AND IN JERRYLAND, JERRY GETS TO MAKE THE RULES!
RICK STU
YOU WON'T HAVE OLD JERRY TO PUSH AROUND ANY MORE!
THIS IS THE START OF A WHOLE NEW ADVENTURE!
JUST ANOTHER CHAPTER IN THE GREAT STORY OF MY LIFE!
SKITTER
SKITTER

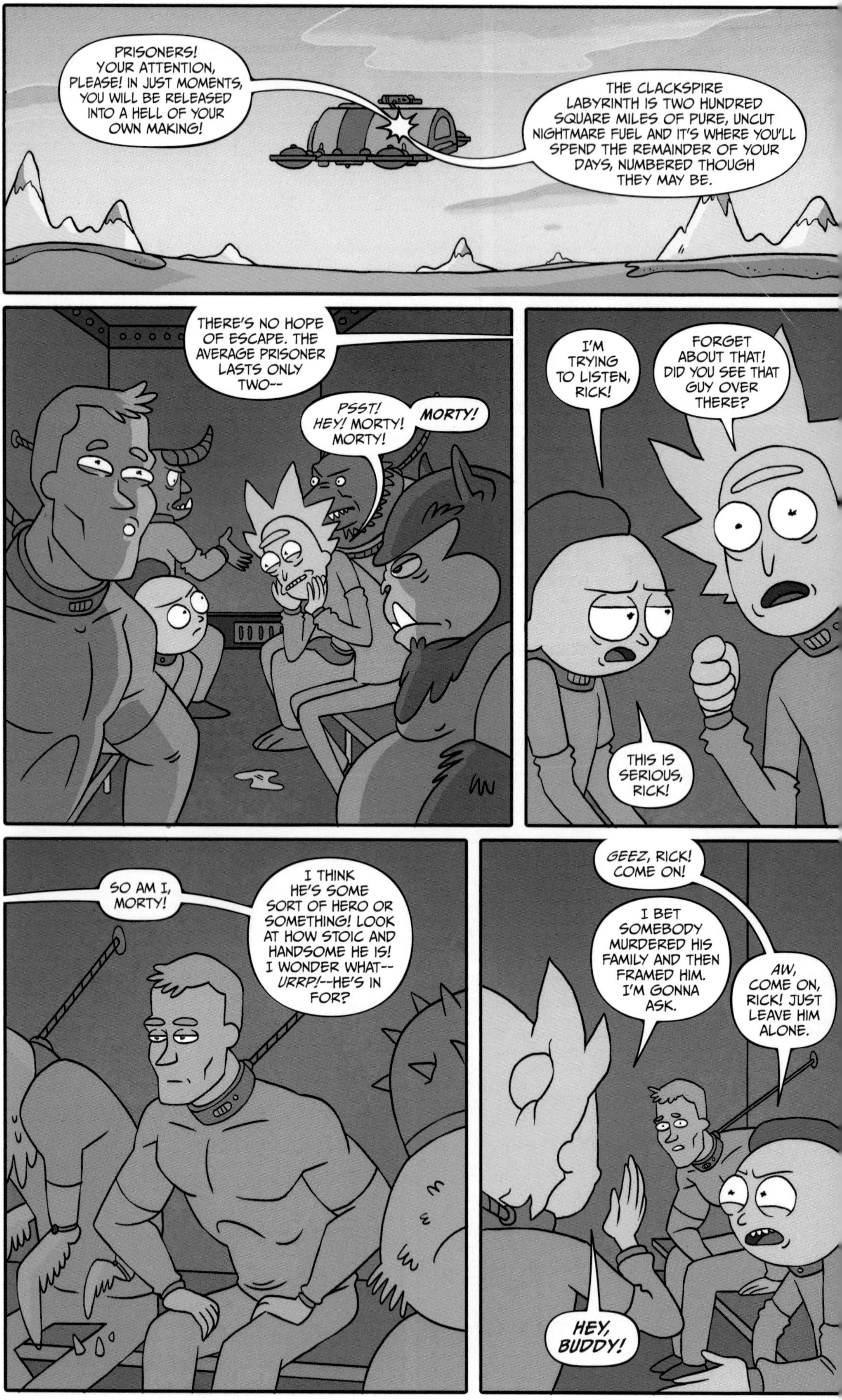

PRISONERS! YOUR ATTENTION, PLEASE! IN JUST MOMENTS, YOU WILL BE RELEASED INTO A HELL OF YOUR OWN MAKING!
THE CLACKSPIRE LABYRINTH IS TWO HUNDRED SQUARE MILES OF PURE, UNCUT NIGHTMARE FUEL AND IT'S WHERE YOU'LL SPEND THE REMAINDER OF YOUR DAYS, NUMBERED THOUGH THEY MAY BE.
THERE'S NO HOPE OF ESCAPE. THE AVERAGE PRISONER LASTS ONLY TWO--
PSST! HEY! MORTY! MORTY!
MORTY!
I'M TRYING TO LISTEN, RICK!
FORGET ABOUT THAT! DID YOU SEE THAT GUY OVER THERE?
THIS IS SERIOUS, RICK!
SO AM I, MORTY!
I THINK HE'S SOME SORT OF HERO OR SOMETHING! LOOK AT HOW STOIC AND HANDSOME HE IS! I WONDER WHAT--URRP!--HE'S IN FOR?
GEEZ, RICK! COME ON!
I BET SOMEBODY MURDERED HIS FAMILY AND THEN FRAMED HIM. I'M GONNA ASK.
AW, COME ON, RICK! JUST LEAVE HIM ALONE.
HEY, BUDDY!

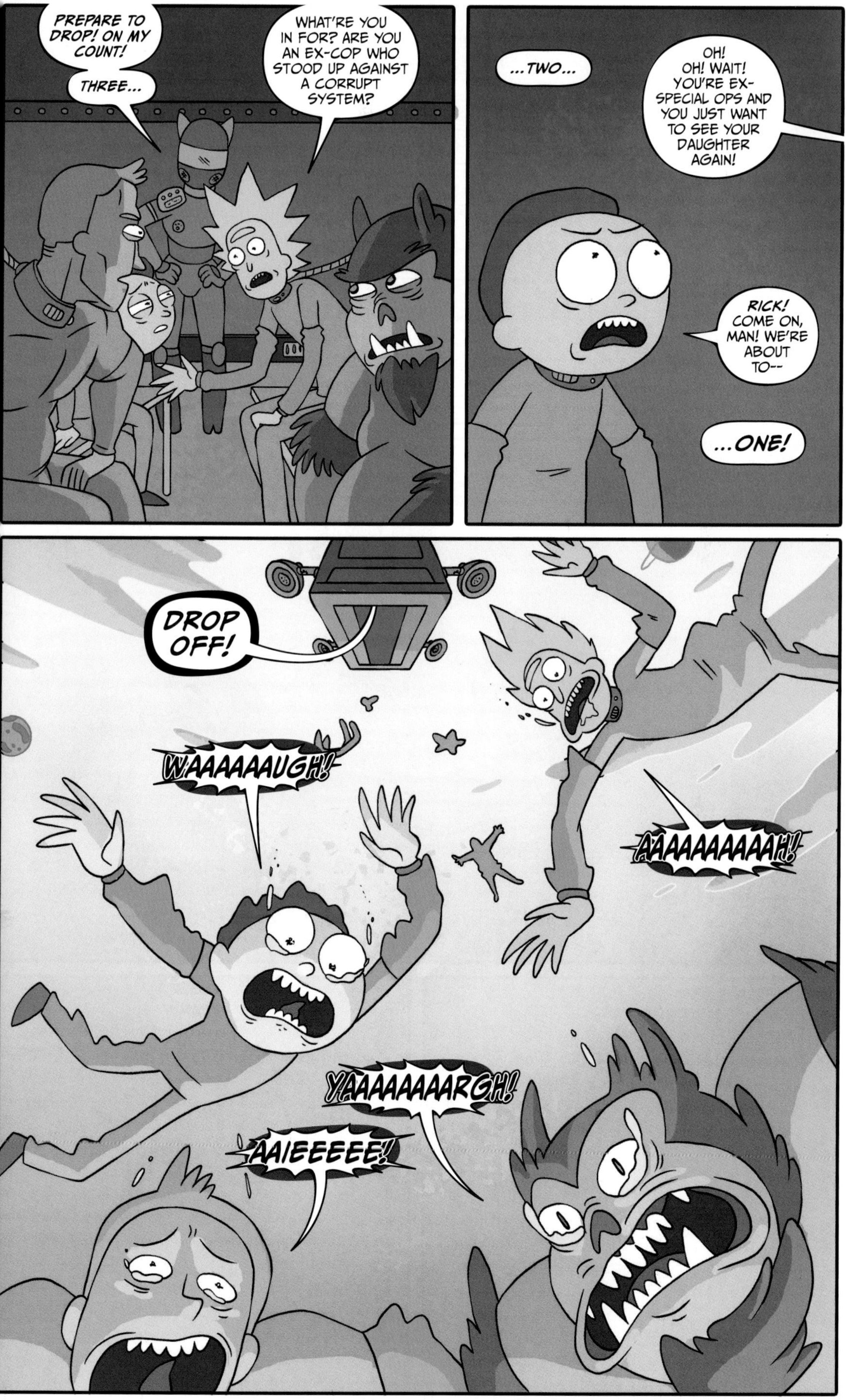
PREPARE TO DROP! ON MY COUNT!
THREE...
WHAT'RE YOU IN FOR? ARE YOU AN EX-COP WHO STOOD UP AGAINST A CORRUPT SYSTEM?
...TWO...
OH! OH! WAIT! YOU'RE EX-SPECIAL OPS AND YOU JUST WANT TO SEE YOUR DAUGHTER AGAIN!
RICK! COME ON, MAN! WE'RE ABOUT TO--
...ONE!
DROP OFF!
WAAAAAAUGH!
AAAAAAAAAAH!
YAAAAAAARGH!
AAIEEEEEE!

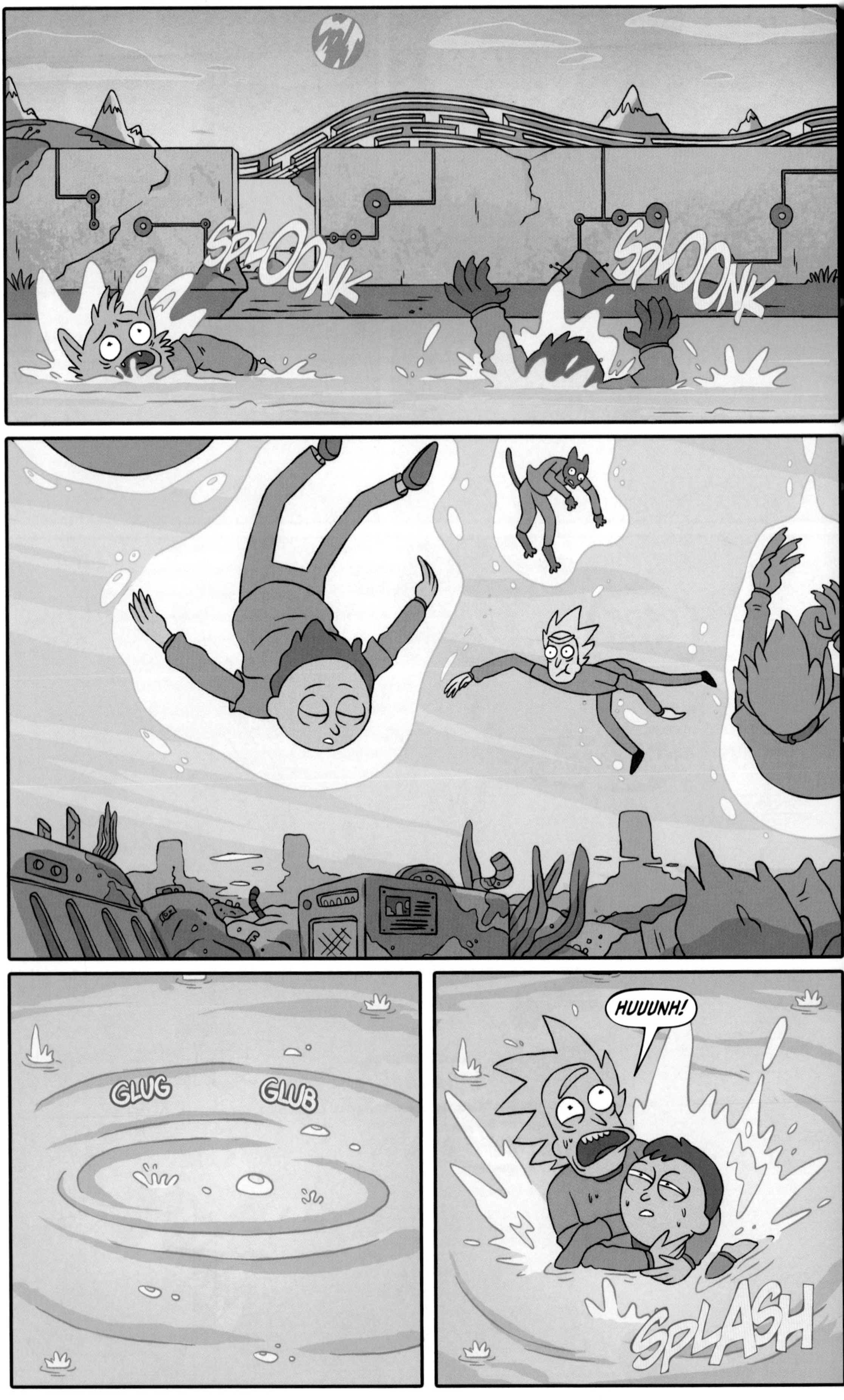
SPLOONK
SPLOONK
GLUG
GLUB
HUUUNH!
SPLASH

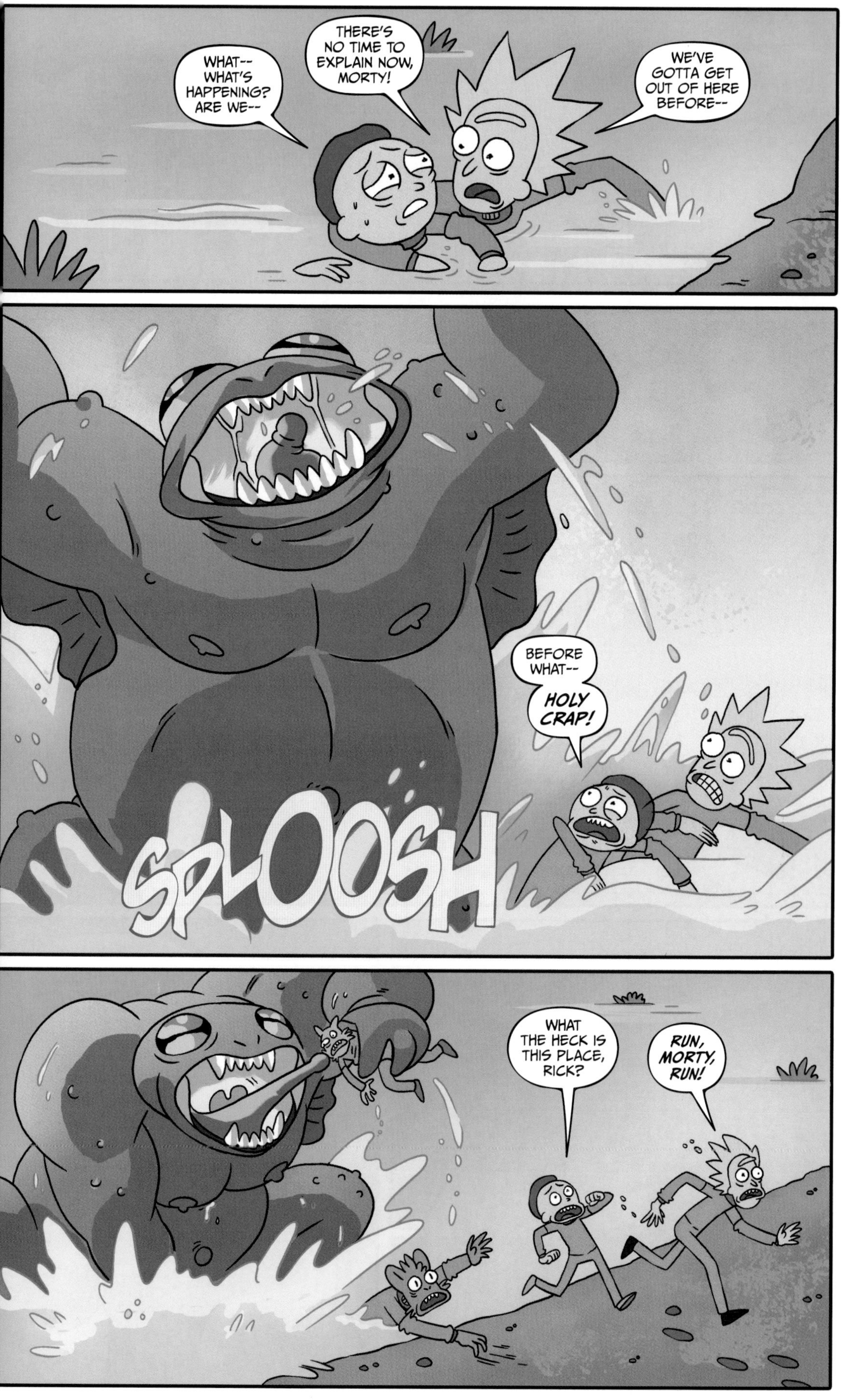
WHAT--
WHAT'S
HAPPENING?
ARE WE--
THERE'S
NO TIME TO
EXPLAIN NOW,
MORTY!
WE'VE
GOTTA GET
OUT OF HERE
BEFORE--
BEFORE
WHAT--
HOLY
CRAP!
SPLOOSH
WHAT
THE HECK IS
THIS PLACE,
RICK?
RUN,
MORTY,
RUN!

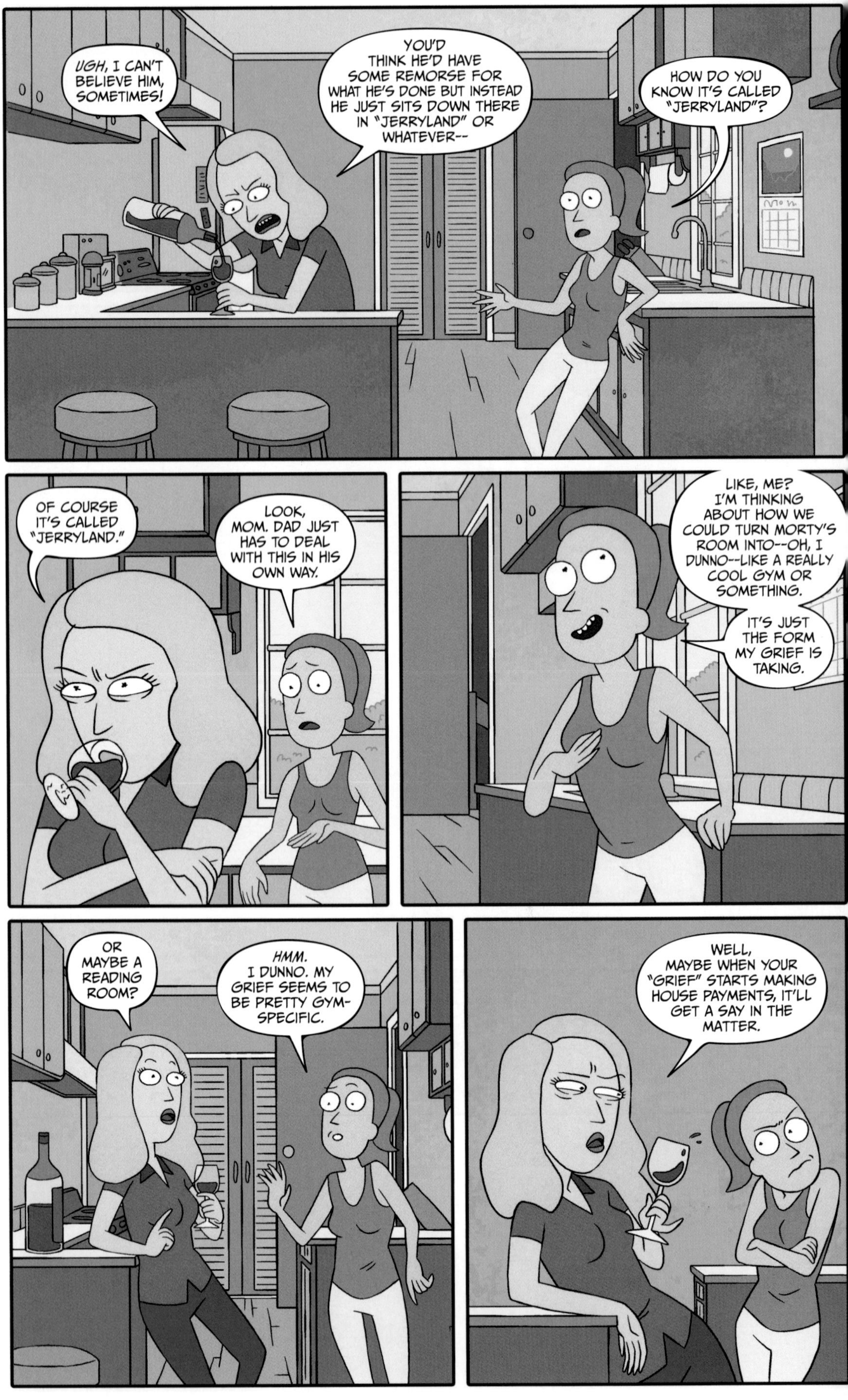

UGH, I CAN'T BELIEVE HIM, SOMETIMES!
YOU'D THINK HE'D HAVE SOME REMORSE FOR WHAT HE'S DONE BUT INSTEAD HE JUST SITS DOWN THERE IN "JERRYLAND" OR WHATEVER--
HOW DO YOU KNOW IT'S CALLED "JERRYLAND"?
OF COURSE IT'S CALLED "JERRYLAND."
LOOK, MOM. DAD JUST HAS TO DEAL WITH THIS IN HIS OWN WAY.
LIKE, ME? I'M THINKING ABOUT HOW WE COULD TURN MORTY'S ROOM INTO--OH, I DUNNO--LIKE A REALLY COOL GYM OR SOMETHING.
IT'S JUST THE FORM MY GRIEF IS TAKING.
OR MAYBE A READING ROOM?
HMM. I DUNNO. MY GRIEF SEEMS TO BE PRETTY GYM-SPECIFIC.
WELL, MAYBE WHEN YOUR "GRIEF" STARTS MAKING HOUSE PAYMENTS, IT'LL GET A SAY IN THE MATTER.

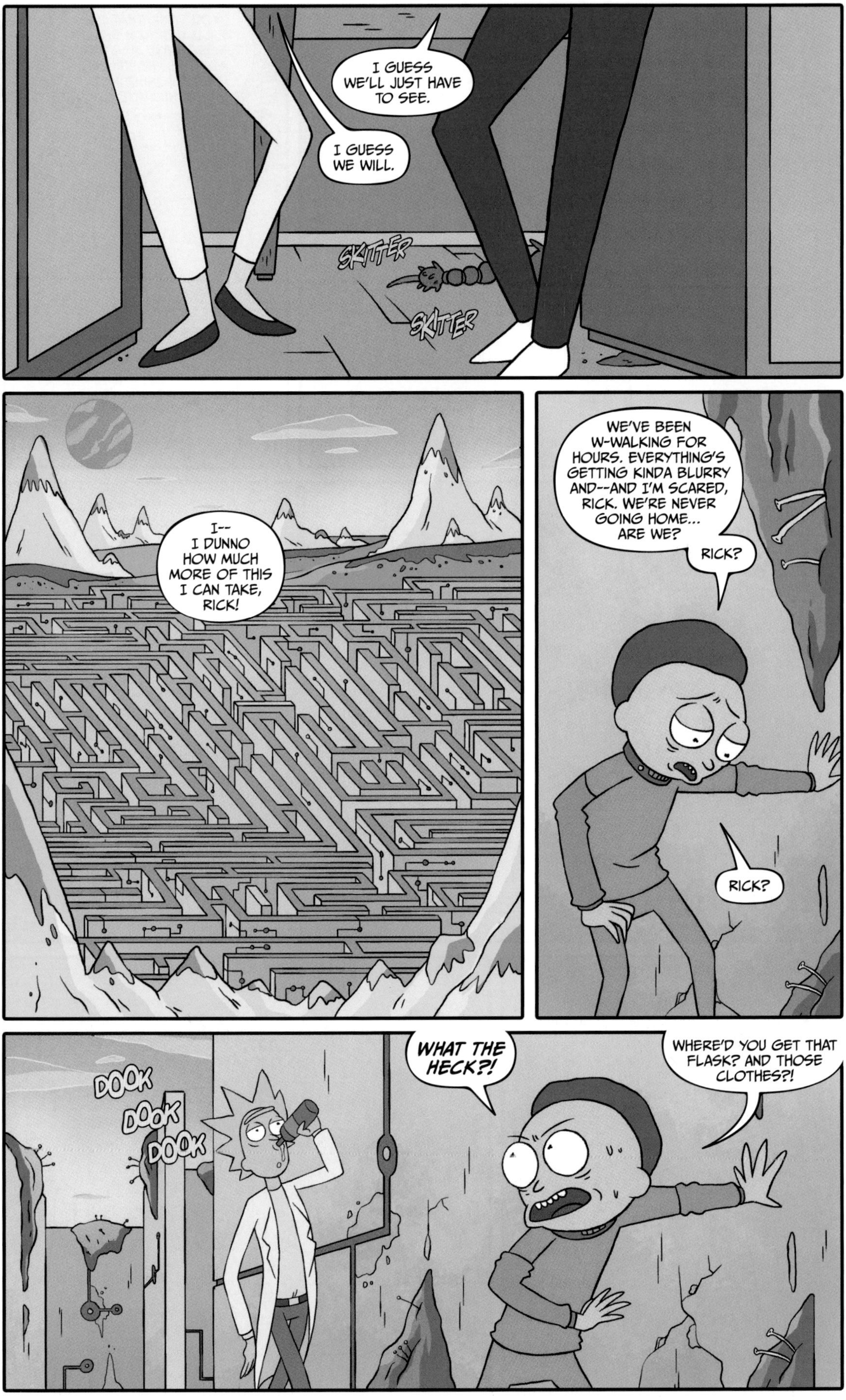
I GUESS WE'LL JUST HAVE TO SEE.
I GUESS WE WILL.
SKITTER
SKITTER
I-- I DUNNO HOW MUCH MORE OF THIS I CAN TAKE, RICK!
WE'VE BEEN W-WALKING FOR HOURS. EVERYTHING'S GETTING KINDA BLURRY AND--AND I'M SCARED, RICK. WE'RE NEVER GOING HOME... ARE WE?
RICK?
RICK?
DOOK
DOOK
DOOK
WHAT THE HECK?!
WHERE'D YOU GET THAT FLASK? AND THOSE CLOTHES?!

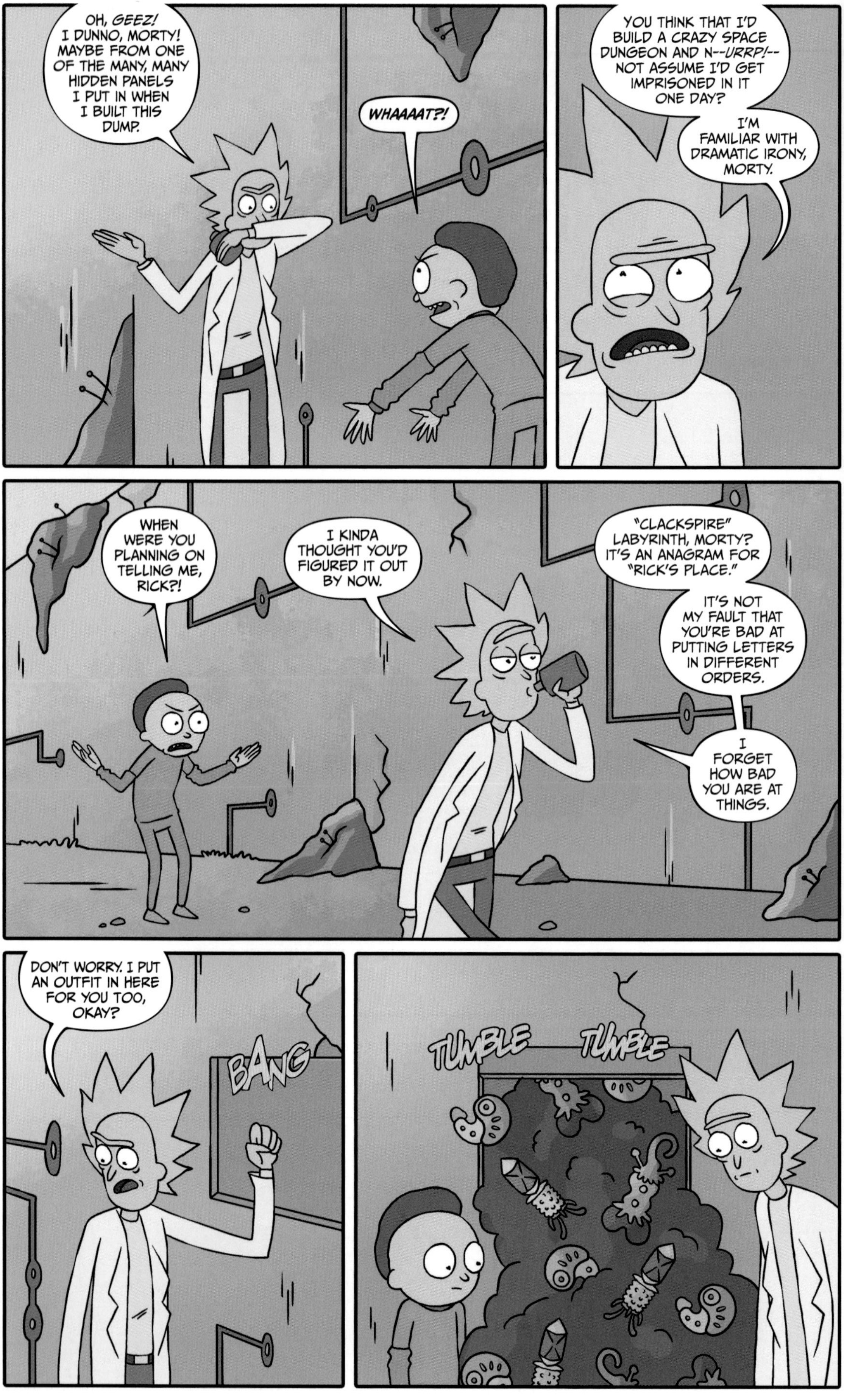
OH, *GEEZ!* I DUNNO, MORTY! MAYBE FROM ONE OF THE MANY, MANY HIDDEN PANELS I PUT IN WHEN I BUILT THIS DUMP.
WHAAAAT?!
YOU THINK THAT I'D BUILD A CRAZY SPACE DUNGEON AND N--*URRP!*--NOT ASSUME I'D GET IMPRISONED IN IT ONE DAY?
I'M FAMILIAR WITH DRAMATIC IRONY, MORTY.
WHEN WERE YOU PLANNING ON TELLING ME, RICK?!
I KINDA THOUGHT YOU'D FIGURED IT OUT BY NOW.
"CLACKSPIRE" LABYRINTH, MORTY? IT'S AN ANAGRAM FOR "RICK'S PLACE."
IT'S NOT MY FAULT THAT YOU'RE BAD AT PUTTING LETTERS IN DIFFERENT ORDERS.
I FORGET HOW BAD YOU ARE AT THINGS.
DON'T WORRY. I PUT AN OUTFIT IN HERE FOR YOU TOO, OKAY?
BANG
TUMBLE TUMBLE

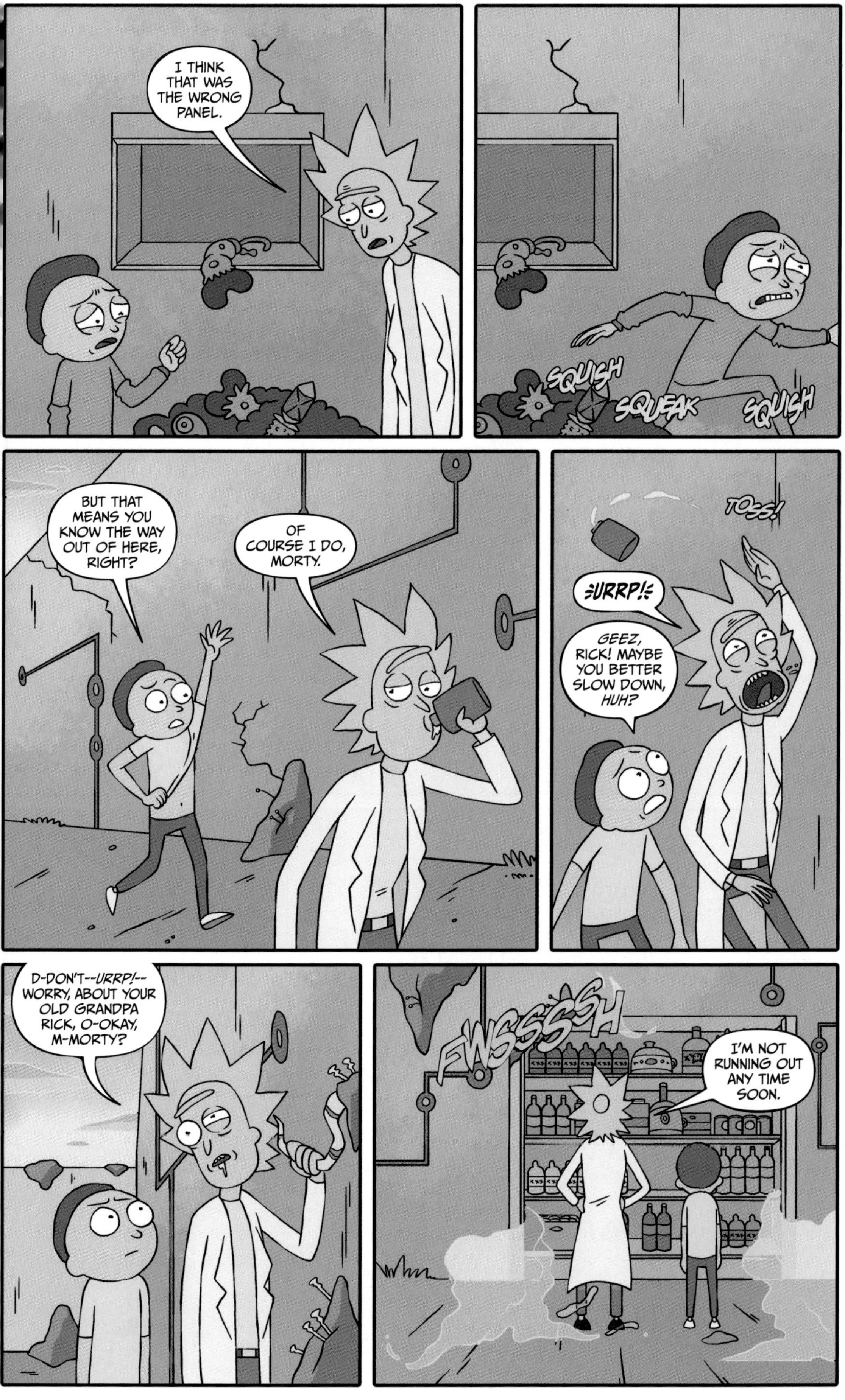
I THINK THAT WAS THE WRONG PANEL.
SQUISH
SQUEAK
SQUISH
BUT THAT MEANS YOU KNOW THE WAY OUT OF HERE, RIGHT?
OF COURSE I DO, MORTY.
TOSS!
URRP!
GEEZ, RICK! MAYBE YOU BETTER SLOW DOWN, HUH?
D-DON'T--URRP!--WORRY, ABOUT YOUR OLD GRANDPA RICK, O-OKAY, M-MORTY?
FWSSSSH
I'M NOT RUNNING OUT ANY TIME SOON.

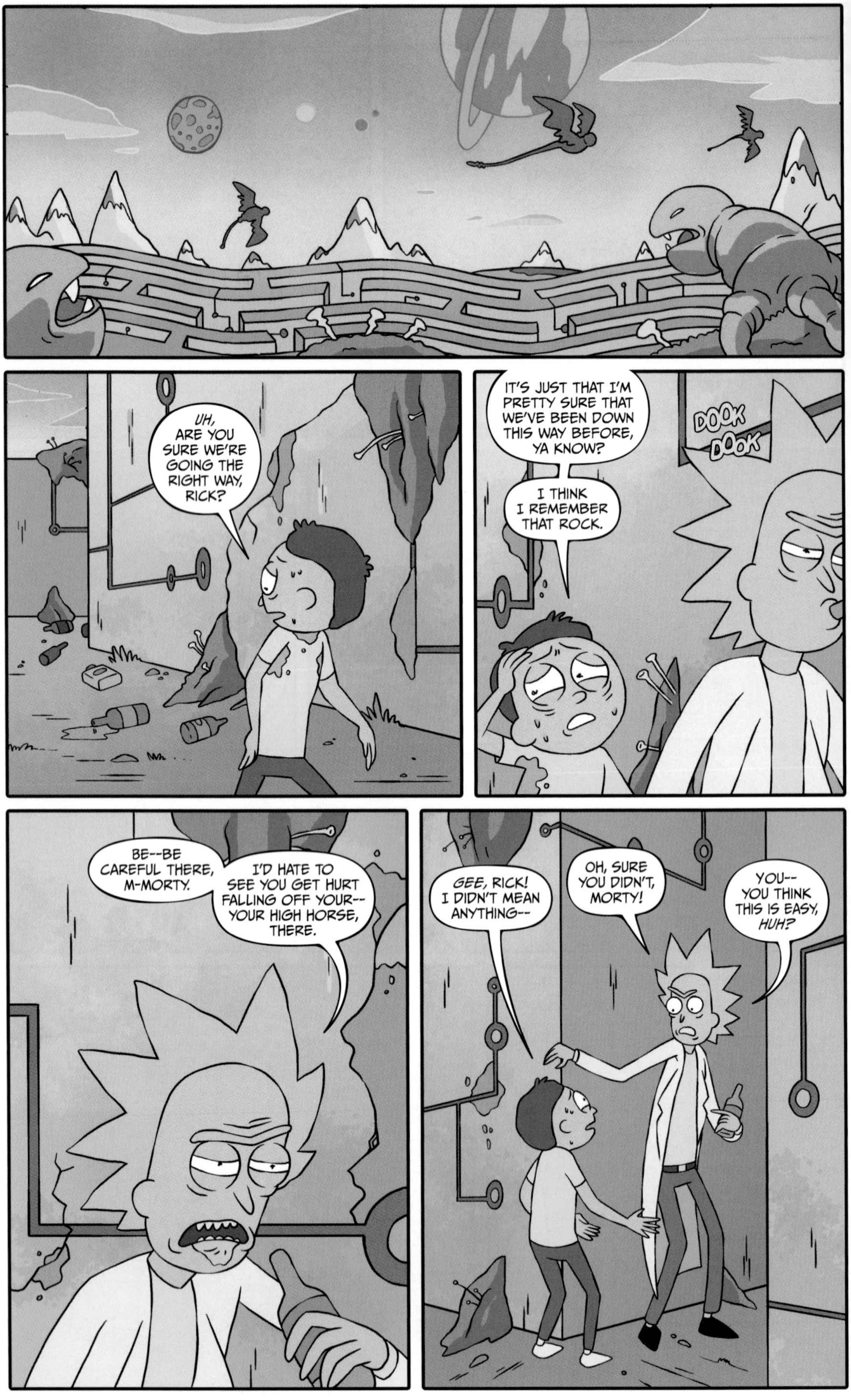
UH, ARE YOU SURE WE'RE GOING THE RIGHT WAY, RICK?
IT'S JUST THAT I'M PRETTY SURE THAT WE'VE BEEN DOWN THIS WAY BEFORE, YA KNOW?
I THINK I REMEMBER THAT ROCK.
DOOK DOOK
BE--BE CAREFUL THERE, M-MORTY.
I'D HATE TO SEE YOU GET HURT FALLING OFF YOUR-- YOUR HIGH HORSE, THERE.
GEE, RICK! I DIDN'T MEAN ANYTHING--
OH, SURE YOU DIDN'T, MORTY!
YOU-- YOU THINK THIS IS EASY, HUH?

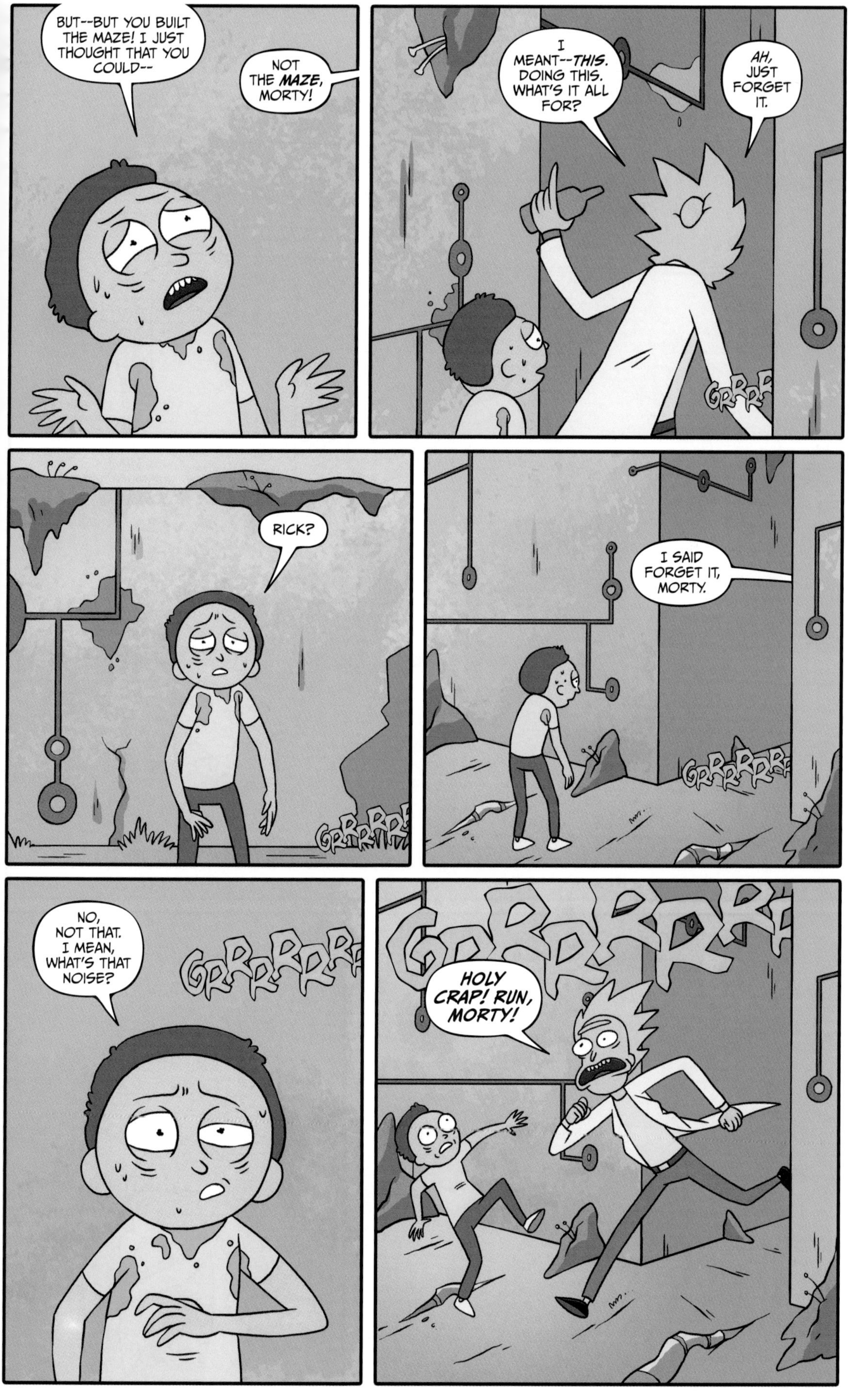
BUT--BUT YOU BUILT THE MAZE! I JUST THOUGHT THAT YOU COULD--
NOT THE *MAZE*, MORTY!
I MEANT--*THIS*. DOING THIS. WHAT'S IT ALL FOR?
AH, JUST FORGET IT.
GRRRR
RICK?
GRRRRRR
I SAID FORGET IT, MORTY.
GRRRRRR
NO, NOT THAT. I MEAN, WHAT'S THAT NOISE?
GRRRRRR
GRRRRRR
HOLY CRAP! RUN, MORTY!

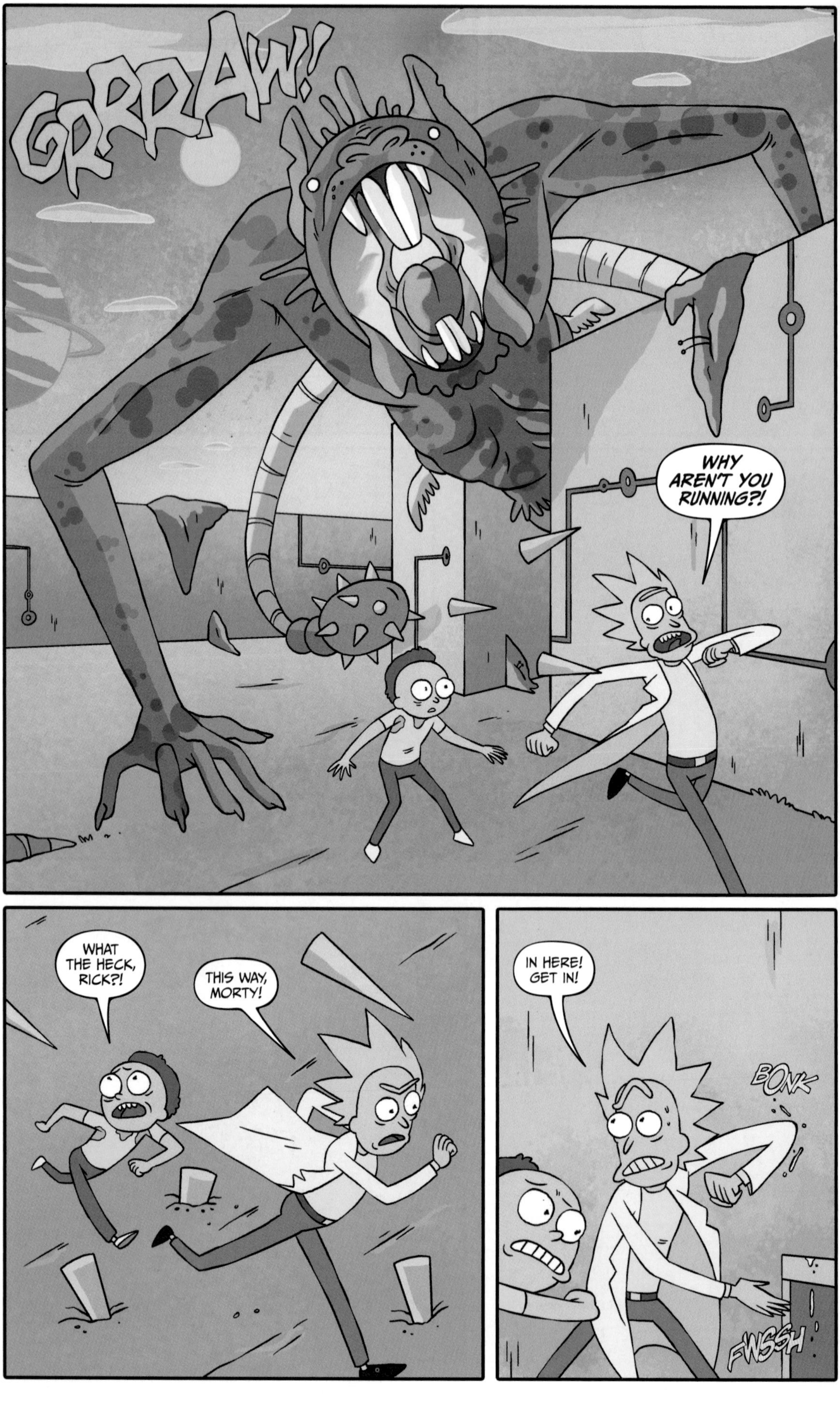
GRRRAW!!
WHY AREN'T YOU RUNNING?!
WHAT THE HECK, RICK?!
THIS WAY, MORTY!
IN HERE! GET IN!
BONK
FWSSH

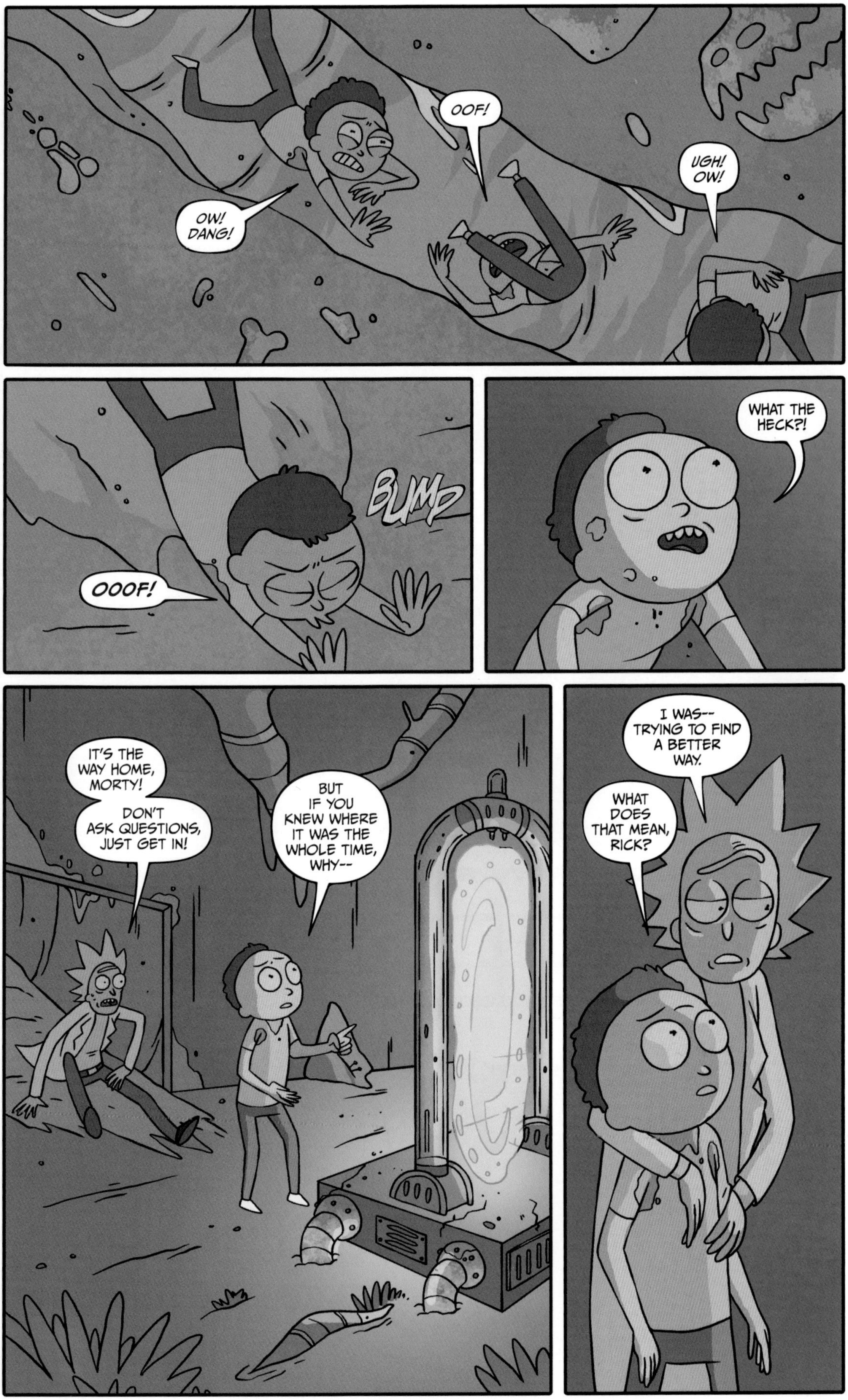
OW! DANG!
OOF!
UGH! OW!
OOOF!
BUMP
WHAT THE HECK?!
IT'S THE WAY HOME, MORTY!
DON'T ASK QUESTIONS, JUST GET IN!
BUT IF YOU KNEW WHERE IT WAS THE WHOLE TIME, WHY--
I WAS-- TRYING TO FIND A BETTER WAY.
WHAT DOES THAT MEAN, RICK?

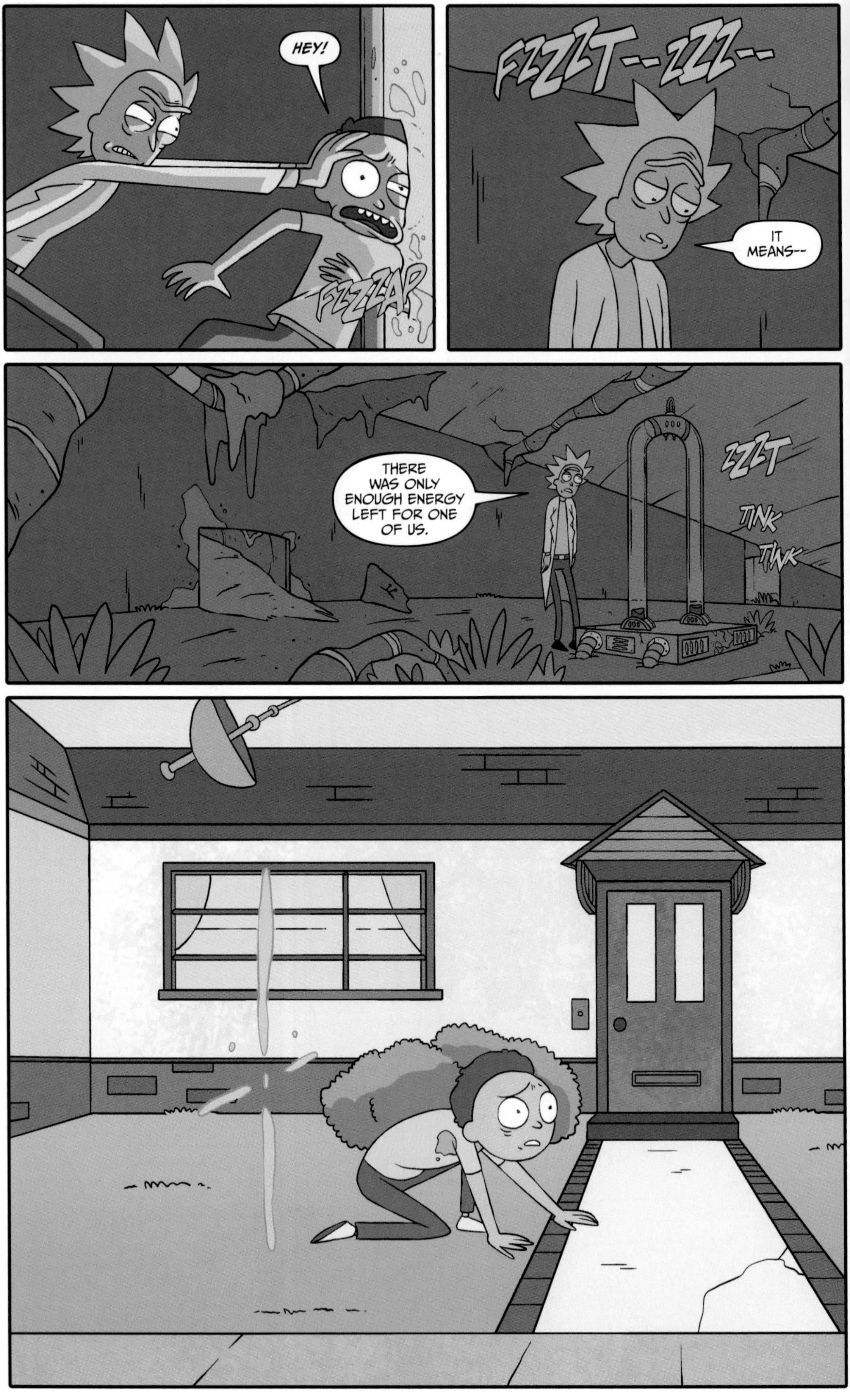
HEY!
FZZZAP
FZZZT--ZZZ--
IT MEANS--
THERE WAS ONLY ENOUGH ENERGY LEFT FOR ONE OF US.
ZZZT
TINK
TINK

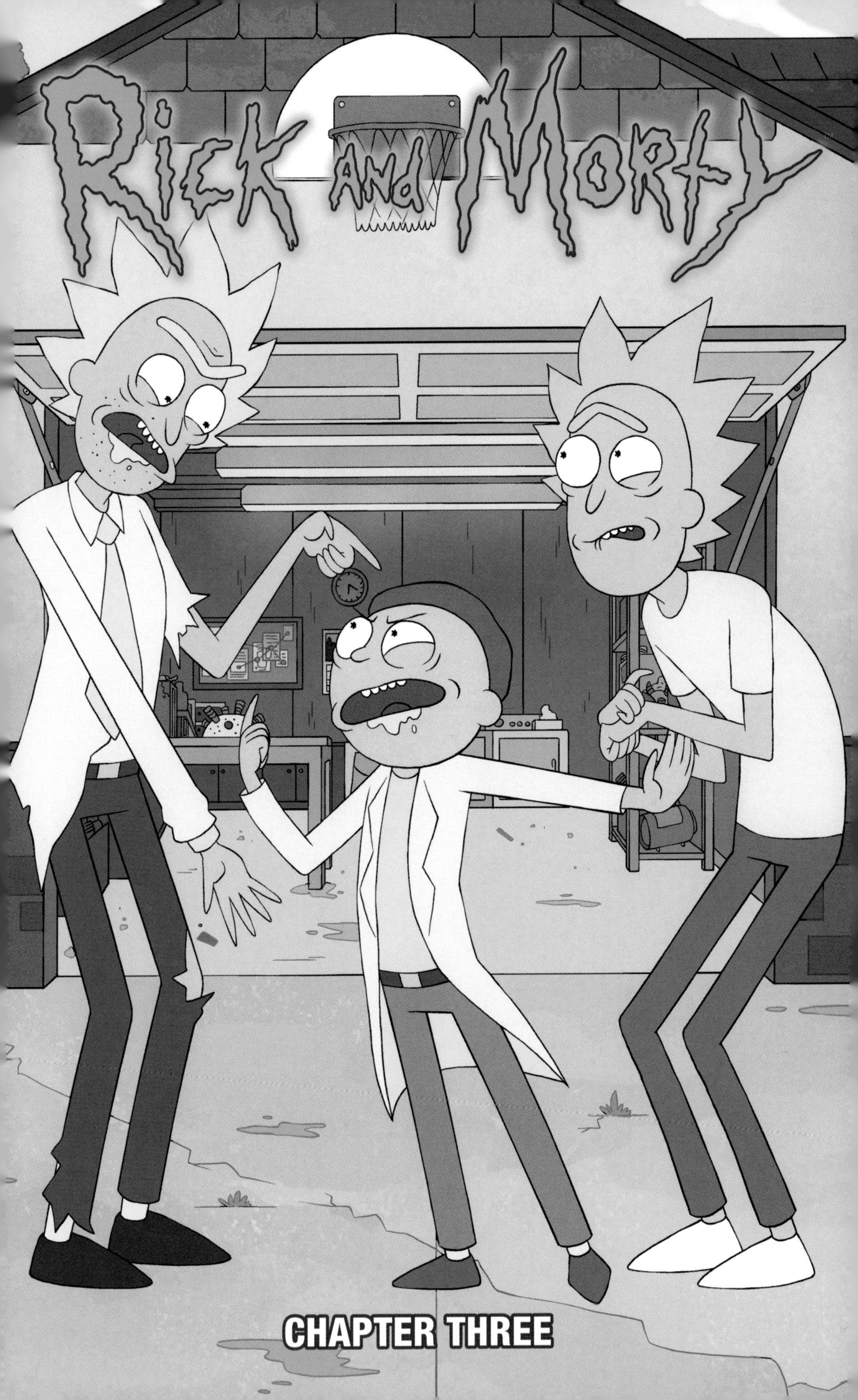
Rick and Morty
CHAPTER THREE

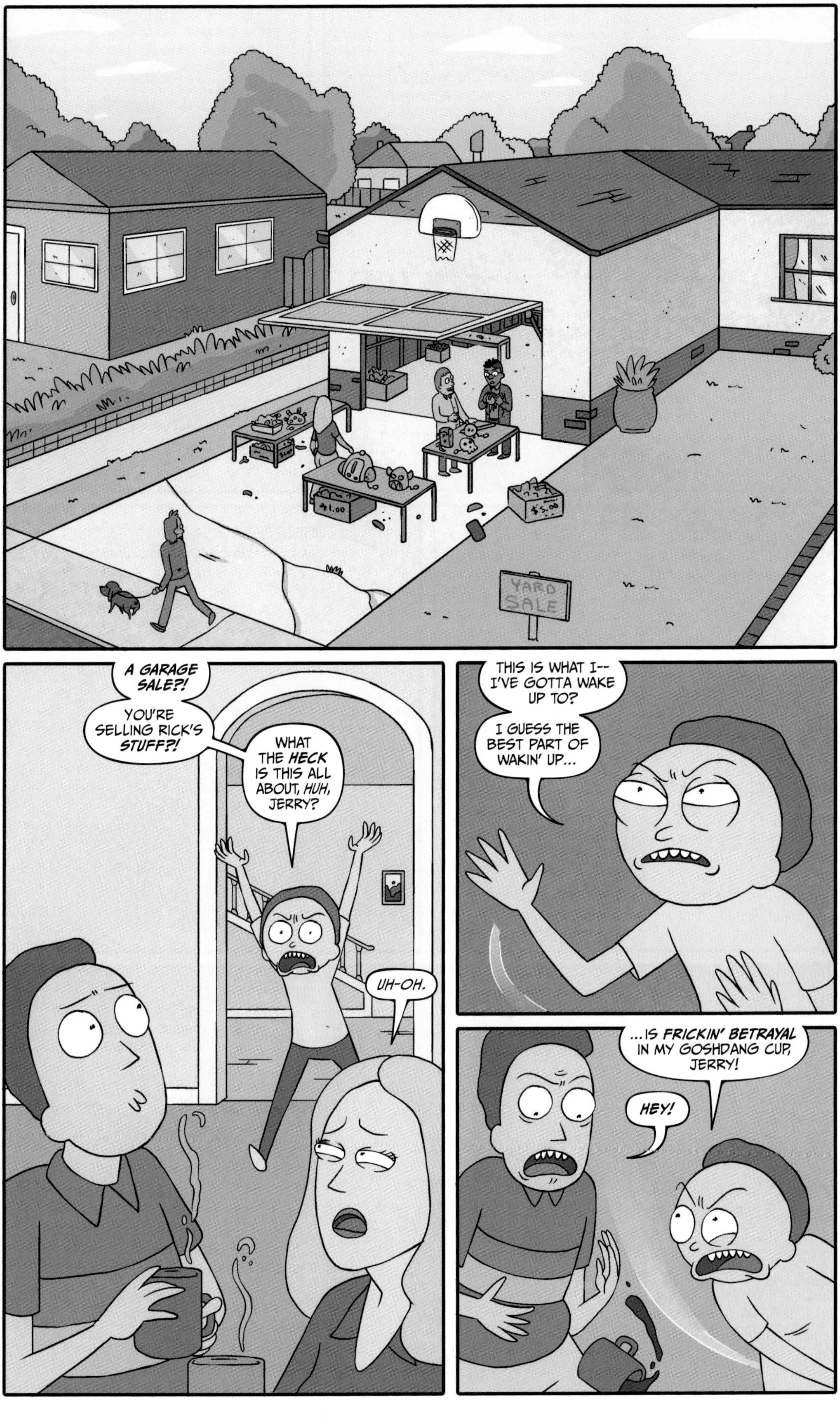
YARD SALE
$1.00
$5.00
A GARAGE SALE?!
YOU'RE SELLING RICK'S STUFF?!
WHAT THE HECK IS THIS ALL ABOUT, HUH, JERRY?
UH-OH.
THIS IS WHAT I-- I'VE GOTTA WAKE UP TO?
I GUESS THE BEST PART OF WAKIN' UP...
...IS FRICKIN' BETRAYAL IN MY GOSHDANG CUP, JERRY!
HEY!

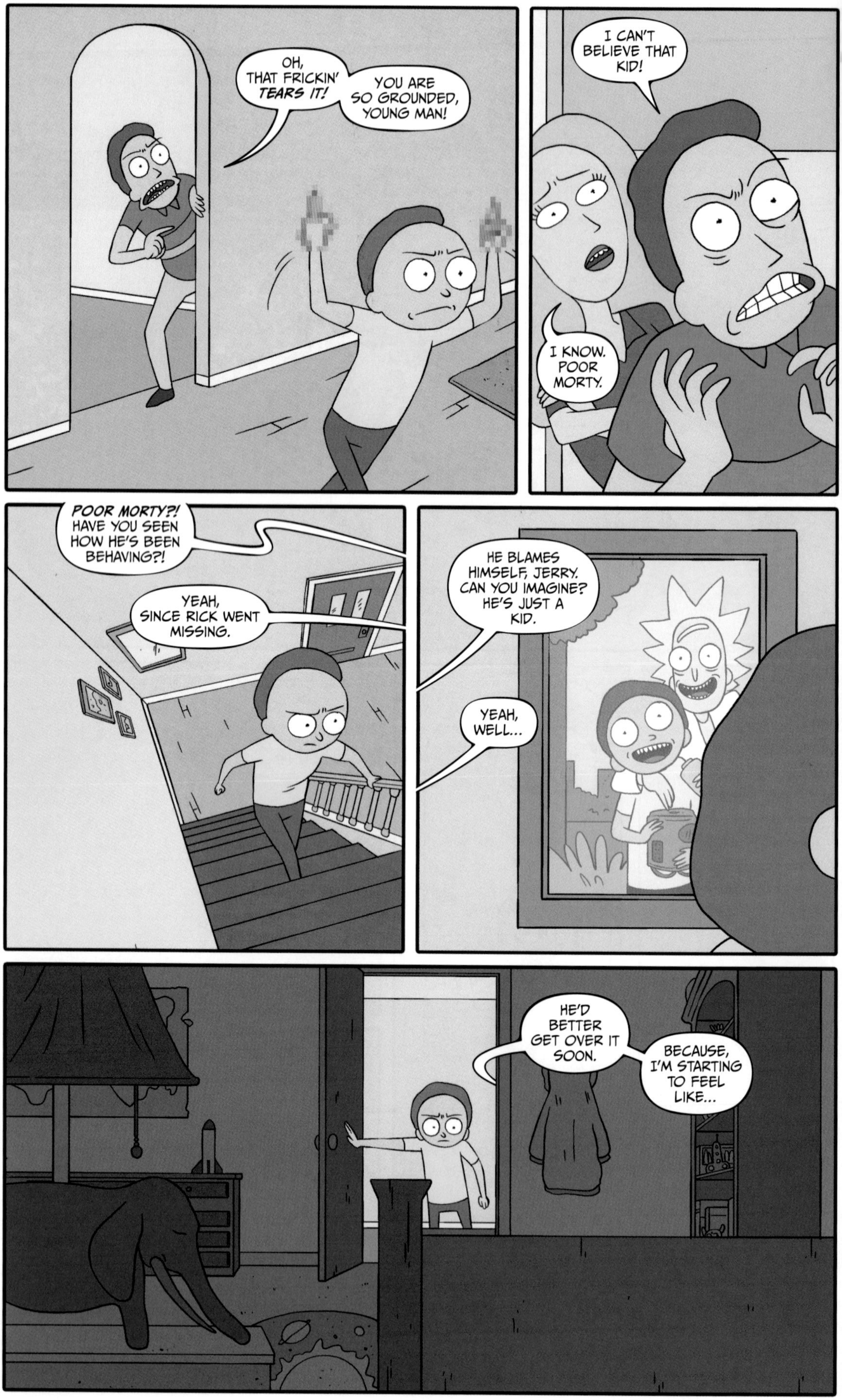
OH, THAT FRICKIN' *TEARS IT!*
YOU ARE SO GROUNDED, YOUNG MAN!
I CAN'T BELIEVE THAT KID!
I KNOW. POOR MORTY.
POOR MORTY?! HAVE YOU SEEN HOW HE'S BEEN BEHAVING?!
YEAH, SINCE RICK WENT MISSING.
HE BLAMES HIMSELF, JERRY. CAN YOU IMAGINE? HE'S JUST A KID.
YEAH, WELL...
HE'D BETTER GET OVER IT SOON.
BECAUSE, I'M STARTING TO FEEL LIKE...

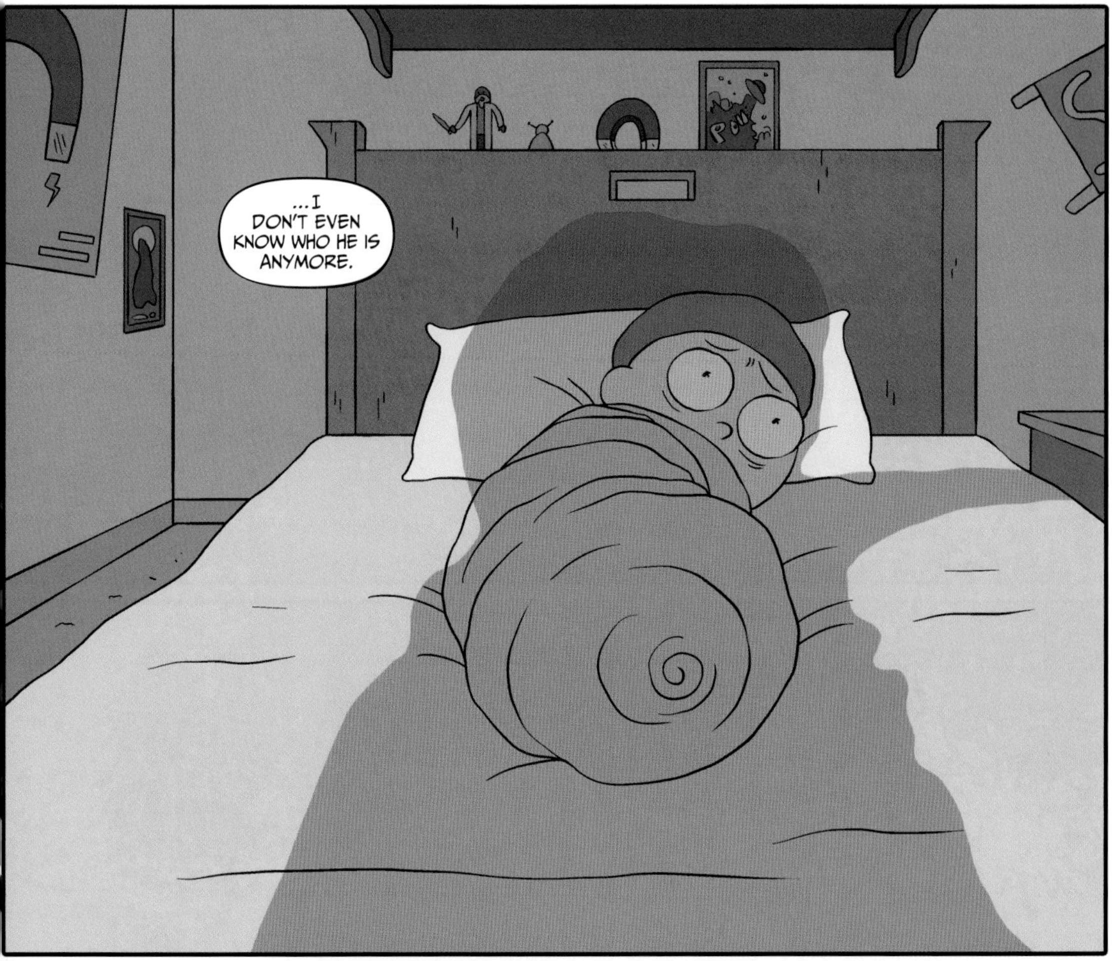
...I DON'T EVEN KNOW WHO HE IS ANYMORE.
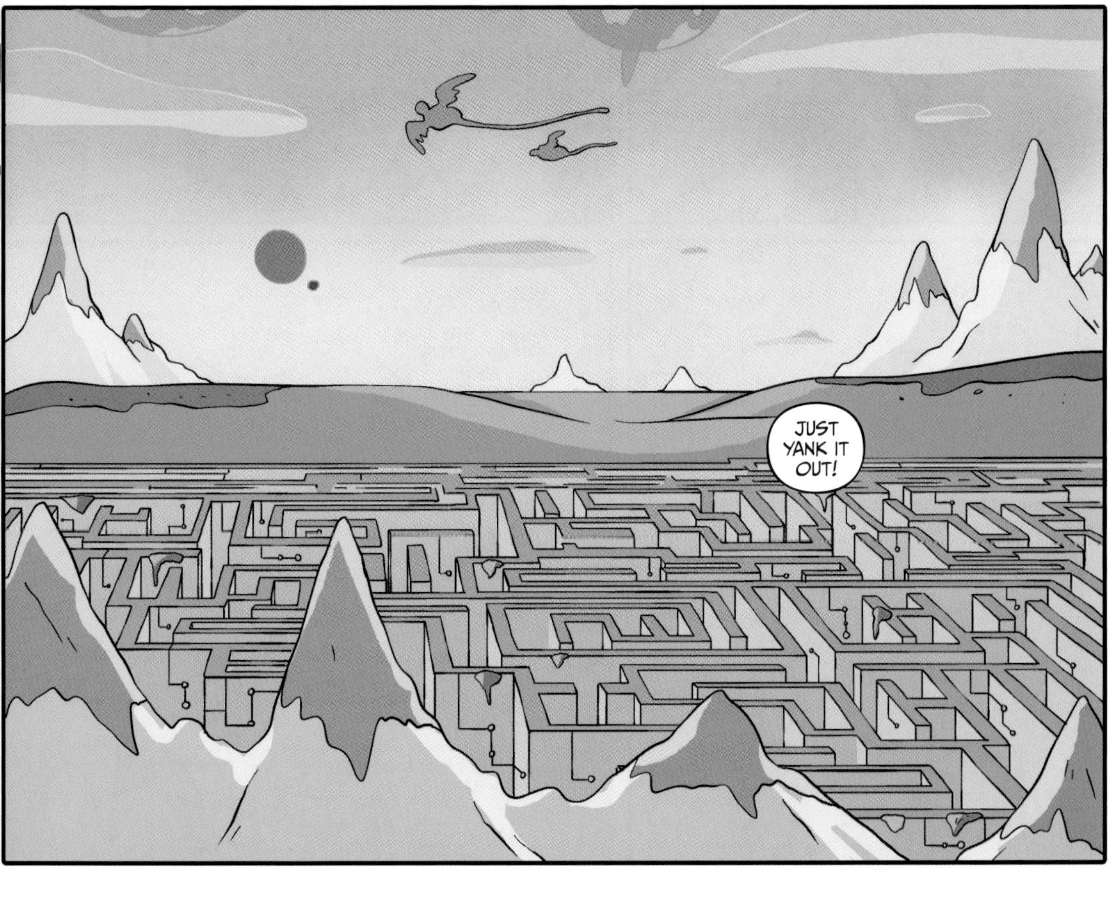
JUST YANK IT OUT!

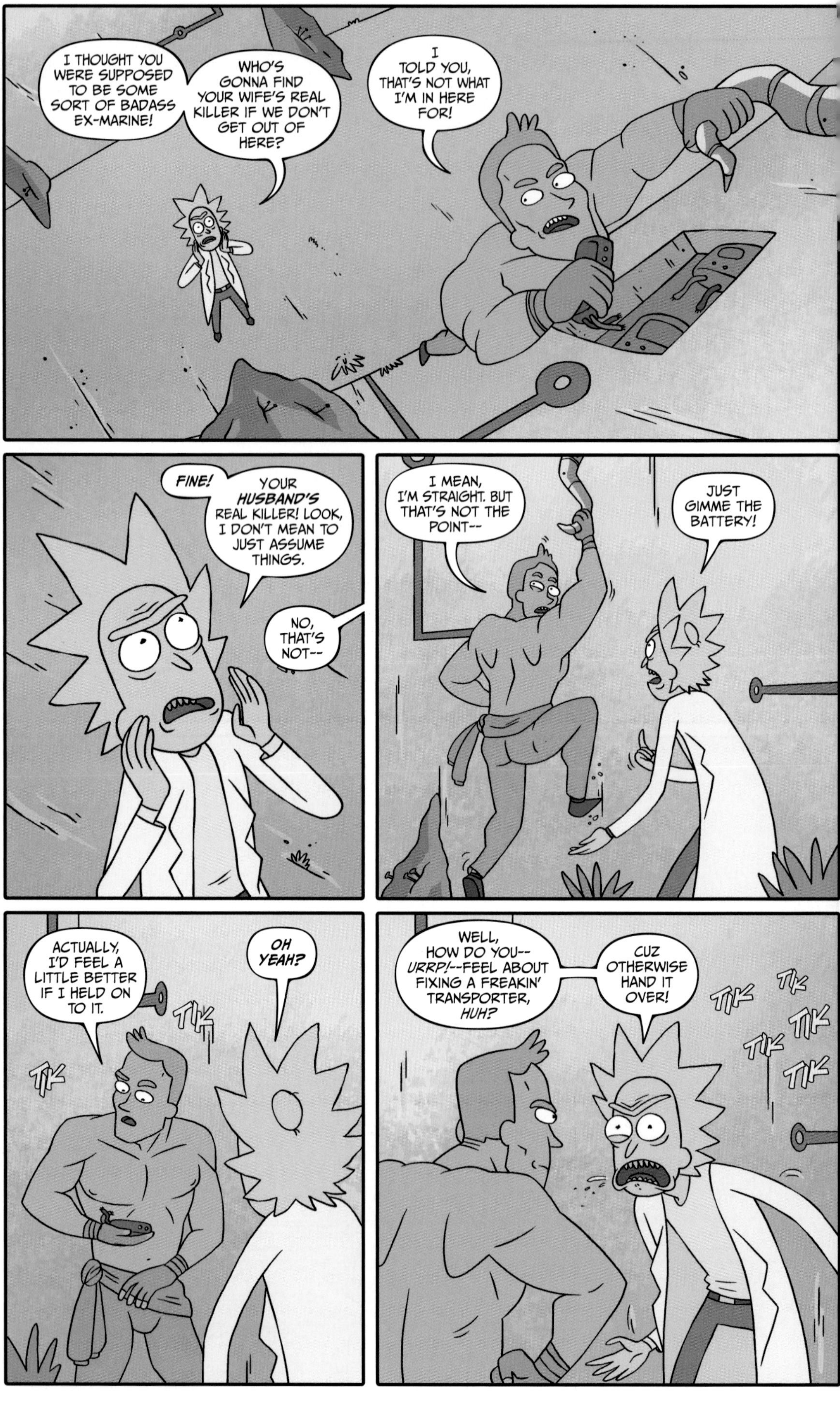
I THOUGHT YOU WERE SUPPOSED TO BE SOME SORT OF BADASS EX-MARINE!
WHO'S GONNA FIND YOUR WIFE'S REAL KILLER IF WE DON'T GET OUT OF HERE?
I TOLD YOU, THAT'S NOT WHAT I'M IN HERE FOR!
FINE!
YOUR HUSBAND'S REAL KILLER! LOOK, I DON'T MEAN TO JUST ASSUME THINGS.
NO, THAT'S NOT--
I MEAN, I'M STRAIGHT. BUT THAT'S NOT THE POINT--
JUST GIMME THE BATTERY!
ACTUALLY, I'D FEEL A LITTLE BETTER IF I HELD ON TO IT.
OH YEAH?
TIK
TIK
WELL, HOW DO YOU--URRP!--FEEL ABOUT FIXING A FREAKIN' TRANSPORTER, HUH?
CUZ OTHERWISE HAND IT OVER!
TIK
TIK
TIK
TIK
TIK

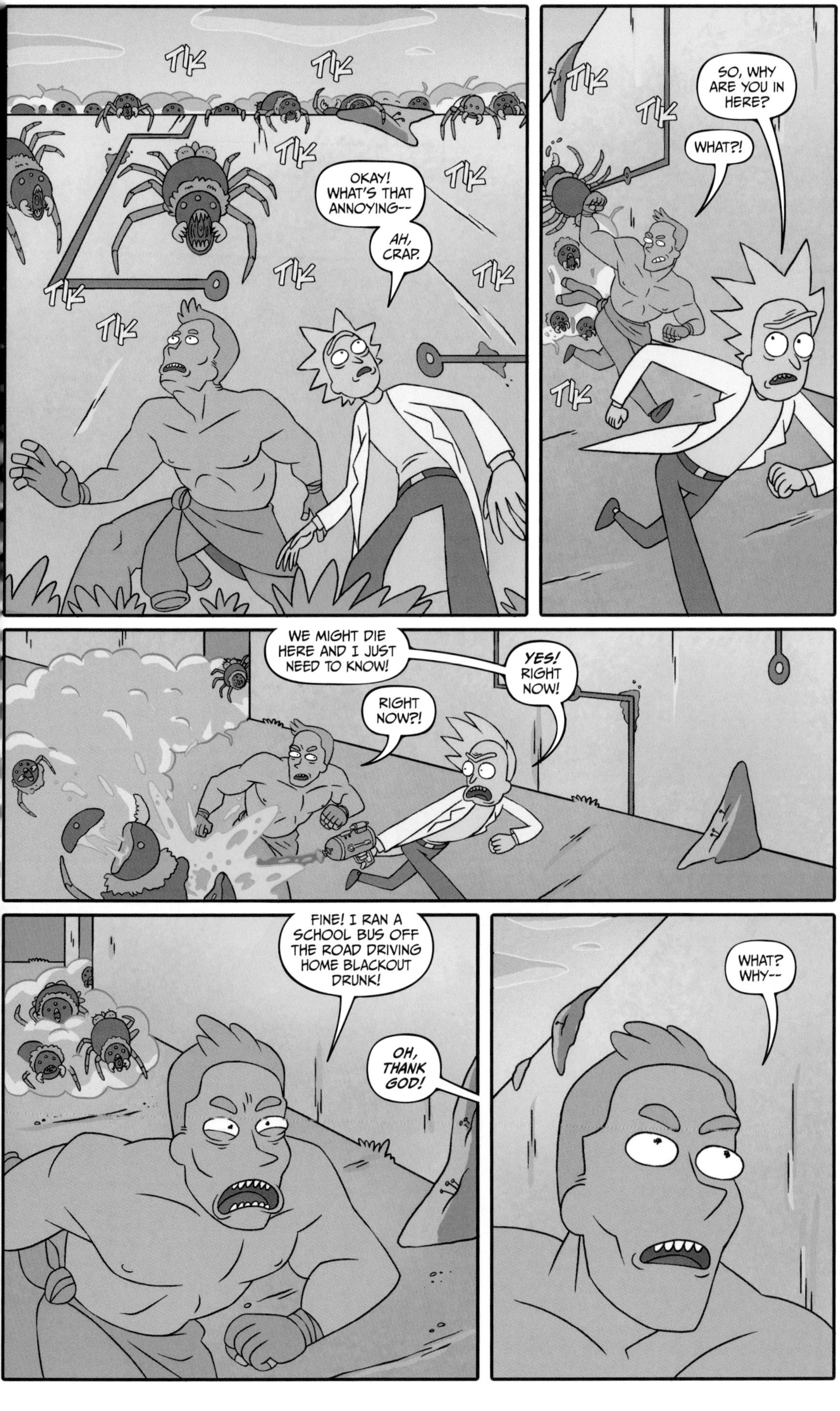
TIK
TIK
TIK
TIK
OKAY! WHAT'S THAT ANNOYING--
AH, CRAP.
TIK
TIK
TIK
TIK
TIK
TIK
SO, WHY ARE YOU IN HERE?
WHAT?!
TIK
WE MIGHT DIE HERE AND I JUST NEED TO KNOW!
RIGHT NOW?!
YES! RIGHT NOW!
FINE! I RAN A SCHOOL BUS OFF THE ROAD DRIVING HOME BLACKOUT DRUNK!
OH, THANK GOD!
WHAT? WHY--

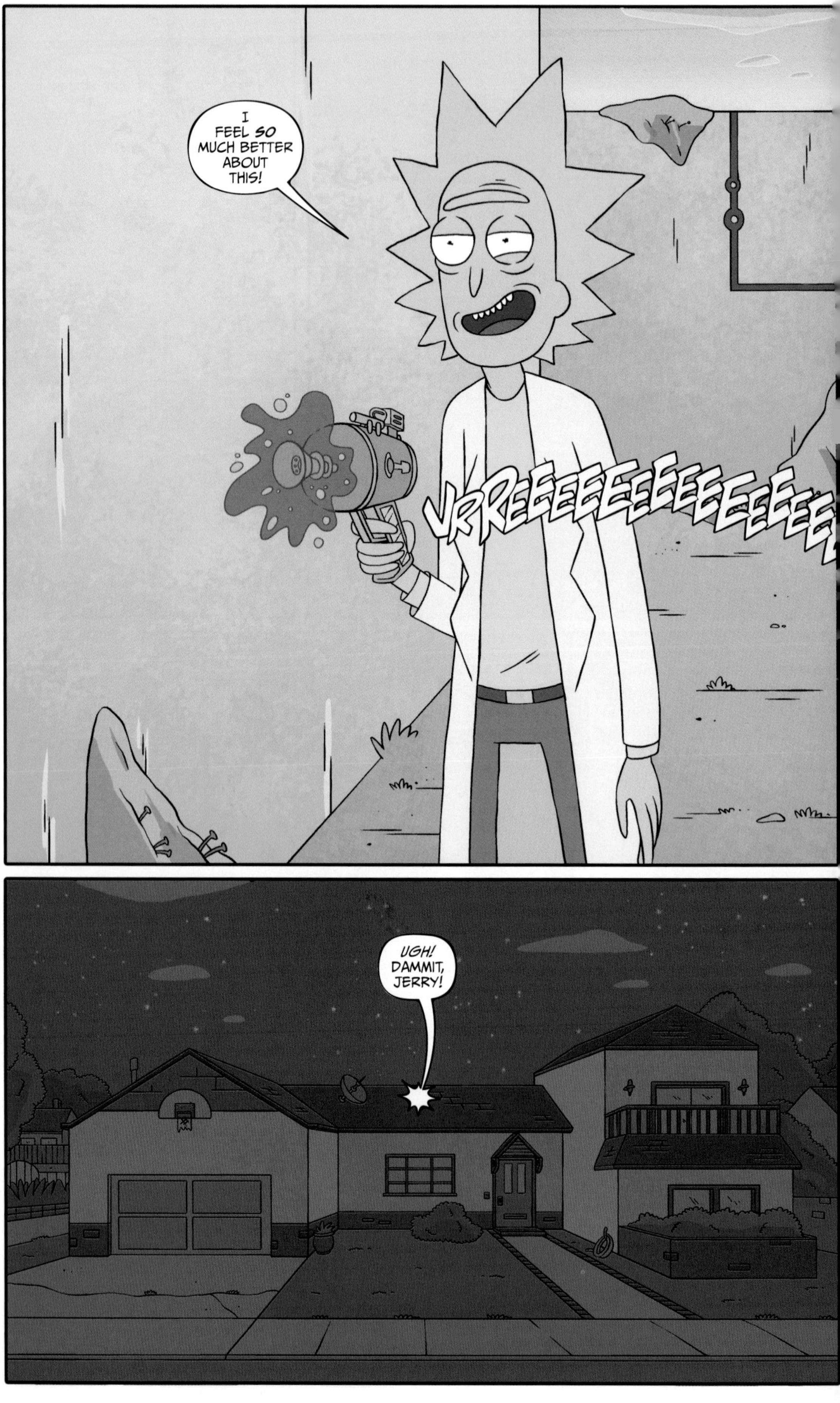
I FEEL SO MUCH BETTER ABOUT THIS!
VRREEEEEEEEEEEEEEE
UGH! DAMMIT, JERRY!

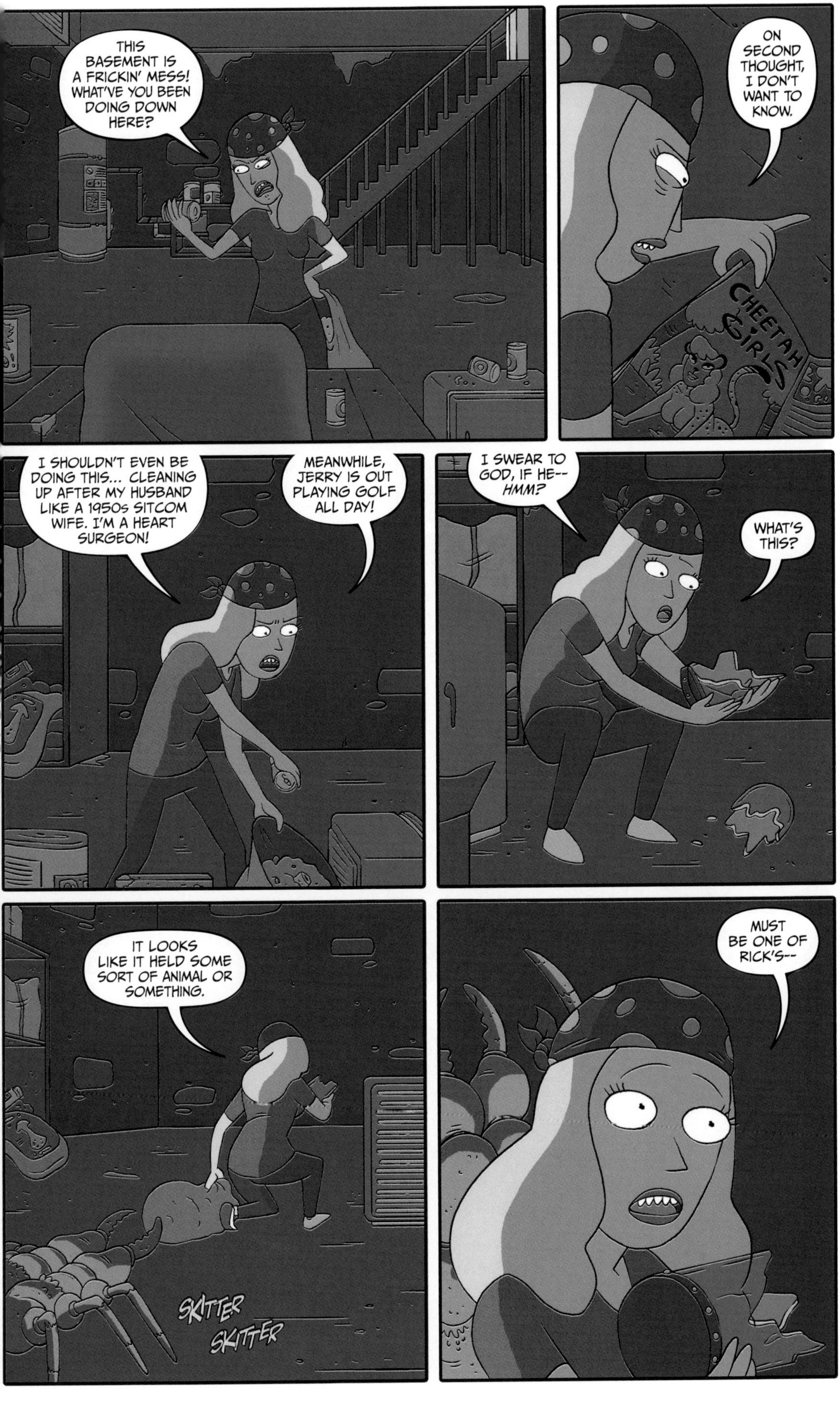
THIS BASEMENT IS A FRICKIN' MESS! WHAT'VE YOU BEEN DOING DOWN HERE?
ON SECOND THOUGHT, I DON'T WANT TO KNOW.
CHEETAH GIRLS
I SHOULDN'T EVEN BE DOING THIS... CLEANING UP AFTER MY HUSBAND LIKE A 1950s SITCOM WIFE. I'M A HEART SURGEON!
MEANWHILE, JERRY IS OUT PLAYING GOLF ALL DAY!
I SWEAR TO GOD, IF HE-- HMM?
WHAT'S THIS?
IT LOOKS LIKE IT HELD SOME SORT OF ANIMAL OR SOMETHING.
SKITTER SKITTER
MUST BE ONE OF RICK'S--

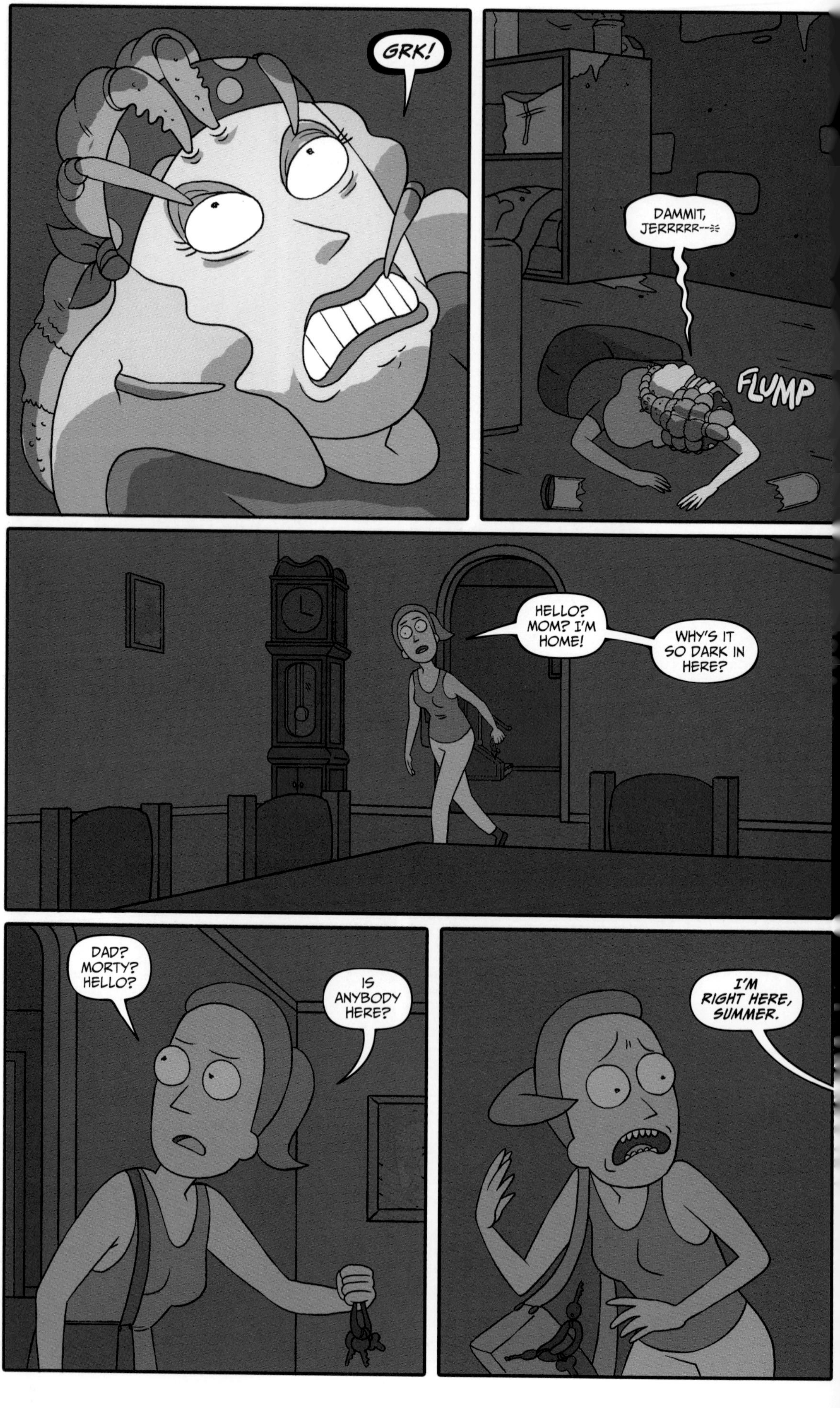
GRK!
DAMMIT, JERRRRR--
FLUMP
HELLO? MOM? I'M HOME!
WHY'S IT SO DARK IN HERE?
DAD? MORTY? HELLO?
IS ANYBODY HERE?
I'M RIGHT HERE, SUMMER.

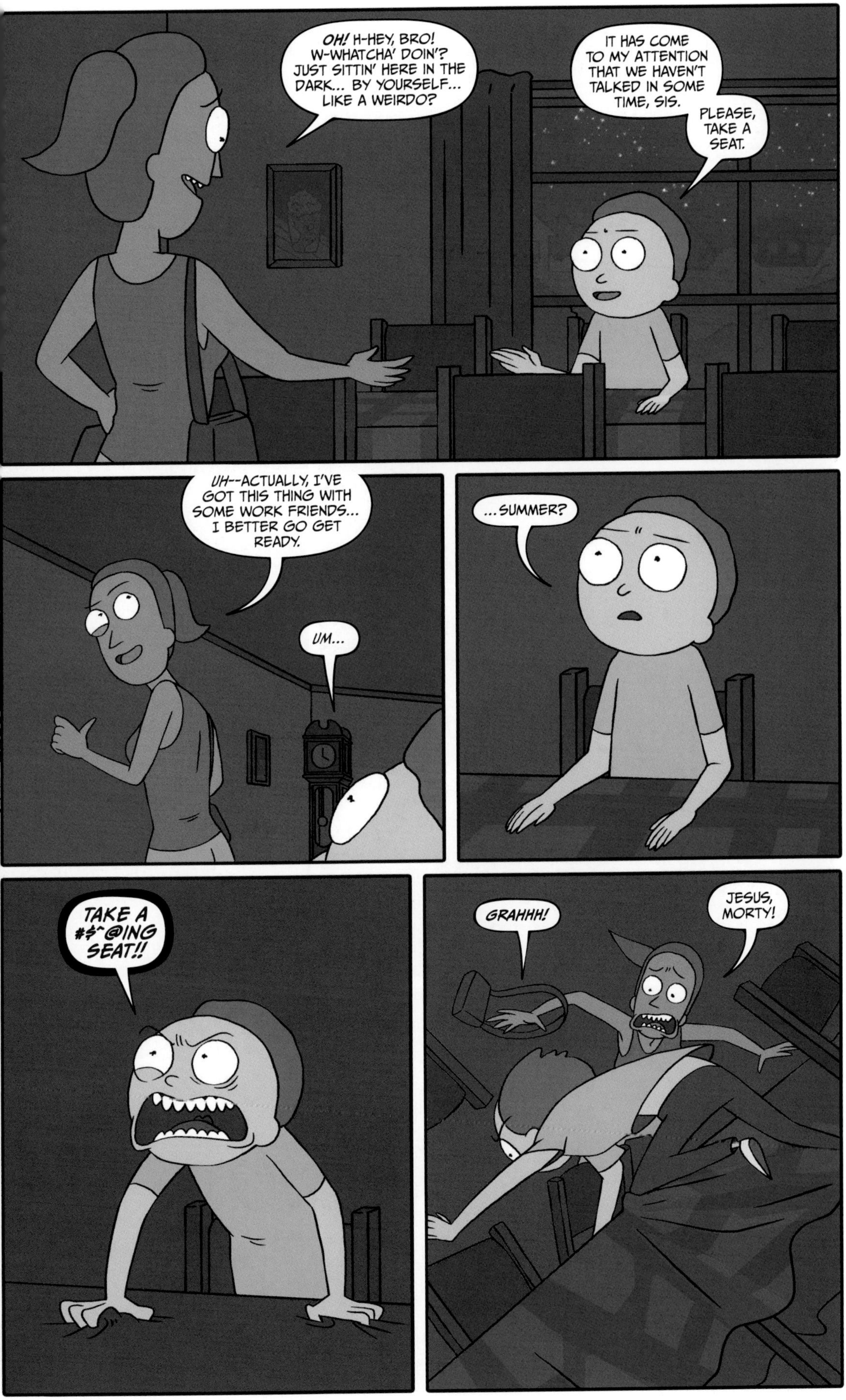
OH! H-HEY, BRO! W-WHATCHA' DOIN'? JUST SITTIN' HERE IN THE DARK... BY YOURSELF... LIKE A WEIRDO?
IT HAS COME TO MY ATTENTION THAT WE HAVEN'T TALKED IN SOME TIME, SIS.
PLEASE, TAKE A SEAT.
UH--ACTUALLY, I'VE GOT THIS THING WITH SOME WORK FRIENDS... I BETTER GO GET READY.
UM...
...SUMMER?
TAKE A #$^@ING SEAT!!
GRAHHH!
JESUS, MORTY!

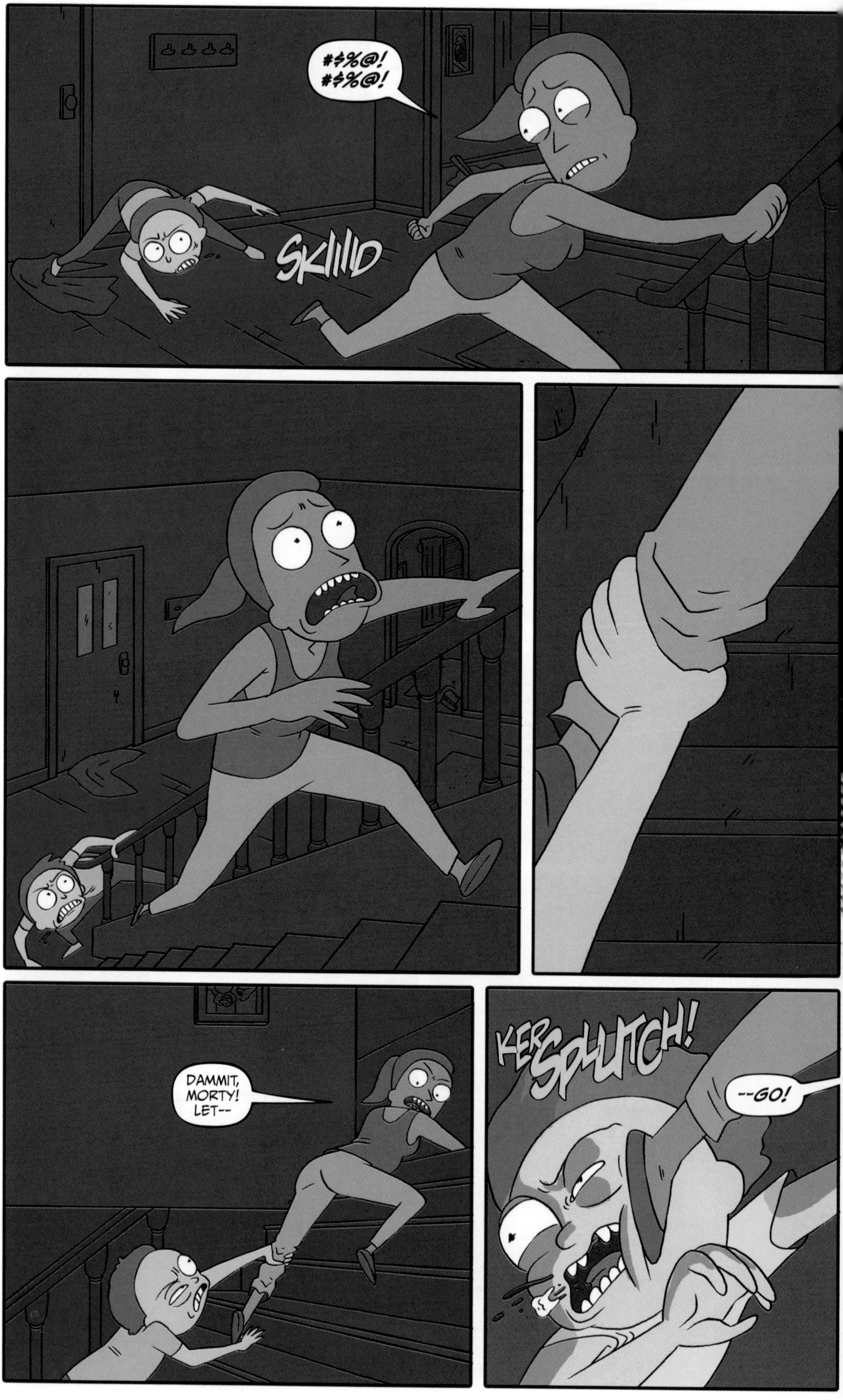
#$%@!
#$%@!
SKIIID
DAMMIT, MORTY! LET--
KERSPLUTCH!
--GO!

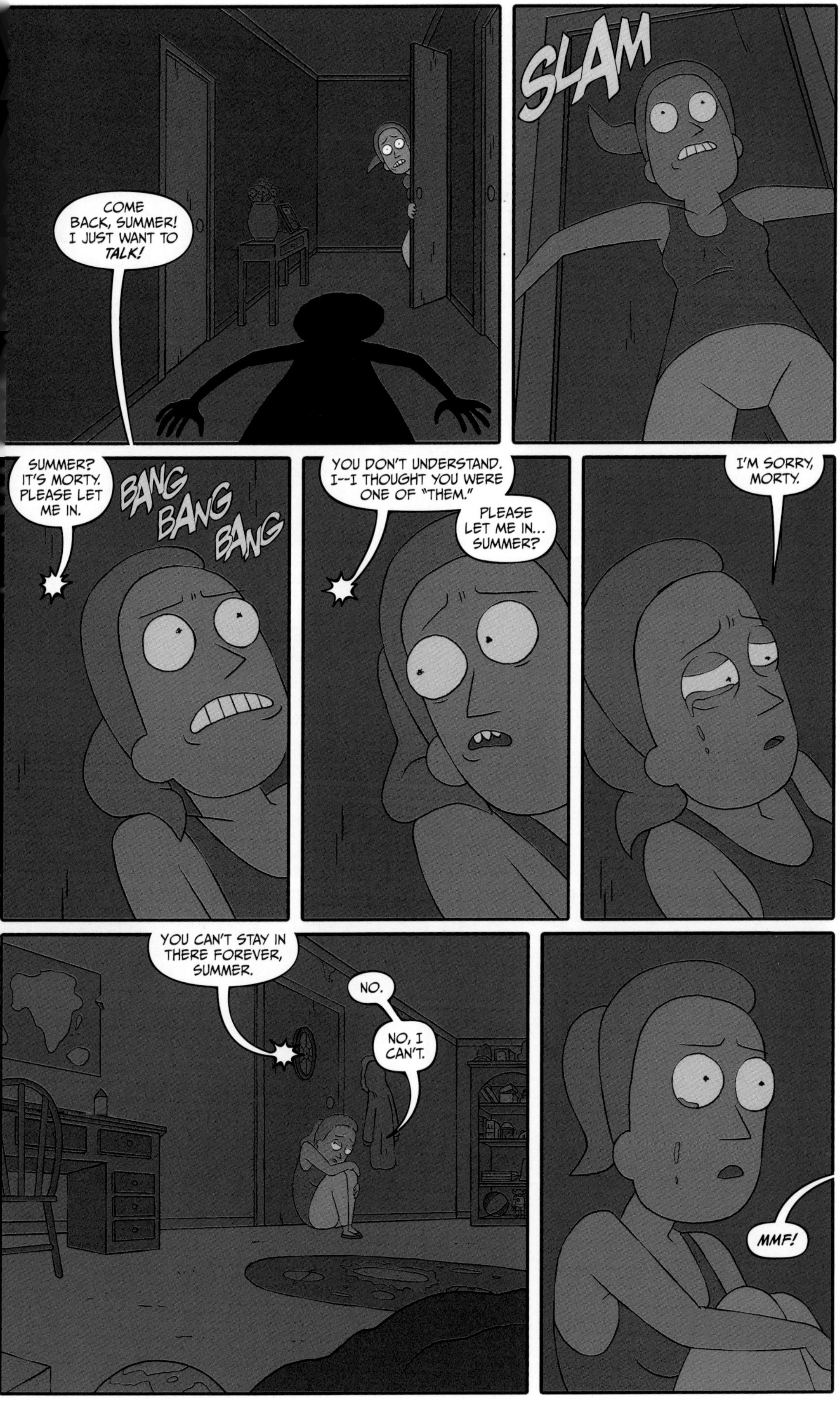
COME BACK, SUMMER! I JUST WANT TO TALK!
SLAM
SUMMER? IT'S MORTY. PLEASE LET ME IN.
BANG BANG BANG
YOU DON'T UNDERSTAND. I--I THOUGHT YOU WERE ONE OF "THEM."
PLEASE LET ME IN... SUMMER?
I'M SORRY, MORTY.
YOU CAN'T STAY IN THERE FOREVER, SUMMER.
NO.
NO, I CAN'T.
MMF!

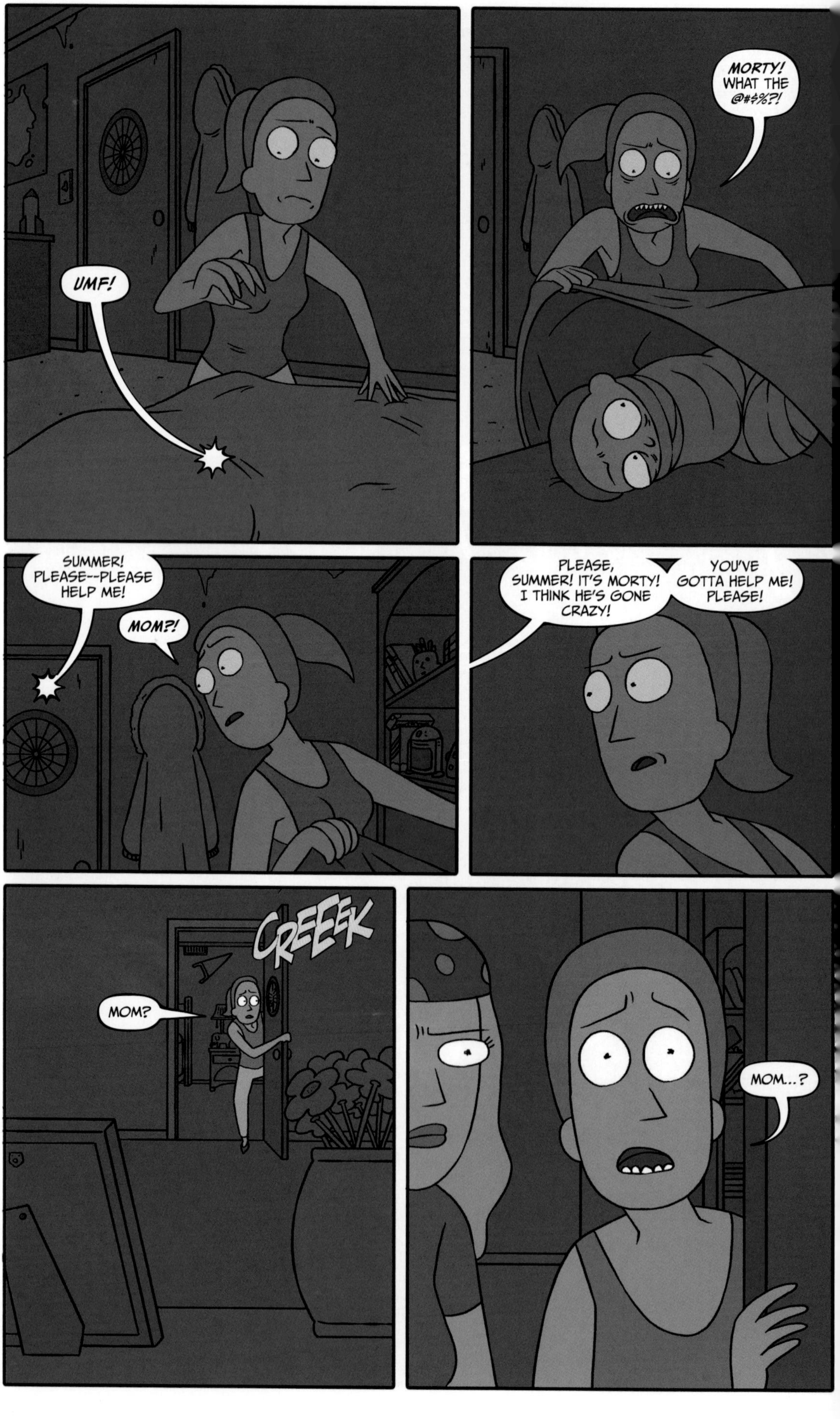
UMF!
MORTY! WHAT THE @#$%?!
SUMMER! PLEASE--PLEASE HELP ME!
MOM?!
PLEASE, SUMMER! IT'S MORTY! I THINK HE'S GONE CRAZY!
YOU'VE GOTTA HELP ME! PLEASE!
CREEEK
MOM?
MOM...?

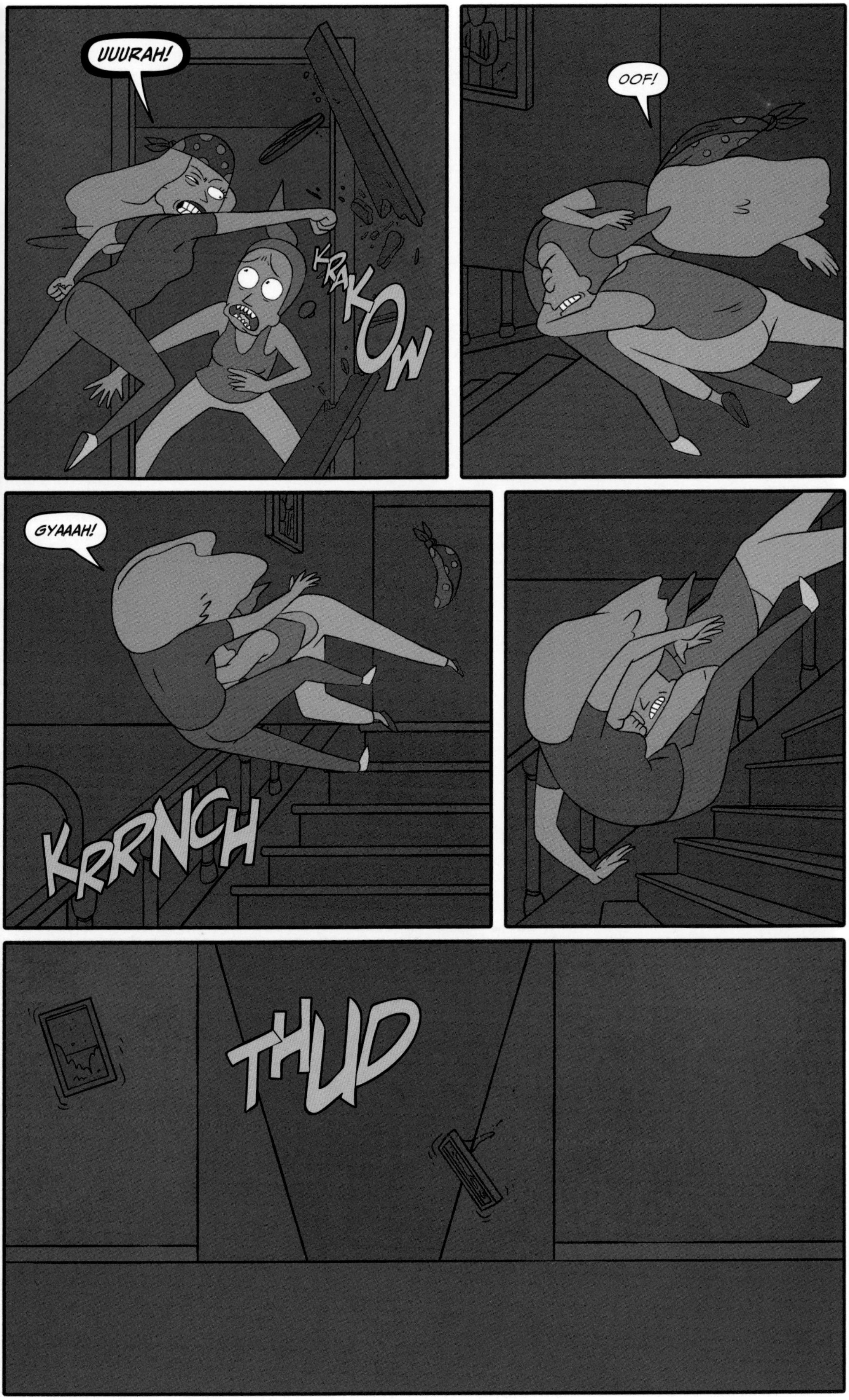
UUURAH!
KRAKOW
OOF!
GYAAAH!
KRRNCH
THUD

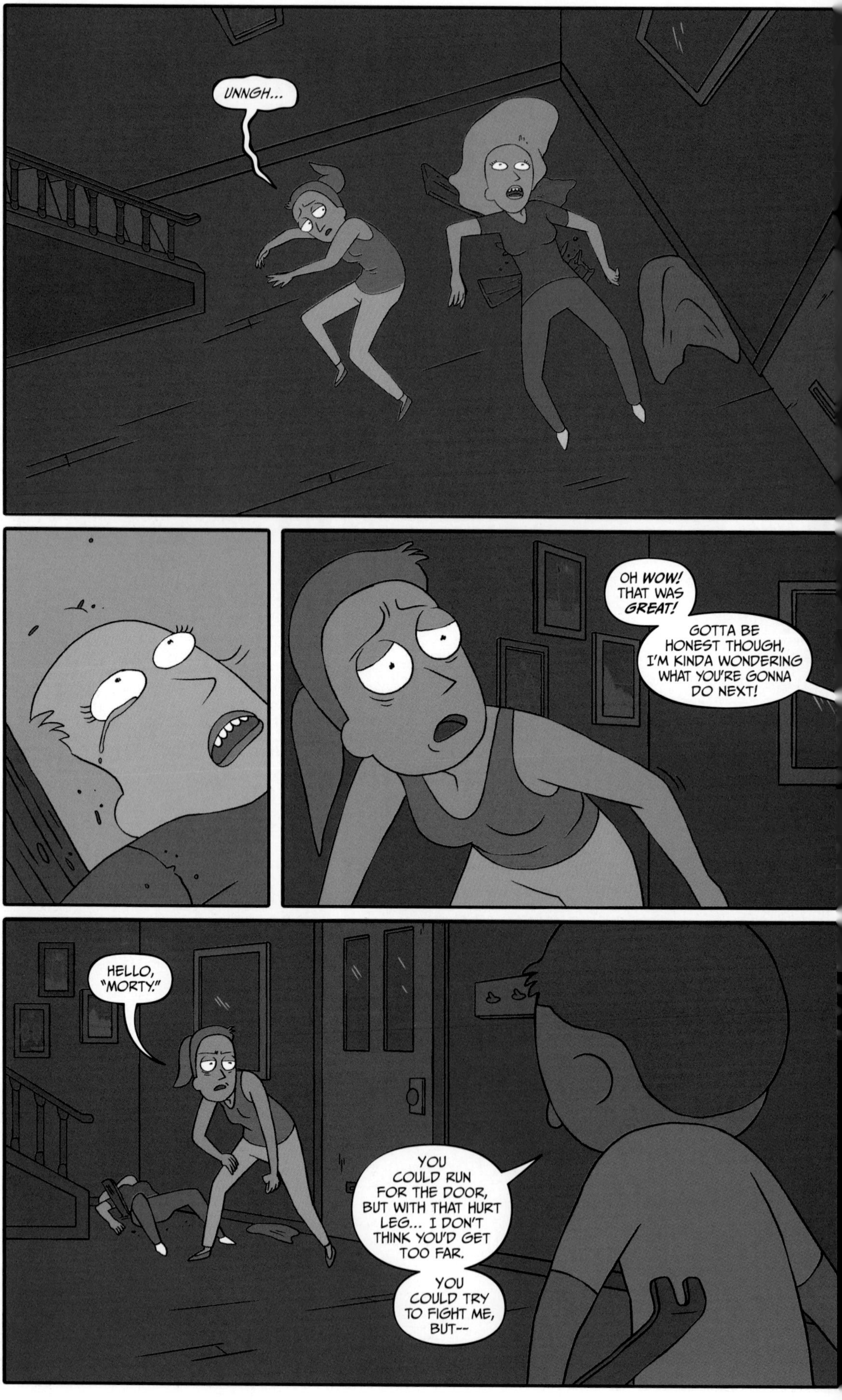
UNNGH...
OH WOW! THAT WAS GREAT!
GOTTA BE HONEST THOUGH, I'M KINDA WONDERING WHAT YOU'RE GONNA DO NEXT!
HELLO, "MORTY."
YOU COULD RUN FOR THE DOOR, BUT WITH THAT HURT LEG... I DON'T THINK YOU'D GET TOO FAR.
YOU COULD TRY TO FIGHT ME, BUT--

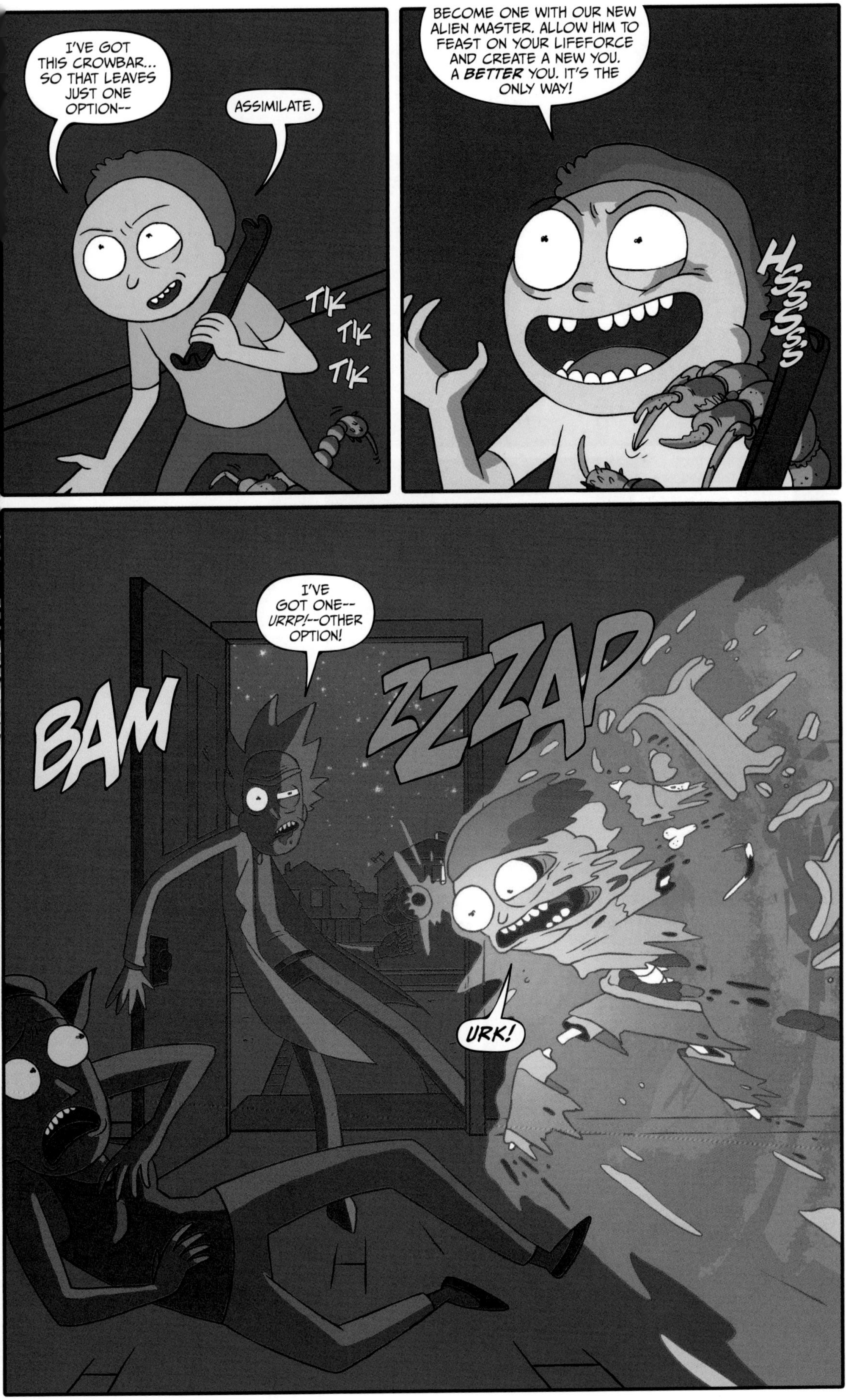
I'VE GOT THIS CROWBAR... SO THAT LEAVES JUST ONE OPTION--
ASSIMILATE.
TIK
TIK
TIK
BECOME ONE WITH OUR NEW ALIEN MASTER. ALLOW HIM TO FEAST ON YOUR LIFEFORCE AND CREATE A NEW YOU. A *BETTER* YOU. IT'S THE ONLY WAY!
HSSSSSS
I'VE GOT ONE-- *URRP!*--OTHER OPTION!
BAM
ZZZAP
URK!

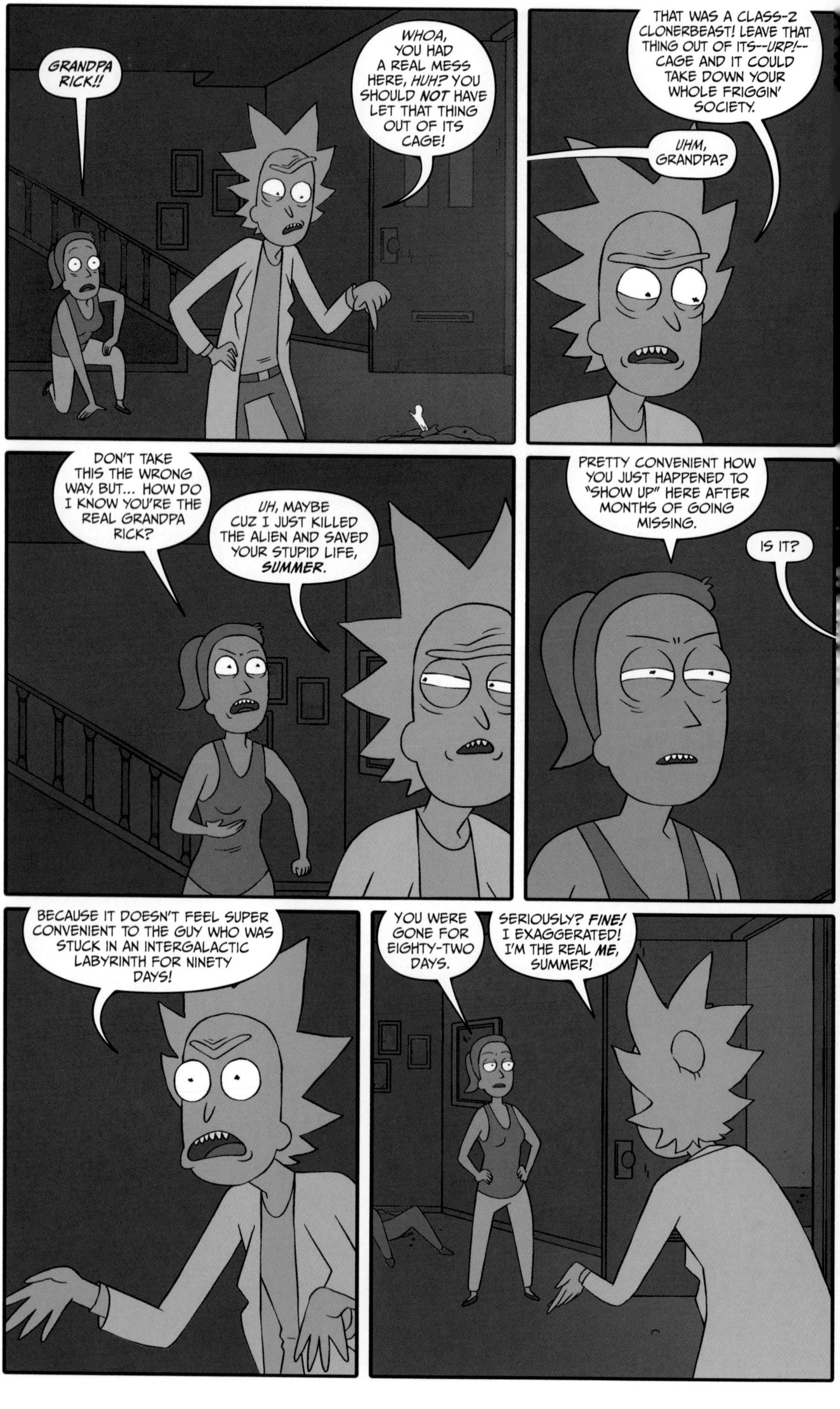
GRANDPA RICK!!
WHOA, YOU HAD A REAL MESS HERE, HUH? YOU SHOULD NOT HAVE LET THAT THING OUT OF ITS CAGE!
THAT WAS A CLASS-2 CLONERBEAST! LEAVE THAT THING OUT OF ITS--URP!-- CAGE AND IT COULD TAKE DOWN YOUR WHOLE FRIGGIN' SOCIETY.
UHM, GRANDPA?
DON'T TAKE THIS THE WRONG WAY, BUT... HOW DO I KNOW YOU'RE THE REAL GRANDPA RICK?
UH, MAYBE CUZ I JUST KILLED THE ALIEN AND SAVED YOUR STUPID LIFE, SUMMER.
PRETTY CONVENIENT HOW YOU JUST HAPPENED TO "SHOW UP" HERE AFTER MONTHS OF GOING MISSING.
IS IT?
BECAUSE IT DOESN'T FEEL SUPER CONVENIENT TO THE GUY WHO WAS STUCK IN AN INTERGALACTIC LABYRINTH FOR NINETY DAYS!
YOU WERE GONE FOR EIGHTY-TWO DAYS.
SERIOUSLY? FINE! I EXAGGERATED! I'M THE REAL ME, SUMMER!

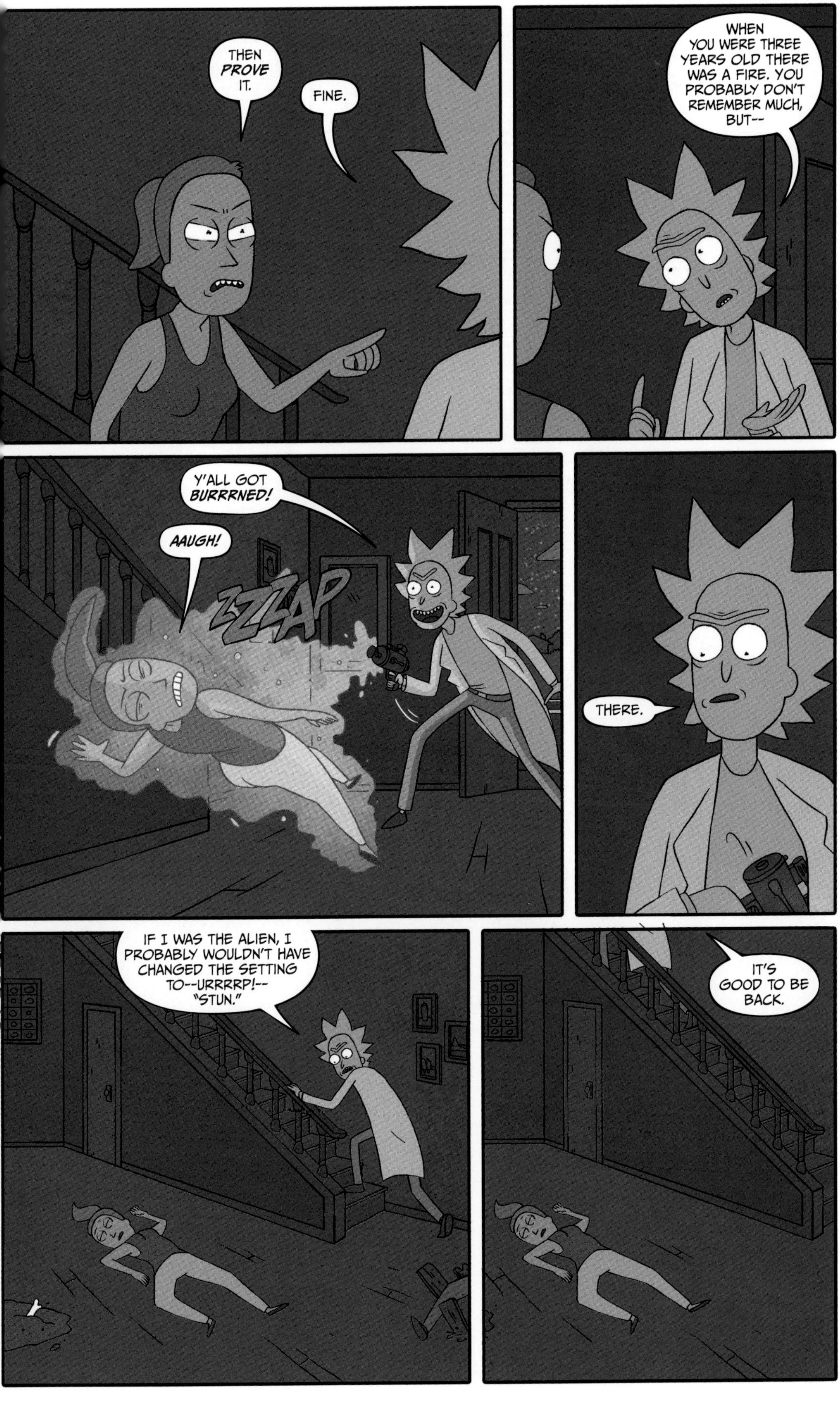
THEN *PROVE* IT.
FINE.
WHEN YOU WERE THREE YEARS OLD THERE WAS A FIRE. YOU PROBABLY DON'T REMEMBER MUCH, BUT--
Y'ALL GOT *BURRRNED!*
AAUGH!
ZZZAP
THERE.
IF I WAS THE ALIEN, I PROBABLY WOULDN'T HAVE CHANGED THE SETTING TO--URRRRP!-- "STUN."
IT'S GOOD TO BE BACK.

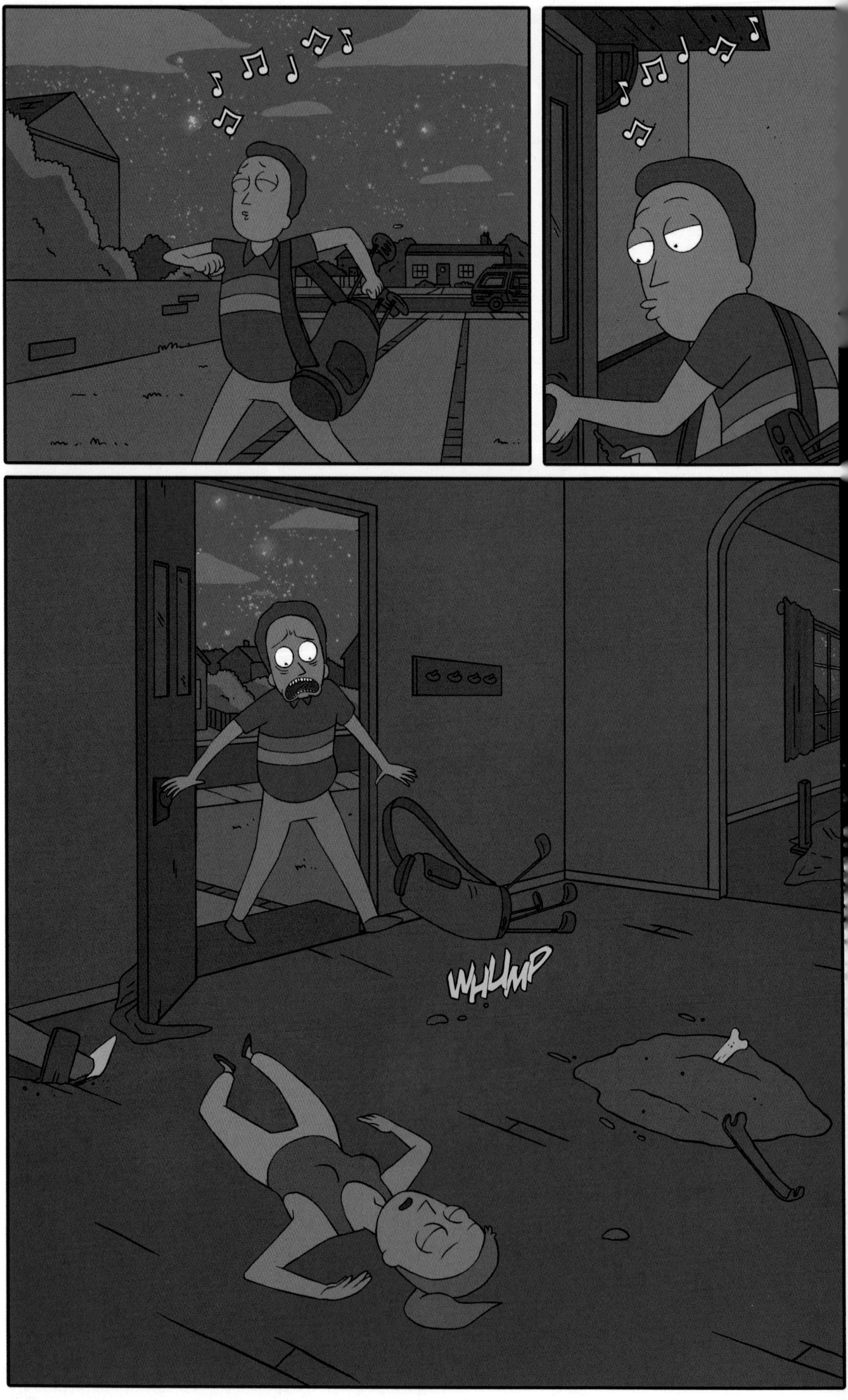
WHUMP

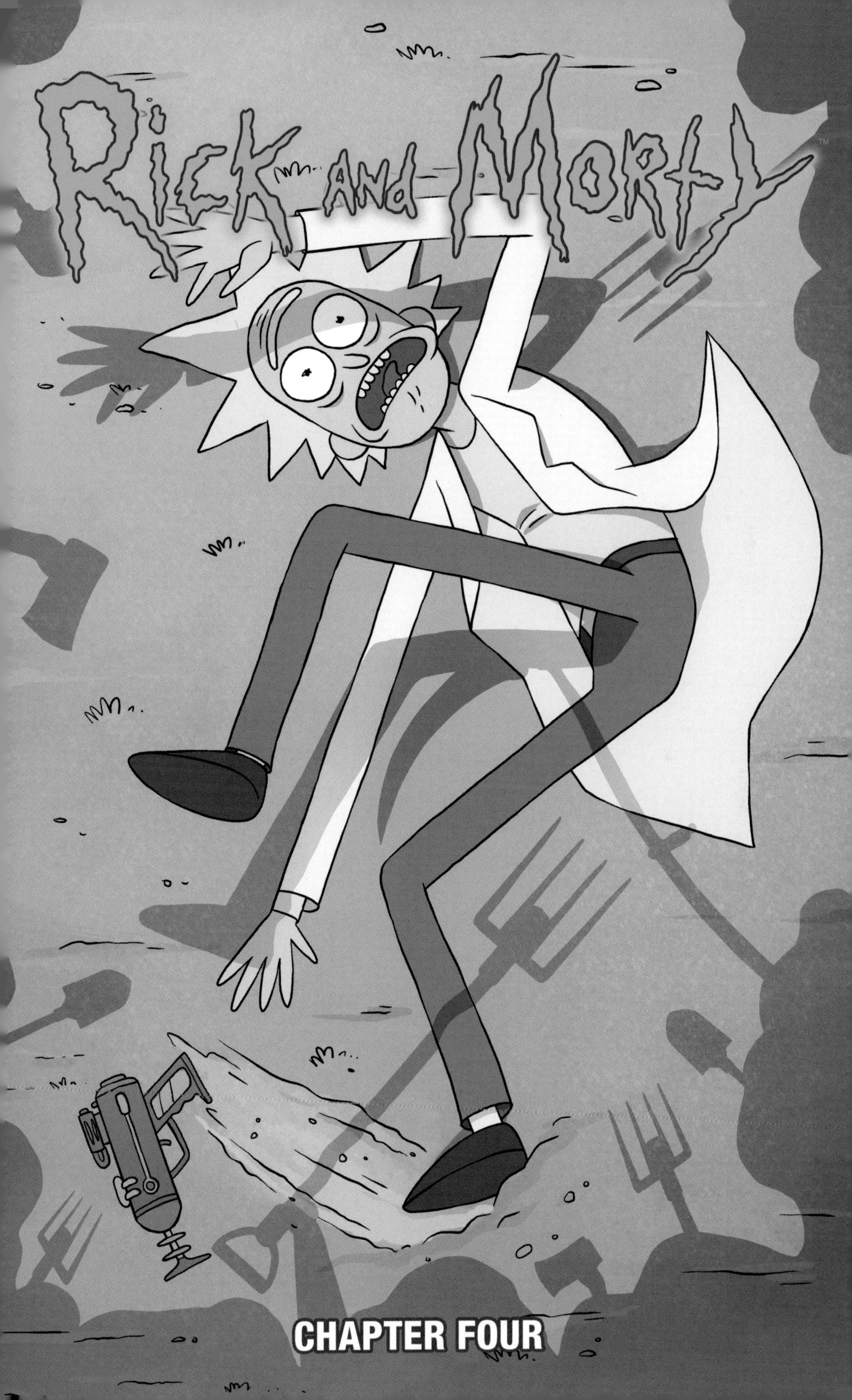
Rick and Morty™

CHAPTER FOUR

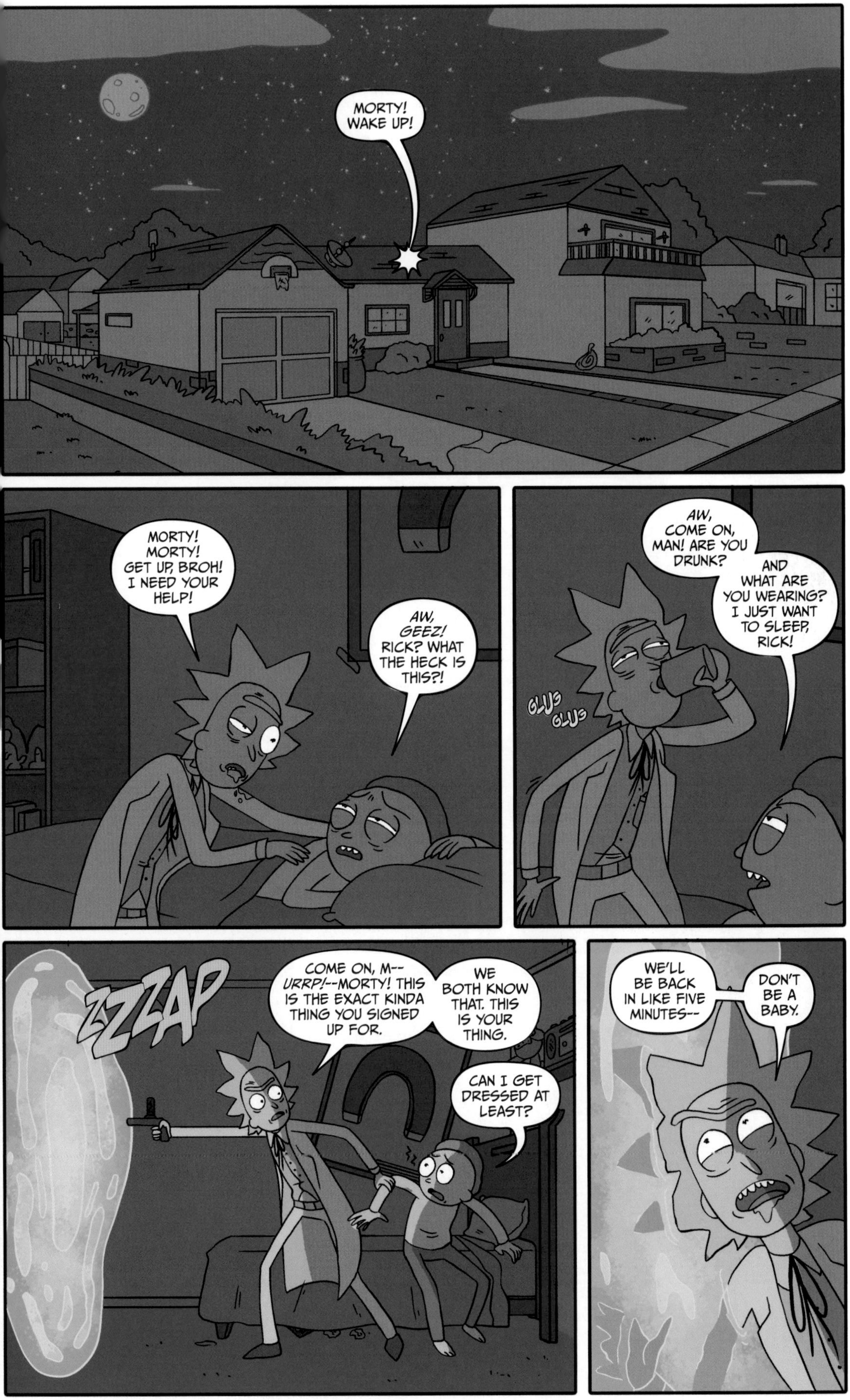
MORTY! WAKE UP!
MORTY! MORTY! GET UP, BROH! I NEED YOUR HELP!
AW, GEEZ! RICK? WHAT THE HECK IS THIS?!
AW, COME ON, MAN! ARE YOU DRUNK?
AND WHAT ARE YOU WEARING? I JUST WANT TO SLEEP, RICK!
GLUG GLUG
ZZZAP
COME ON, M-- URRP!--MORTY! THIS IS THE EXACT KINDA THING YOU SIGNED UP FOR.
WE BOTH KNOW THAT. THIS IS YOUR THING.
CAN I GET DRESSED AT LEAST?
WE'LL BE BACK IN LIKE FIVE MINUTES--
DON'T BE A BABY.

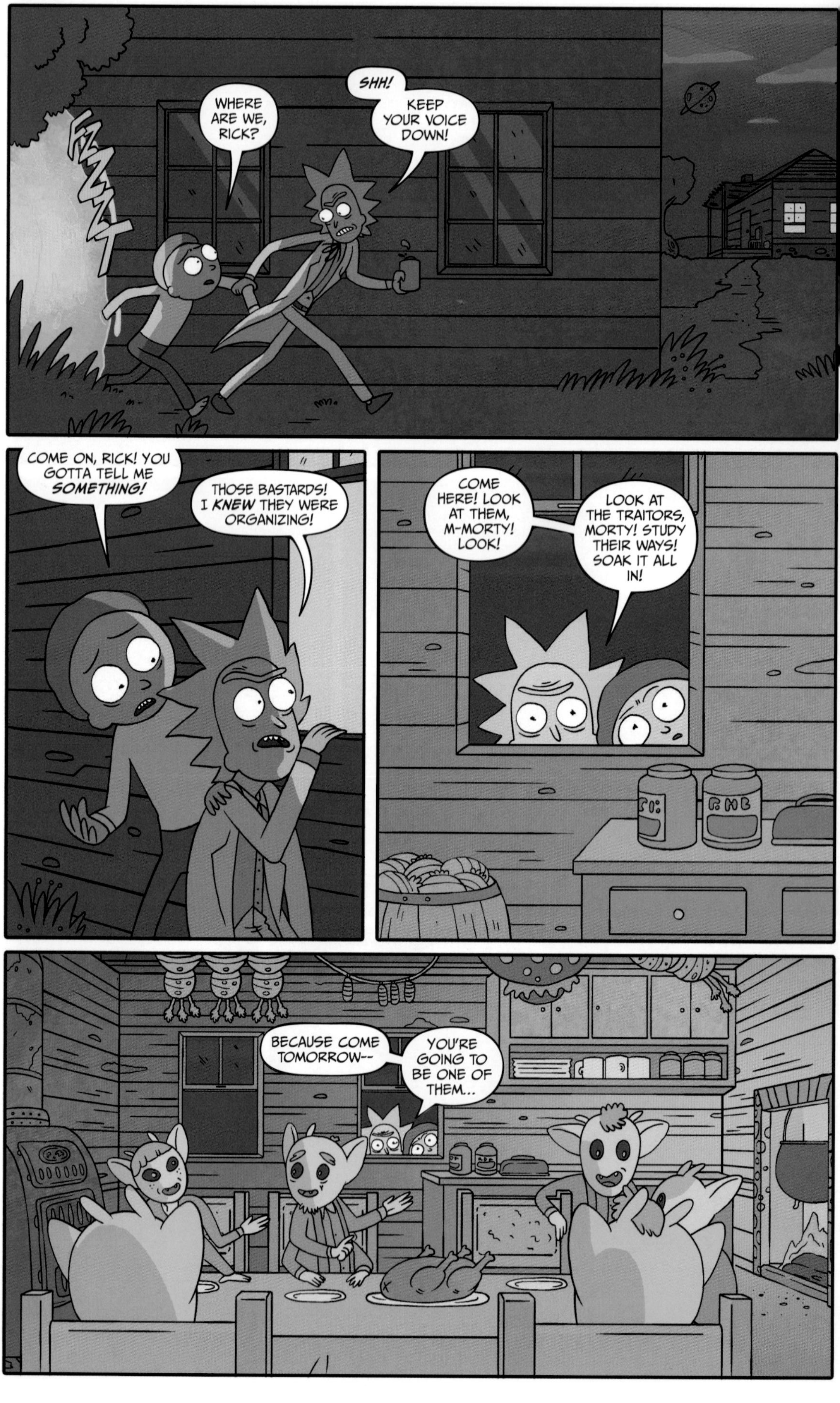
FZZZT
WHERE ARE WE, RICK?
SHH!
KEEP YOUR VOICE DOWN!
COME ON, RICK! YOU GOTTA TELL ME SOMETHING!
THOSE BASTARDS! I KNEW THEY WERE ORGANIZING!
COME HERE! LOOK AT THEM, M-MORTY! LOOK!
LOOK AT THE TRAITORS, MORTY! STUDY THEIR WAYS! SOAK IT ALL IN!
BECAUSE COME TOMORROW--
YOU'RE GOING TO BE ONE OF THEM...

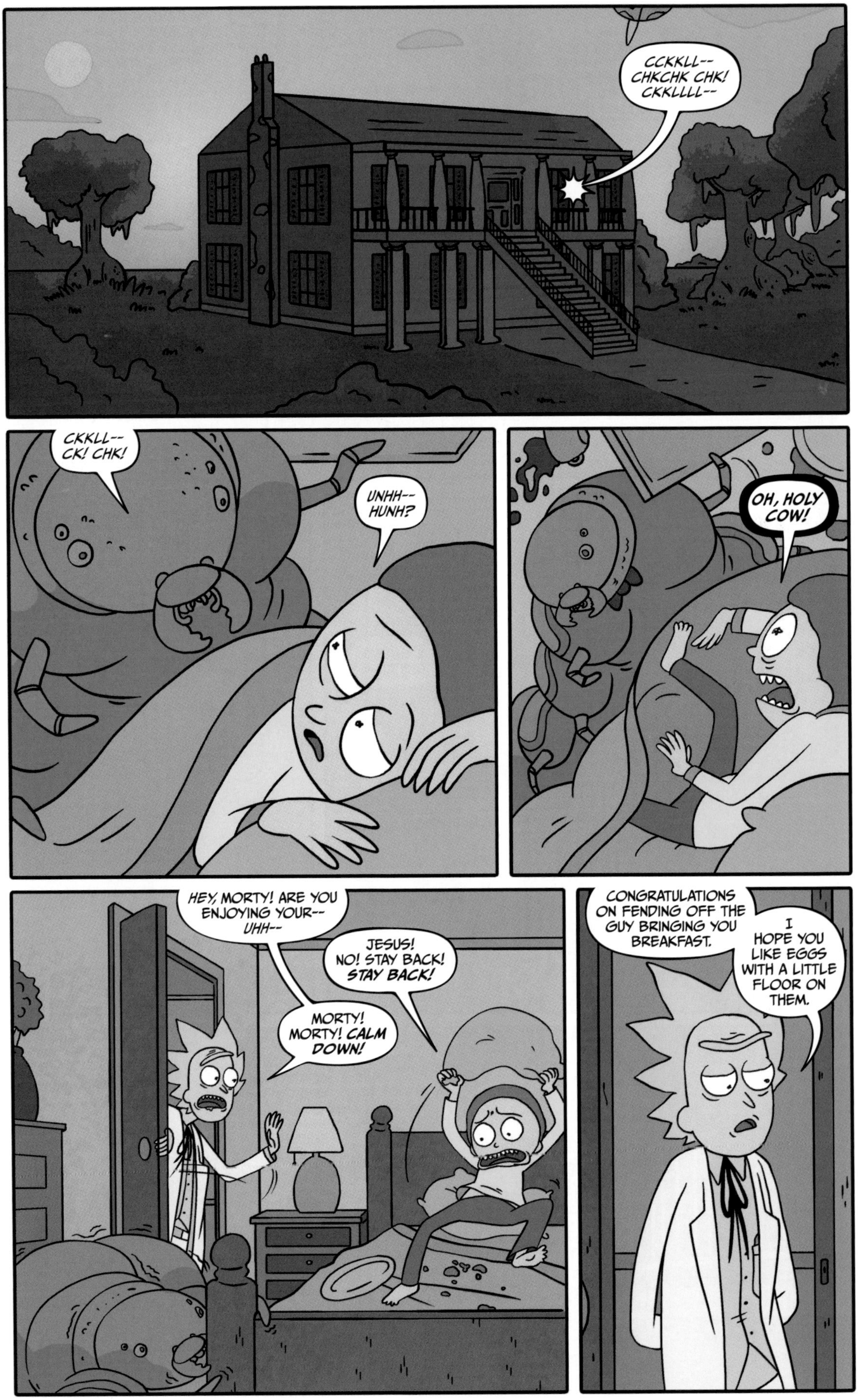
CCKKLL--
CHKCHK CHK!
CKKLLLL--
CKKLL--
CK! CHK!
UNHH--
HUNH?
OH, HOLY
COW!
HEY, MORTY! ARE YOU
ENJOYING YOUR--
UHH--
JESUS!
NO! STAY BACK!
STAY BACK!
MORTY!
MORTY! CALM
DOWN!
CONGRATULATIONS
ON FENDING OFF THE
GUY BRINGING YOU
BREAKFAST.
I
HOPE YOU
LIKE EGGS
WITH A LITTLE
FLOOR ON
THEM.

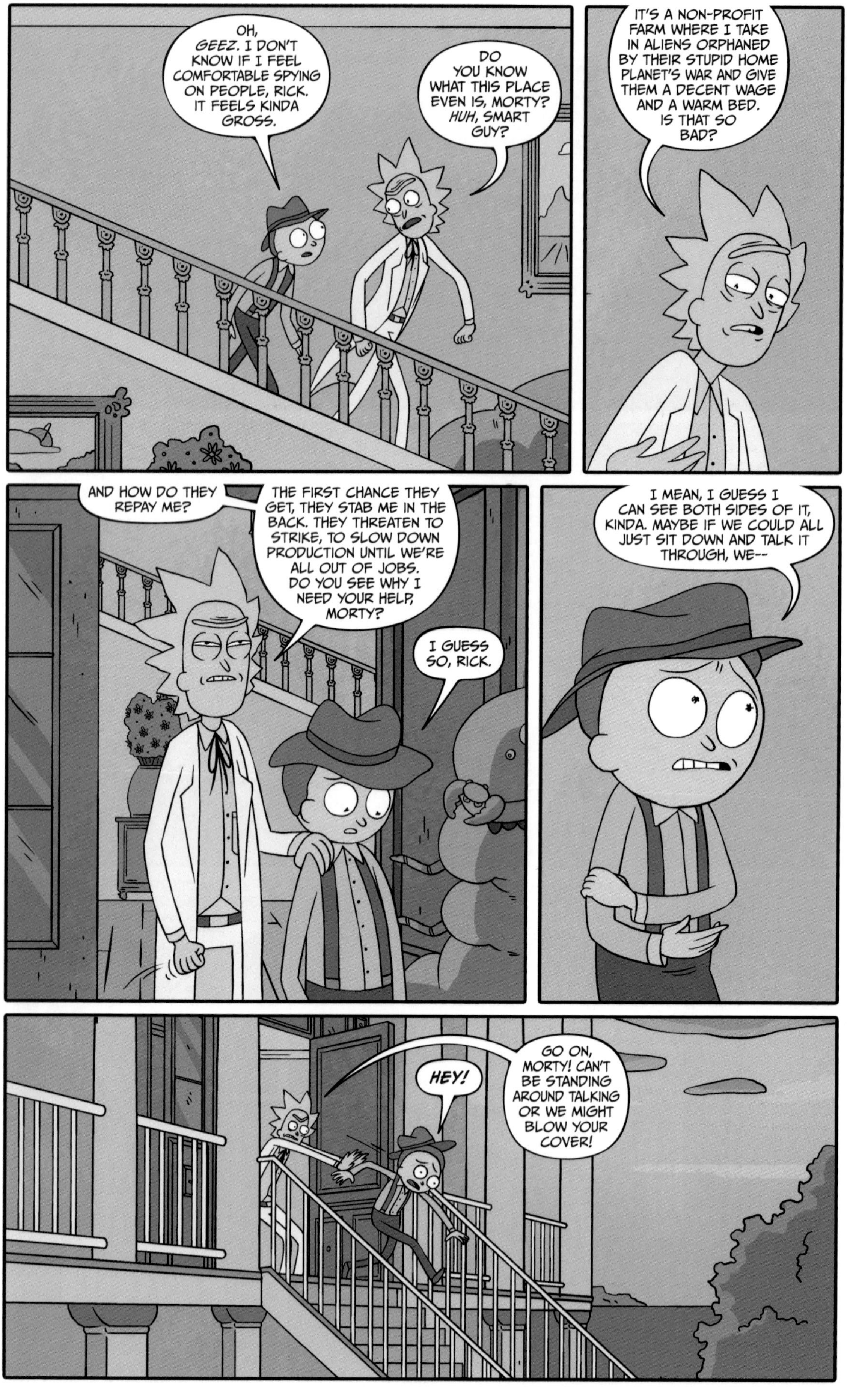
OH, GEEZ. I DON'T KNOW IF I FEEL COMFORTABLE SPYING ON PEOPLE, RICK. IT FEELS KINDA GROSS.
DO YOU KNOW WHAT THIS PLACE EVEN IS, MORTY? HUH, SMART GUY?
IT'S A NON-PROFIT FARM WHERE I TAKE IN ALIENS ORPHANED BY THEIR STUPID HOME PLANET'S WAR AND GIVE THEM A DECENT WAGE AND A WARM BED. IS THAT SO BAD?
AND HOW DO THEY REPAY ME?
THE FIRST CHANCE THEY GET, THEY STAB ME IN THE BACK. THEY THREATEN TO STRIKE, TO SLOW DOWN PRODUCTION UNTIL WE'RE ALL OUT OF JOBS. DO YOU SEE WHY I NEED YOUR HELP, MORTY?
I GUESS SO, RICK.
I MEAN, I GUESS I CAN SEE BOTH SIDES OF IT, KINDA. MAYBE IF WE COULD ALL JUST SIT DOWN AND TALK IT THROUGH, WE--
GO ON, MORTY! CAN'T BE STANDING AROUND TALKING OR WE MIGHT BLOW YOUR COVER!
HEY!

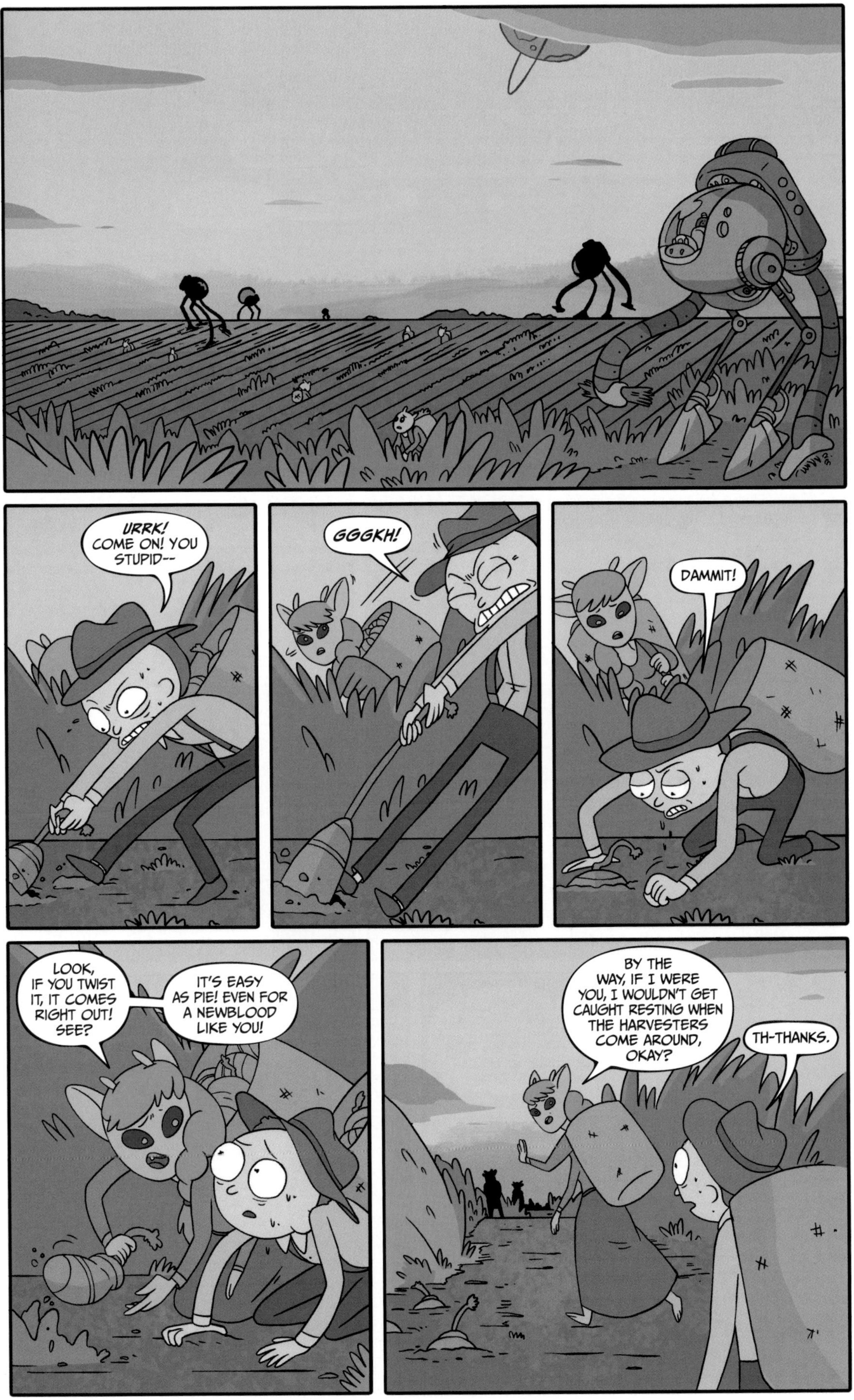
URRK! COME ON! YOU STUPID--
GGGKH!
DAMMIT!
LOOK, IF YOU TWIST IT, IT COMES RIGHT OUT! SEE?
IT'S EASY AS PIE! EVEN FOR A NEWBLOOD LIKE YOU!
BY THE WAY, IF I WERE YOU, I WOULDN'T GET CAUGHT RESTING WHEN THE HARVESTERS COME AROUND, OKAY?
TH-THANKS.

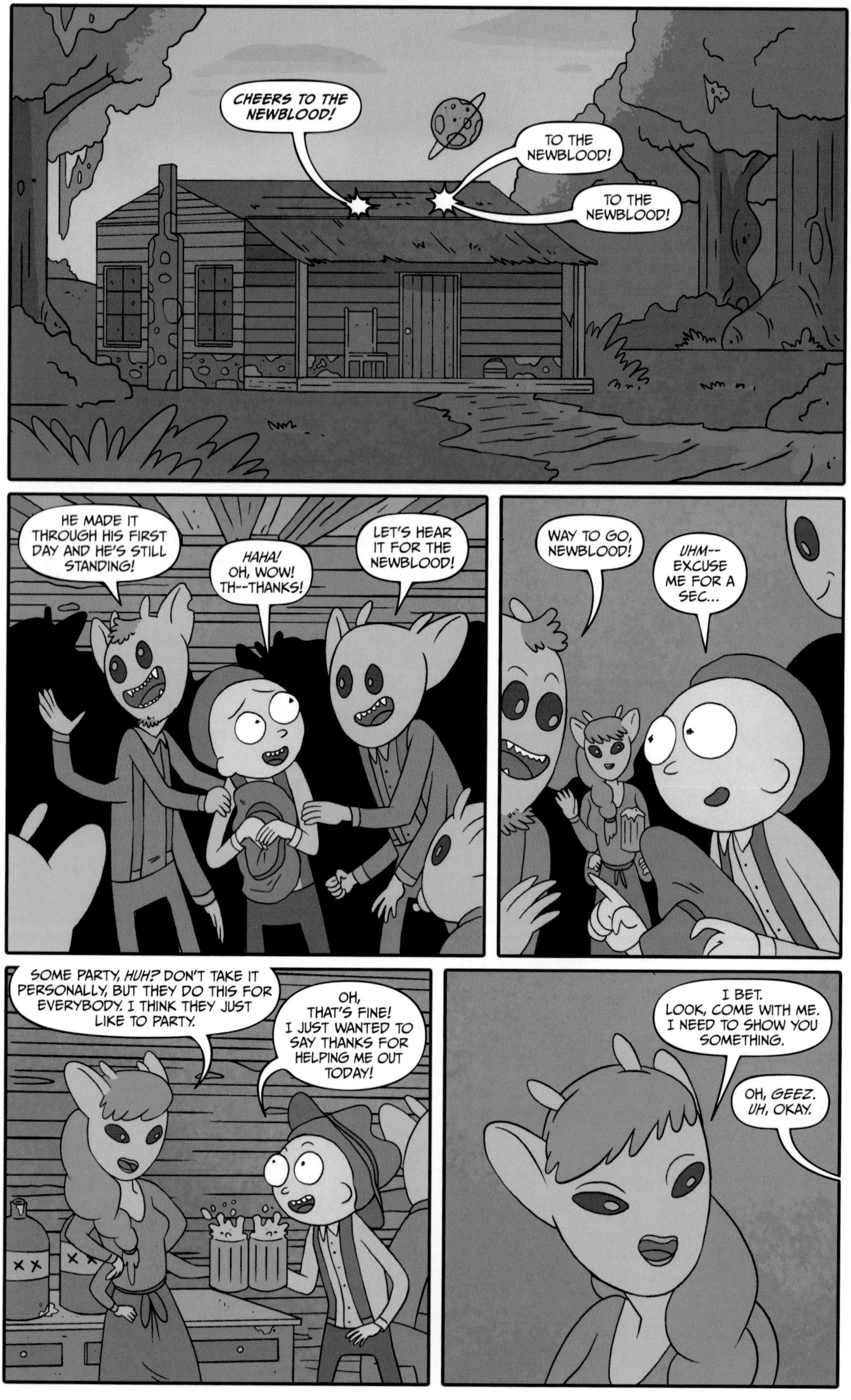
CHEERS TO THE NEWBLOOD!
TO THE NEWBLOOD!
TO THE NEWBLOOD!
HE MADE IT THROUGH HIS FIRST DAY AND HE'S STILL STANDING!
HAHA! OH, WOW! TH--THANKS!
LET'S HEAR IT FOR THE NEWBLOOD!
WAY TO GO, NEWBLOOD!
UHM-- EXCUSE ME FOR A SEC...
SOME PARTY, HUH? DON'T TAKE IT PERSONALLY, BUT THEY DO THIS FOR EVERYBODY. I THINK THEY JUST LIKE TO PARTY.
OH, THAT'S FINE! I JUST WANTED TO SAY THANKS FOR HELPING ME OUT TODAY!
I BET. LOOK, COME WITH ME. I NEED TO SHOW YOU SOMETHING.
OH, GEEZ. UH, OKAY.

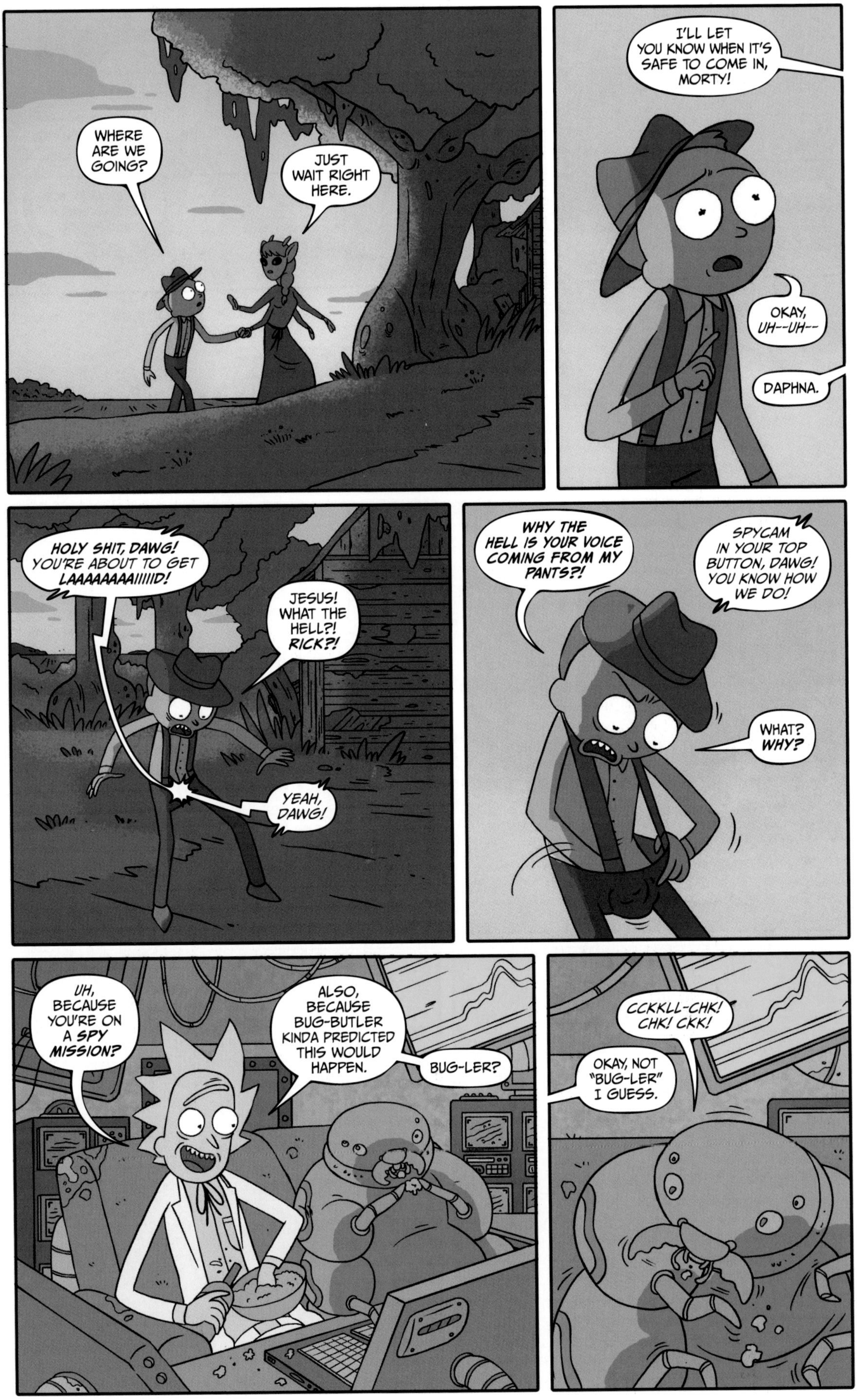

WHERE ARE WE GOING?
JUST WAIT RIGHT HERE.
I'LL LET YOU KNOW WHEN IT'S SAFE TO COME IN, MORTY!
OKAY, UH--UH--
DAPHNA.
HOLY SHIT, DAWG! YOU'RE ABOUT TO GET LAAAAAAAAIIIIID!
JESUS! WHAT THE HELL?! RICK?!
YEAH, DAWG!
WHY THE HELL IS YOUR VOICE COMING FROM MY PANTS?!
SPYCAM IN YOUR TOP BUTTON, DAWG! YOU KNOW HOW WE DO!
WHAT? WHY?
UH, BECAUSE YOU'RE ON A SPY MISSION?
ALSO, BECAUSE BUG-BUTLER KINDA PREDICTED THIS WOULD HAPPEN.
BUG-LER?
CCKKLL-CHK! CHK! CKK!
OKAY, NOT "BUG-LER" I GUESS.

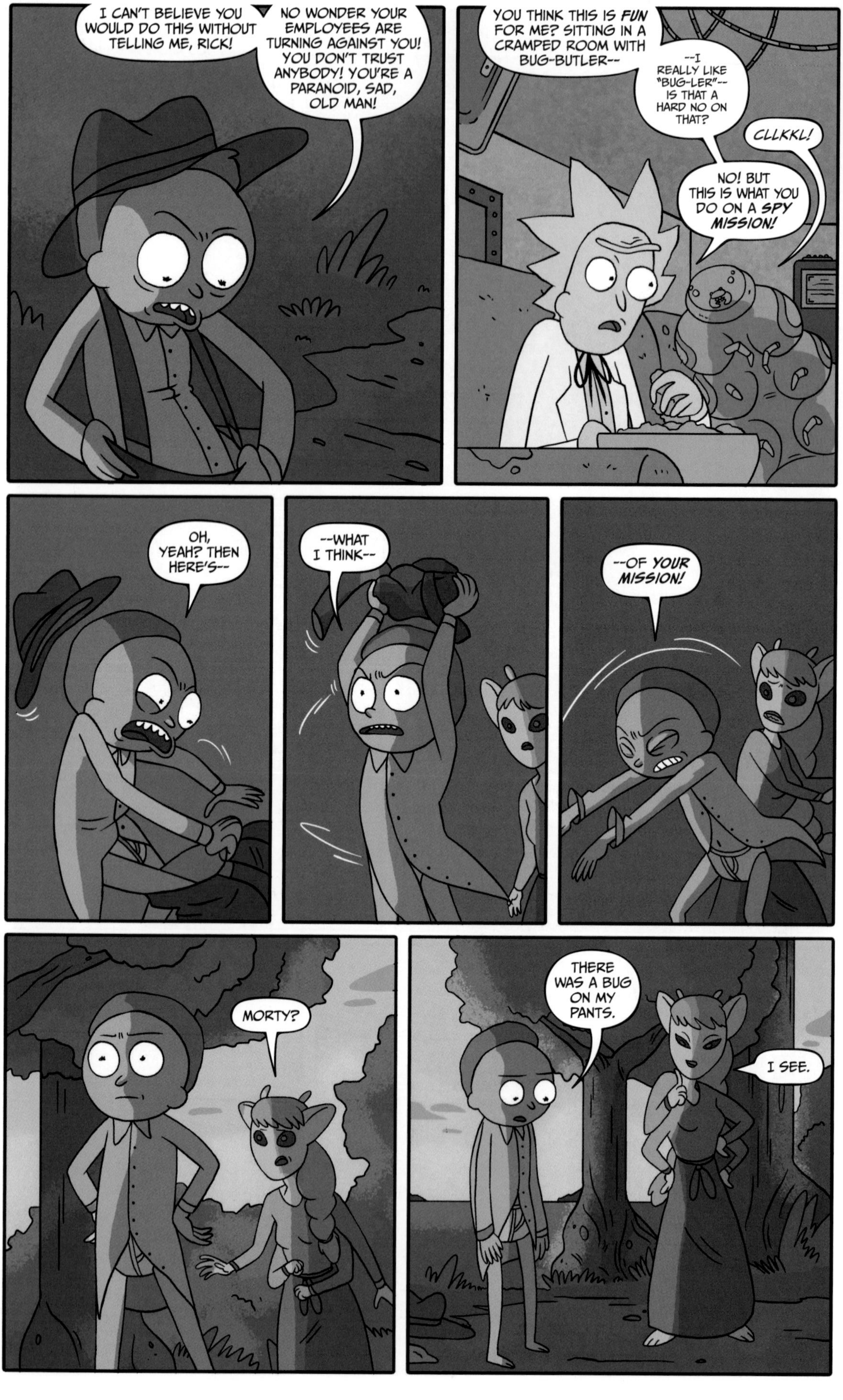
I CAN'T BELIEVE YOU WOULD DO THIS WITHOUT TELLING ME, RICK!
NO WONDER YOUR EMPLOYEES ARE TURNING AGAINST YOU! YOU DON'T TRUST ANYBODY! YOU'RE A PARANOID, SAD, OLD MAN!
YOU THINK THIS IS FUN FOR ME? SITTING IN A CRAMPED ROOM WITH BUG-BUTLER--
--I REALLY LIKE "BUG-LER"-- IS THAT A HARD NO ON THAT?
CLLKKL!
NO! BUT THIS IS WHAT YOU DO ON A SPY MISSION!
OH, YEAH? THEN HERE'S--
--WHAT I THINK--
--OF YOUR MISSION!
MORTY?
THERE WAS A BUG ON MY PANTS.
I SEE.

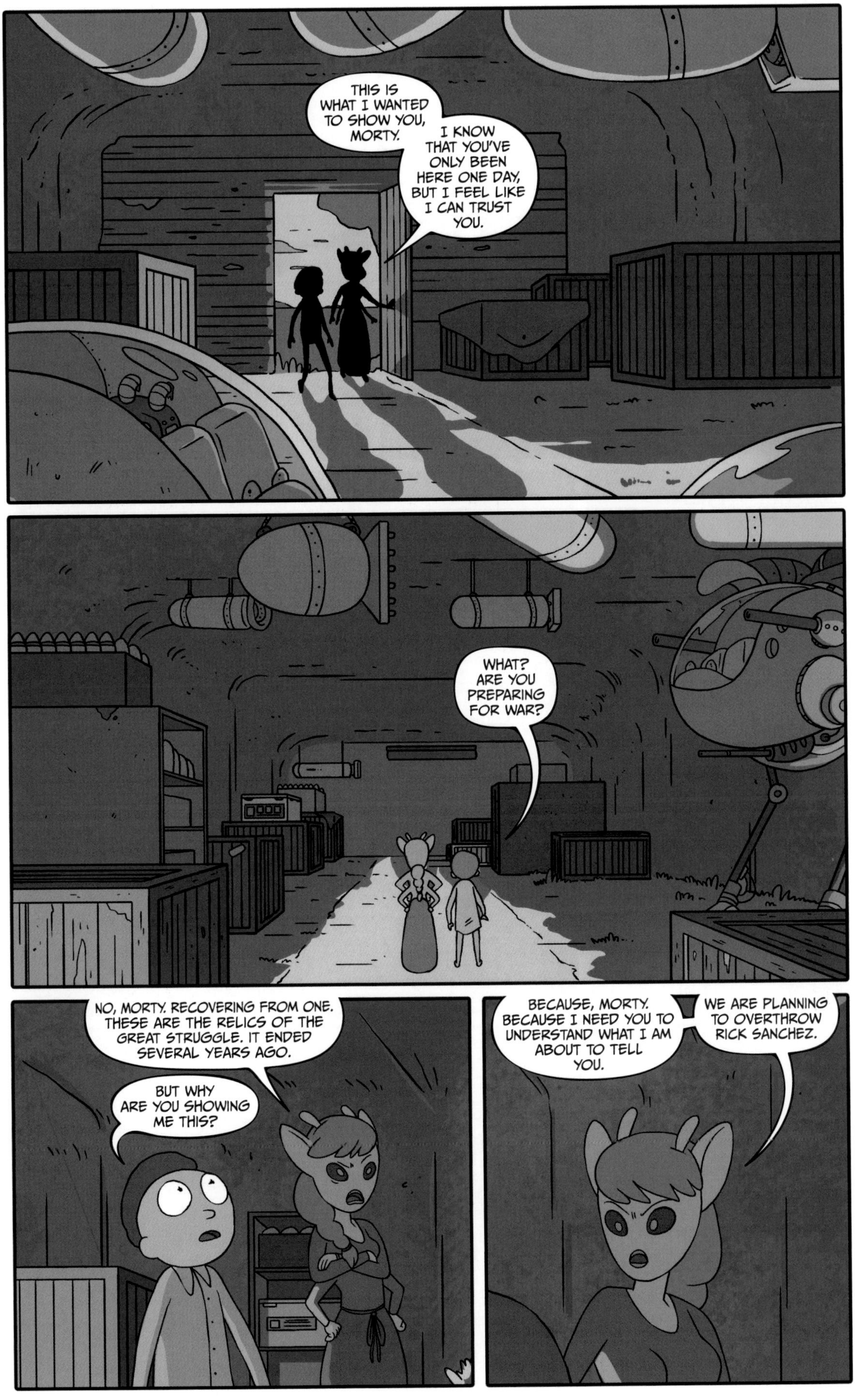
THIS IS WHAT I WANTED TO SHOW YOU, MORTY.
I KNOW THAT YOU'VE ONLY BEEN HERE ONE DAY, BUT I FEEL LIKE I CAN TRUST YOU.
WHAT? ARE YOU PREPARING FOR WAR?
NO, MORTY. RECOVERING FROM ONE. THESE ARE THE RELICS OF THE GREAT STRUGGLE. IT ENDED SEVERAL YEARS AGO.
BUT WHY ARE YOU SHOWING ME THIS?
BECAUSE, MORTY. BECAUSE I NEED YOU TO UNDERSTAND WHAT I AM ABOUT TO TELL YOU.
WE ARE PLANNING TO OVERTHROW RICK SANCHEZ.

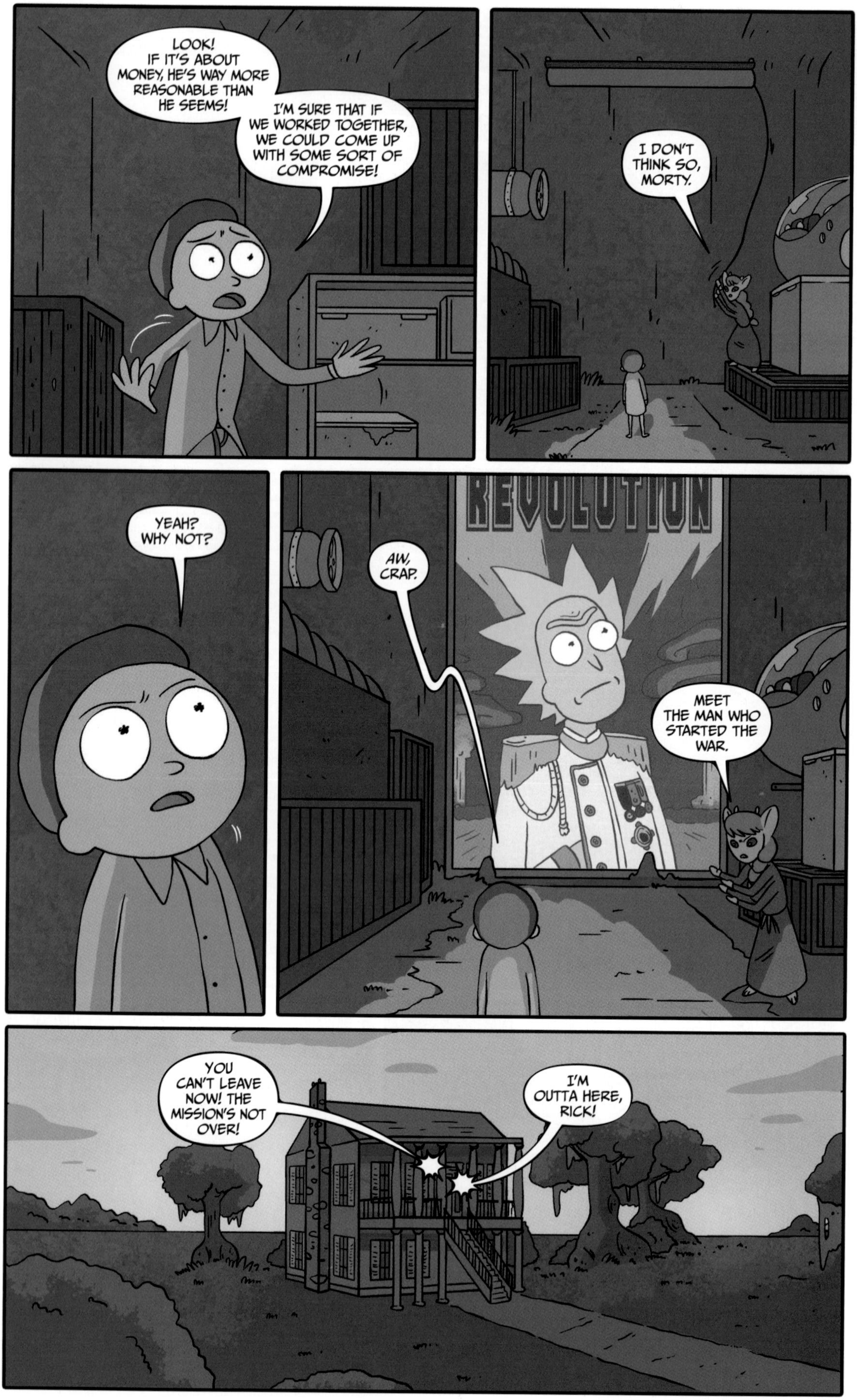
LOOK! IF IT'S ABOUT MONEY, HE'S WAY MORE REASONABLE THAN HE SEEMS!
I'M SURE THAT IF WE WORKED TOGETHER, WE COULD COME UP WITH SOME SORT OF COMPROMISE!
I DON'T THINK SO, MORTY.
YEAH? WHY NOT?
AW, CRAP.
REVOLUTION
MEET THE MAN WHO STARTED THE WAR.
YOU CAN'T LEAVE NOW! THE MISSION'S NOT OVER!
I'M OUTTA HERE, RICK!

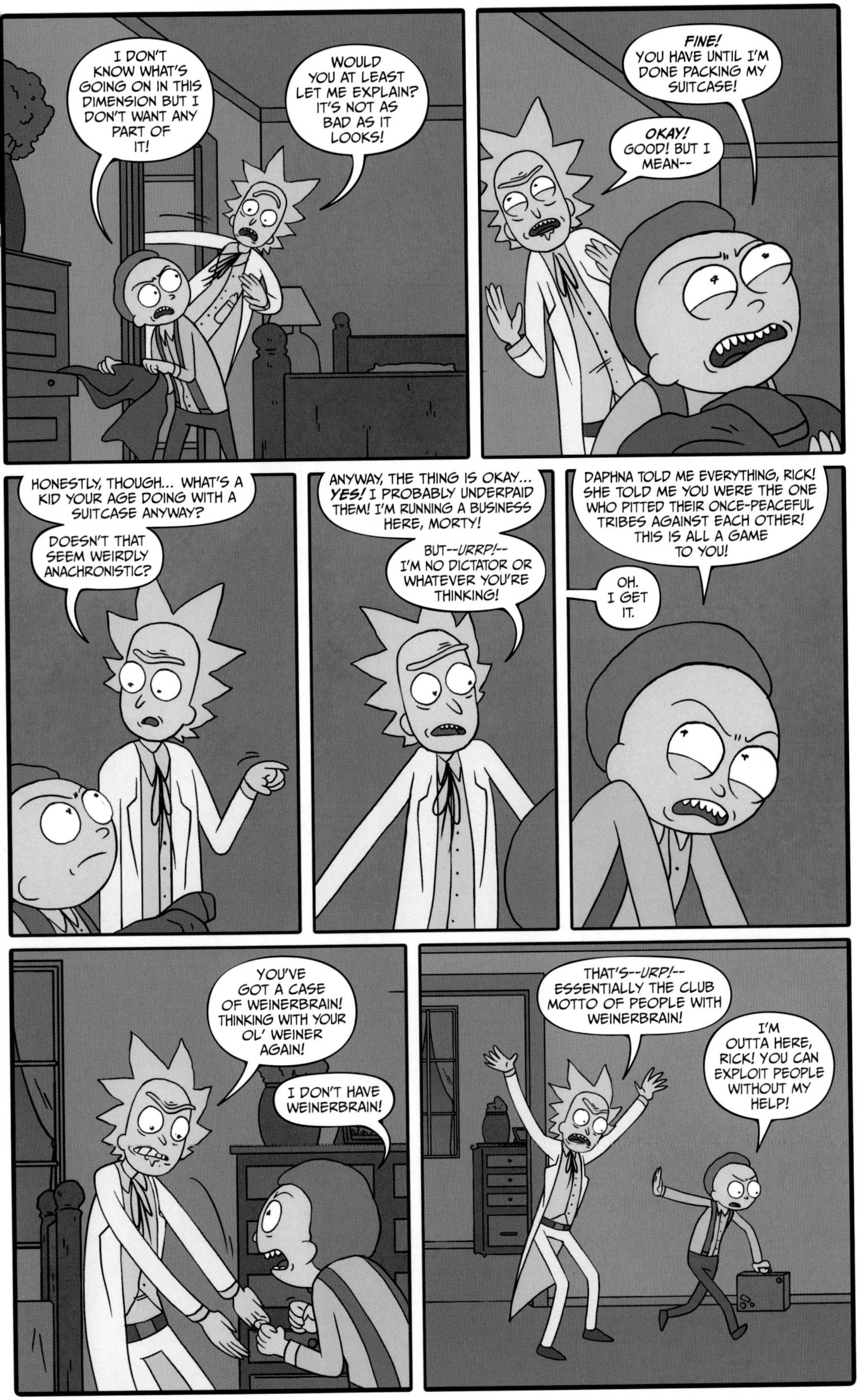
I DON'T KNOW WHAT'S GOING ON IN THIS DIMENSION BUT I DON'T WANT ANY PART OF IT!
WOULD YOU AT LEAST LET ME EXPLAIN? IT'S NOT AS BAD AS IT LOOKS!
FINE! YOU HAVE UNTIL I'M DONE PACKING MY SUITCASE!
OKAY! GOOD! BUT I MEAN--
HONESTLY, THOUGH... WHAT'S A KID YOUR AGE DOING WITH A SUITCASE ANYWAY?
DOESN'T THAT SEEM WEIRDLY ANACHRONISTIC?
ANYWAY, THE THING IS OKAY... YES! I PROBABLY UNDERPAID THEM! I'M RUNNING A BUSINESS HERE, MORTY!
BUT--URRP!-- I'M NO DICTATOR OR WHATEVER YOU'RE THINKING!
DAPHNA TOLD ME EVERYTHING, RICK! SHE TOLD ME YOU WERE THE ONE WHO PITTED THEIR ONCE-PEACEFUL TRIBES AGAINST EACH OTHER! THIS IS ALL A GAME TO YOU!
OH. I GET IT.
YOU'VE GOT A CASE OF WEINERBRAIN! THINKING WITH YOUR OL' WEINER AGAIN!
I DON'T HAVE WEINERBRAIN!
THAT'S--URP!-- ESSENTIALLY THE CLUB MOTTO OF PEOPLE WITH WEINERBRAIN!
I'M OUTTA HERE, RICK! YOU CAN EXPLOIT PEOPLE WITHOUT MY HELP!

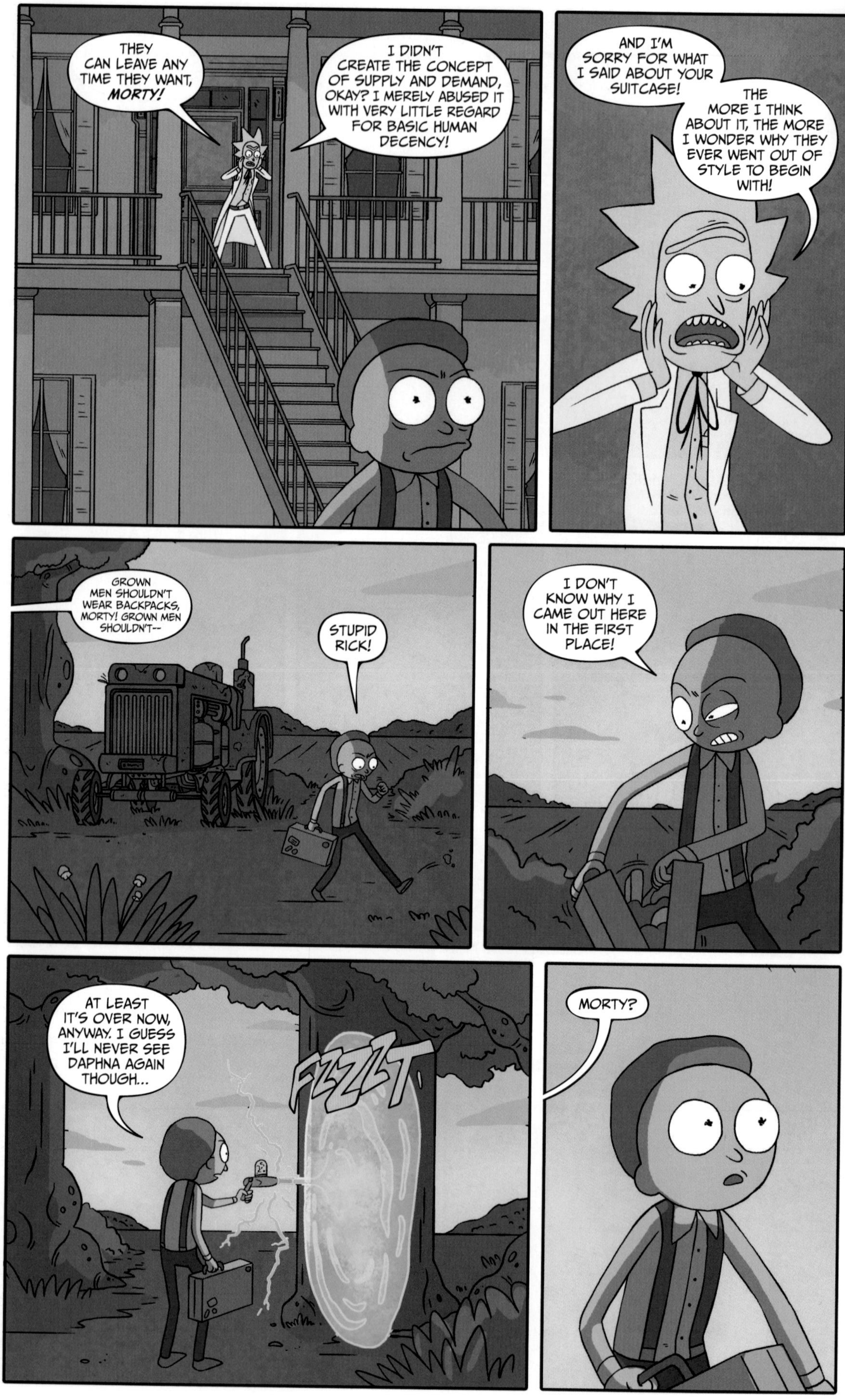
THEY CAN LEAVE ANY TIME THEY WANT, MORTY!
I DIDN'T CREATE THE CONCEPT OF SUPPLY AND DEMAND, OKAY? I MERELY ABUSED IT WITH VERY LITTLE REGARD FOR BASIC HUMAN DECENCY!
AND I'M SORRY FOR WHAT I SAID ABOUT YOUR SUITCASE!
THE MORE I THINK ABOUT IT, THE MORE I WONDER WHY THEY EVER WENT OUT OF STYLE TO BEGIN WITH!
GROWN MEN SHOULDN'T WEAR BACKPACKS, MORTY! GROWN MEN SHOULDN'T--
STUPID RICK!
I DON'T KNOW WHY I CAME OUT HERE IN THE FIRST PLACE!
AT LEAST IT'S OVER NOW, ANYWAY. I GUESS I'LL NEVER SEE DAPHNA AGAIN THOUGH...
FZZZT
MORTY?

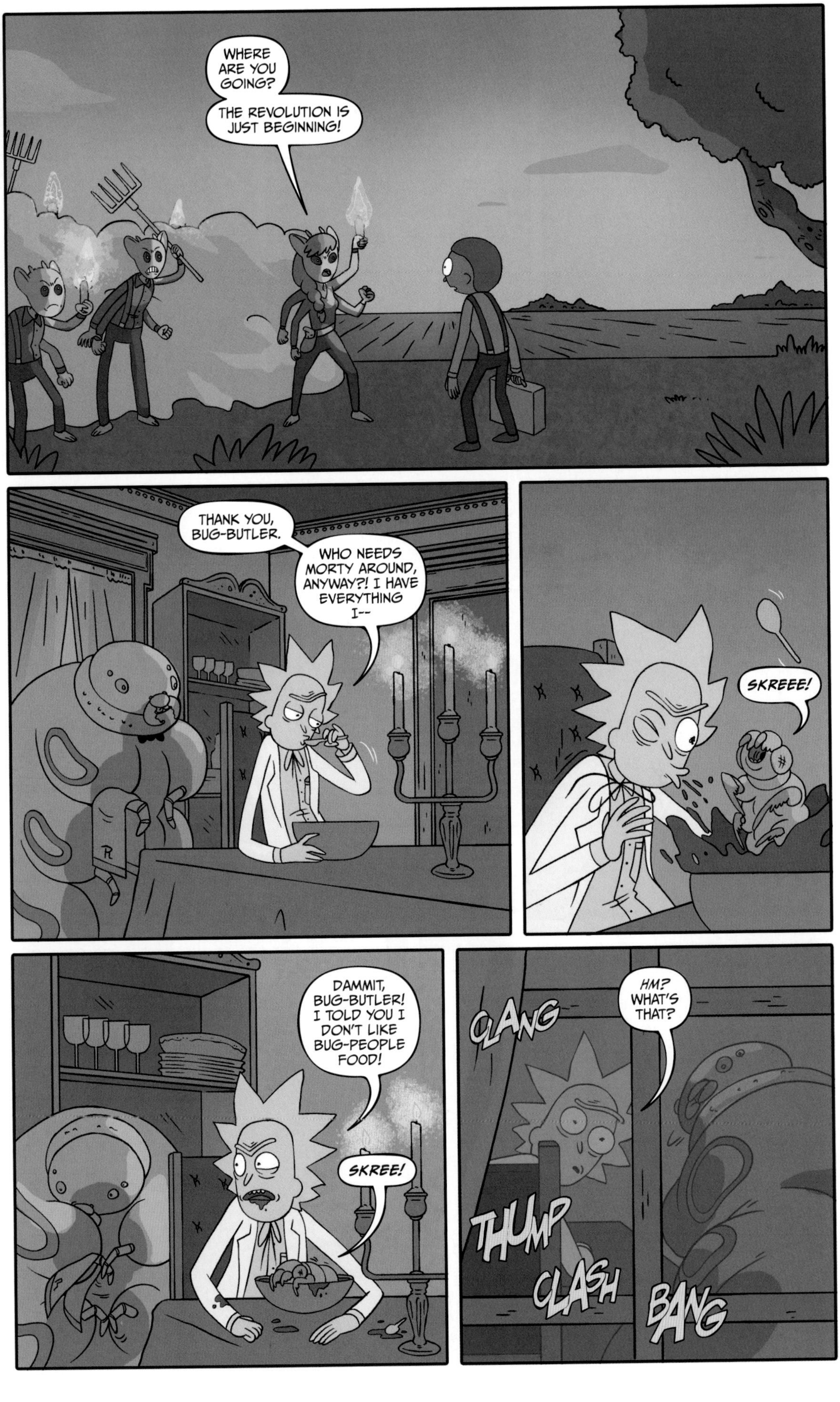
WHERE ARE YOU GOING?
THE REVOLUTION IS JUST BEGINNING!
THANK YOU, BUG-BUTLER.
WHO NEEDS MORTY AROUND, ANYWAY?! I HAVE EVERYTHING I--
SKREEE!
DAMMIT, BUG-BUTLER! I TOLD YOU I DON'T LIKE BUG-PEOPLE FOOD!
SKREE!
CLANG
HM? WHAT'S THAT?
THUMP
CLASH
BANG

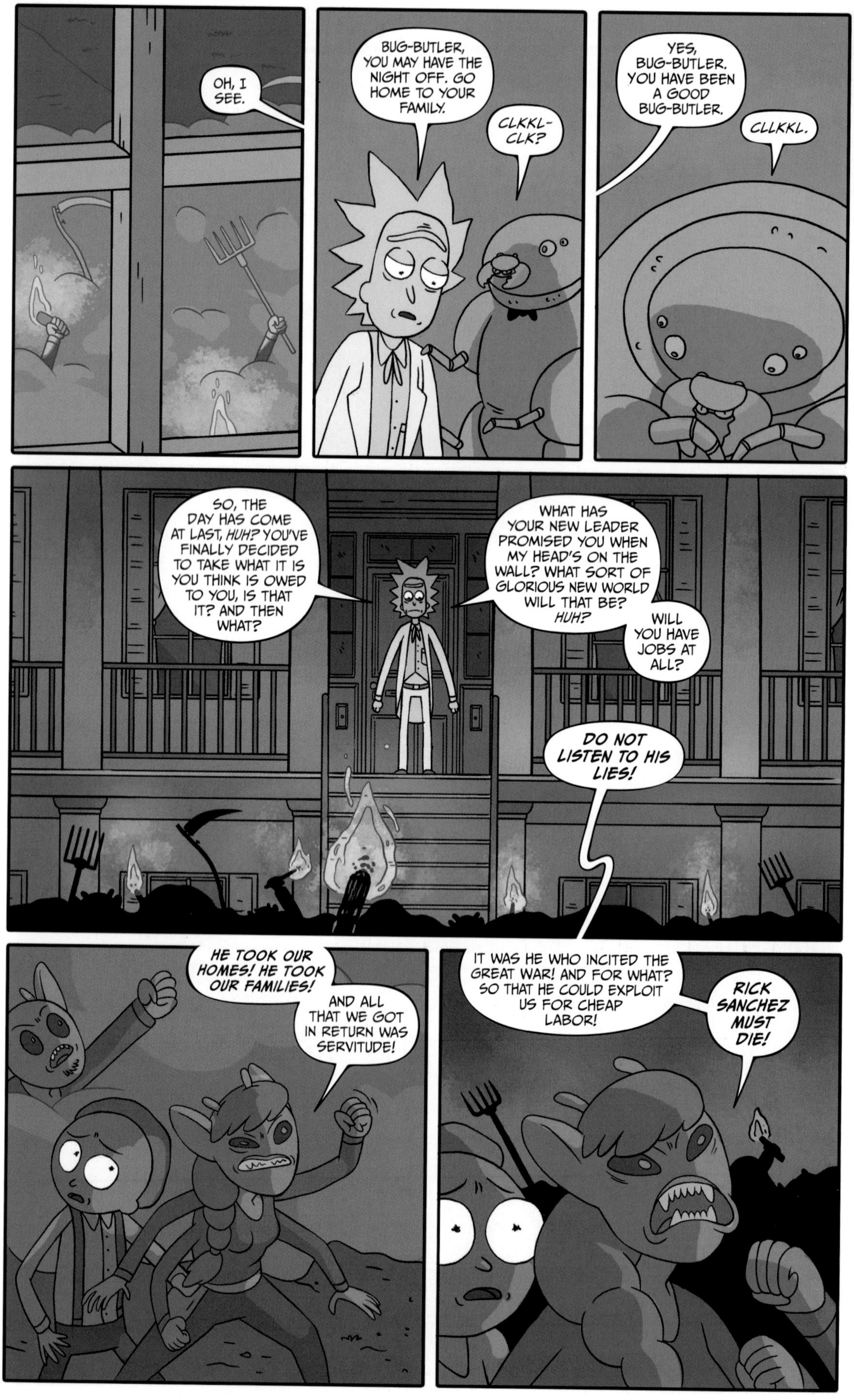
OH, I SEE.
BUG-BUTLER, YOU MAY HAVE THE NIGHT OFF. GO HOME TO YOUR FAMILY.
CLKKL-CLK?
YES, BUG-BUTLER. YOU HAVE BEEN A GOOD BUG-BUTLER.
CLLKKL.
SO, THE DAY HAS COME AT LAST, HUH? YOU'VE FINALLY DECIDED TO TAKE WHAT IT IS YOU THINK IS OWED TO YOU, IS THAT IT? AND THEN WHAT?
WHAT HAS YOUR NEW LEADER PROMISED YOU WHEN MY HEAD'S ON THE WALL? WHAT SORT OF GLORIOUS NEW WORLD WILL THAT BE? HUH?
WILL YOU HAVE JOBS AT ALL?
DO NOT LISTEN TO HIS LIES!
IT WAS HE WHO INCITED THE GREAT WAR! AND FOR WHAT? SO THAT HE COULD EXPLOIT US FOR CHEAP LABOR!
HE TOOK OUR HOMES! HE TOOK OUR FAMILIES!
AND ALL THAT WE GOT IN RETURN WAS SERVITUDE!
RICK SANCHEZ MUST DIE!

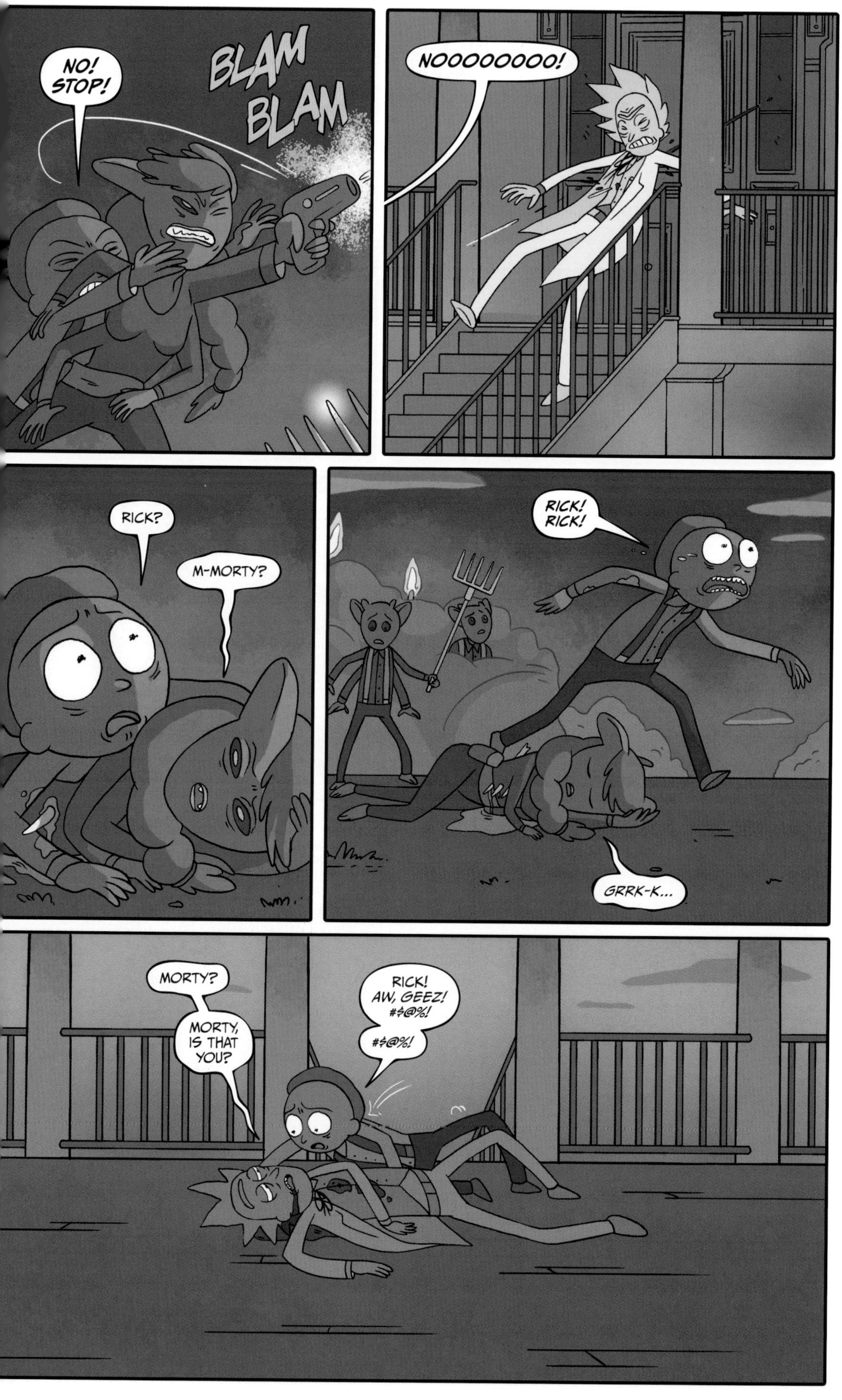
NO! STOP!
BLAM BLAM
NOOOOOOOO!
RICK?
M-MORTY?
RICK! RICK!
GRRK-K...
MORTY?
MORTY, IS THAT YOU?
RICK! AW, GEEZ! #$@%!
#$@%!

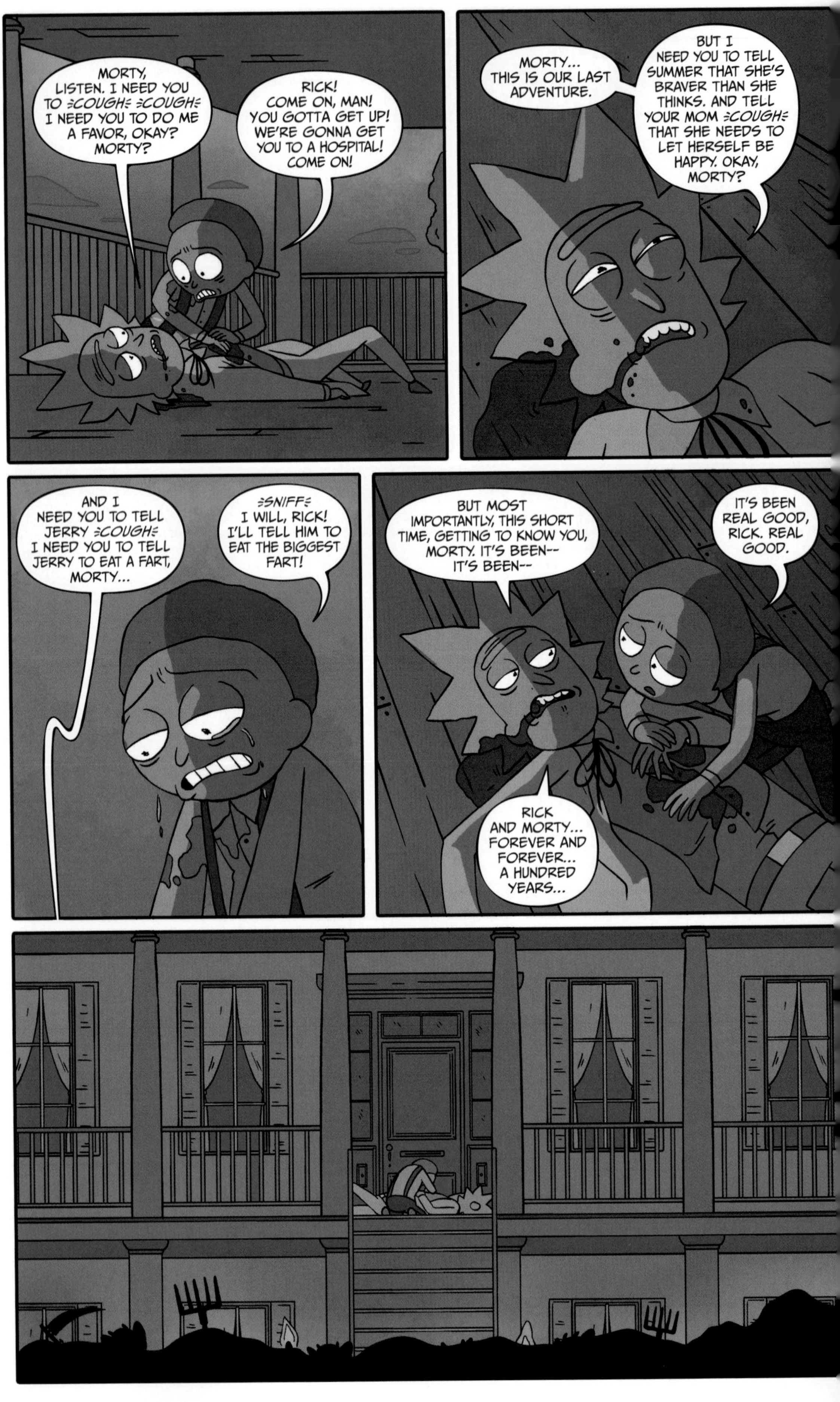
MORTY, LISTEN. I NEED YOU TO ≈COUGH≈ ≈COUGH≈ I NEED YOU TO DO ME A FAVOR, OKAY? MORTY?
RICK! COME ON, MAN! YOU GOTTA GET UP! WE'RE GONNA GET YOU TO A HOSPITAL! COME ON!
MORTY... THIS IS OUR LAST ADVENTURE.
BUT I NEED YOU TO TELL SUMMER THAT SHE'S BRAVER THAN SHE THINKS. AND TELL YOUR MOM ≈COUGH≈ THAT SHE NEEDS TO LET HERSELF BE HAPPY. OKAY, MORTY?
AND I NEED YOU TO TELL JERRY ≈COUGH≈ I NEED YOU TO TELL JERRY TO EAT A FART, MORTY...
≈SNIFF≈ I WILL, RICK! I'LL TELL HIM TO EAT THE BIGGEST FART!
BUT MOST IMPORTANTLY, THIS SHORT TIME, GETTING TO KNOW YOU, MORTY. IT'S BEEN-- IT'S BEEN--
IT'S BEEN REAL GOOD, RICK. REAL GOOD.
RICK AND MORTY... FOREVER AND FOREVER... A HUNDRED YEARS...

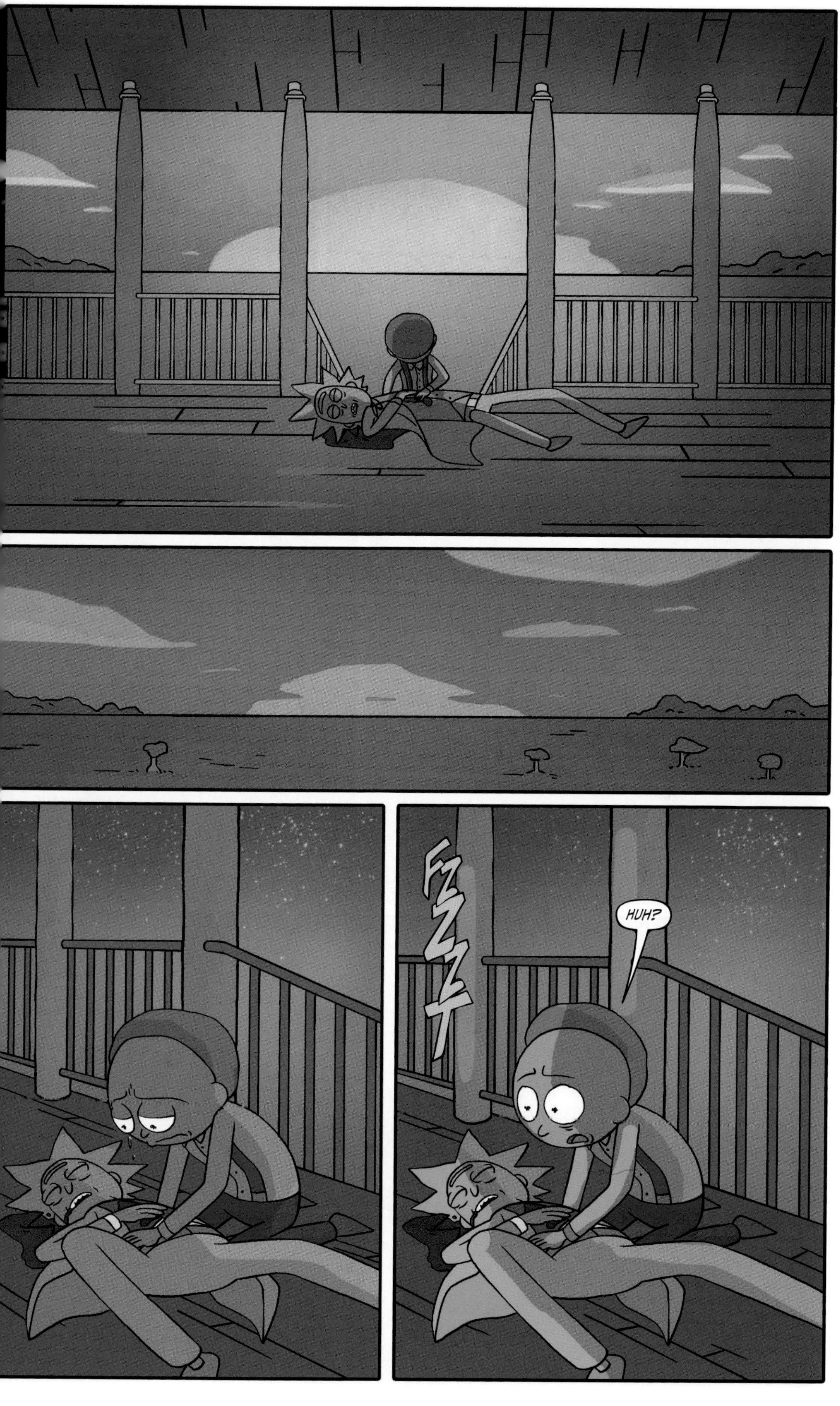
FZZZT
HUH?

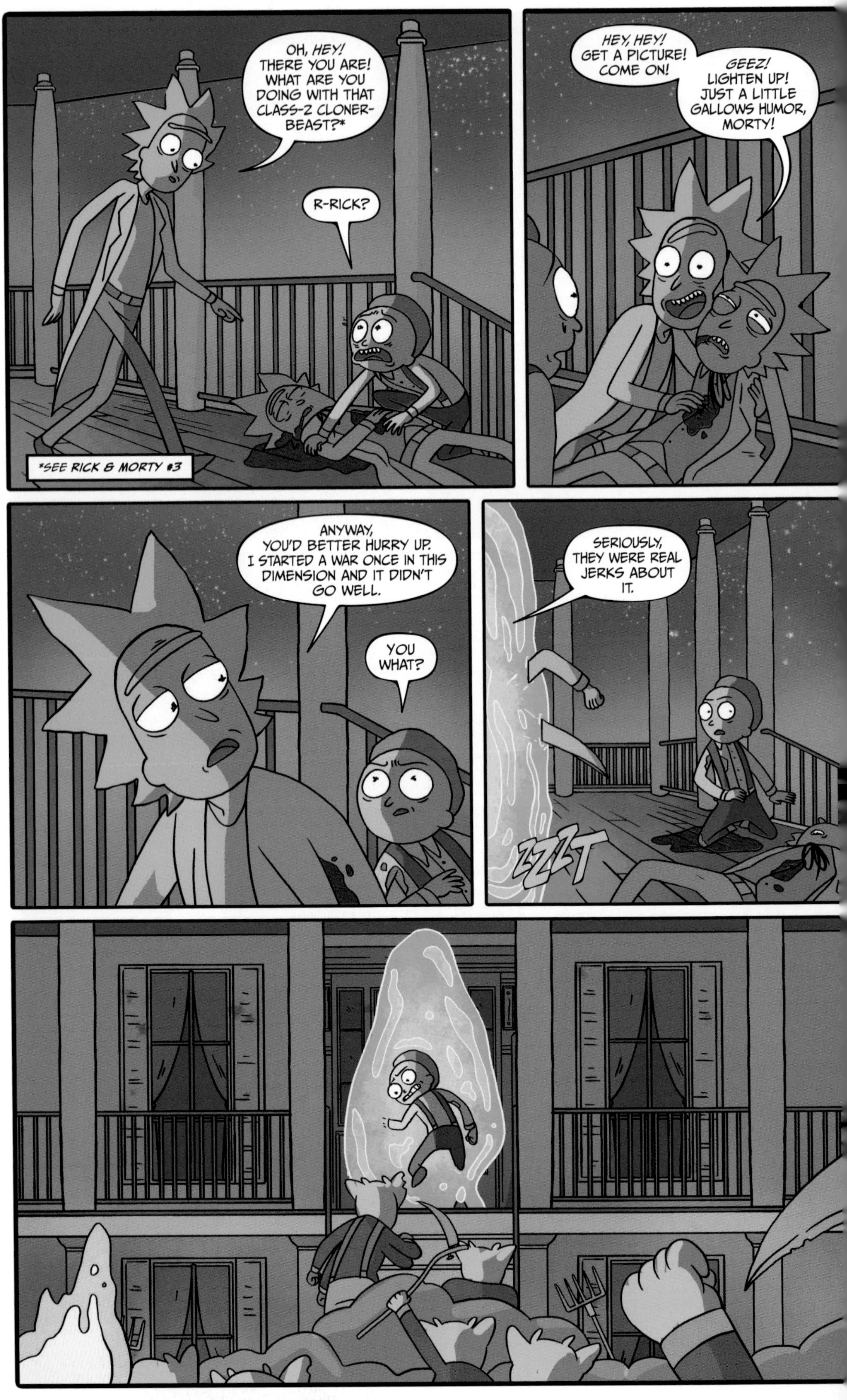
OH, HEY! THERE YOU ARE! WHAT ARE YOU DOING WITH THAT CLASS-2 CLONER-BEAST?*
R-RICK?
*SEE RICK & MORTY #3
HEY, HEY! GET A PICTURE! COME ON!
GEEZ! LIGHTEN UP! JUST A LITTLE GALLOWS HUMOR, MORTY!
ANYWAY, YOU'D BETTER HURRY UP. I STARTED A WAR ONCE IN THIS DIMENSION AND IT DIDN'T GO WELL.
YOU WHAT?
SERIOUSLY, THEY WERE REAL JERKS ABOUT IT.
ZZZT

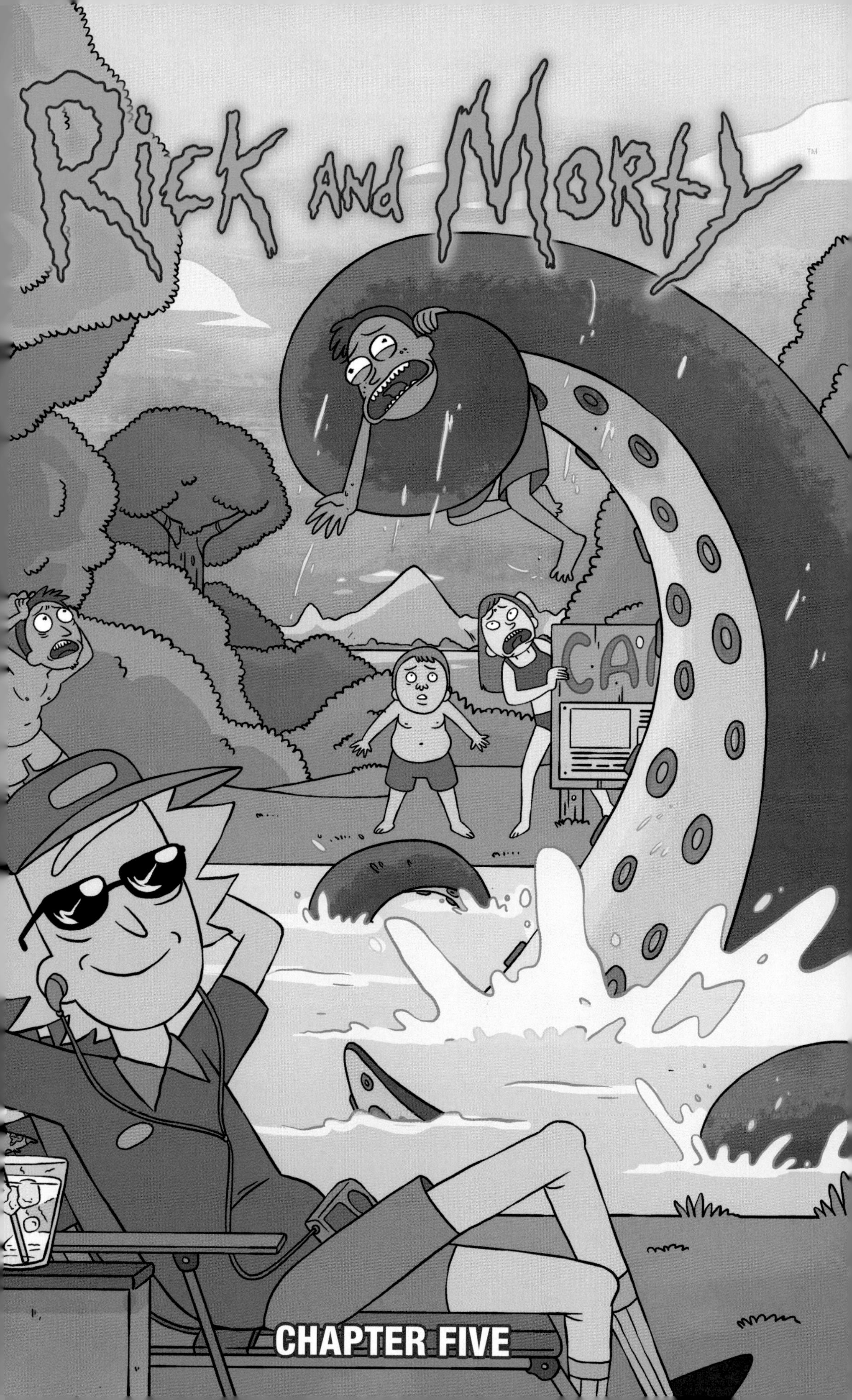
RICK AND MORTY™
CHAPTER FIVE

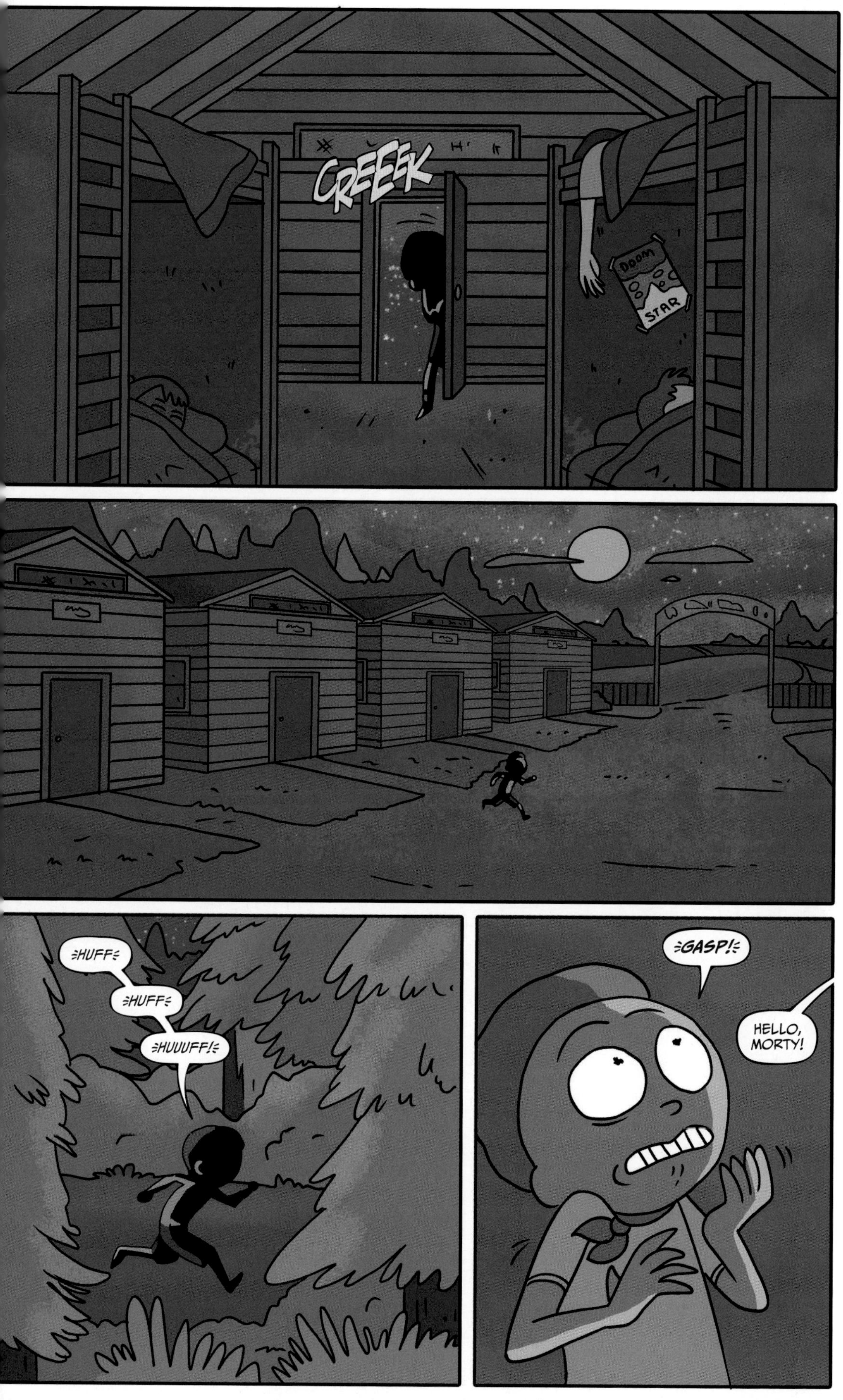
CREEEK
DOOM STAR
HUFF
HUFF
HUUUFF!
GASP!
HELLO, MORTY!

RICK?!

SNEAKIN' OUTTA YOUR BUNK AT NIGHT TO--TO MEET G--URRP!--GIRLS AGAIN, EH, MORTY?

WH--WHAT ARE YOU DOING HERE AT CAMP CAMPERSON, THE SUMMER CAMP THAT I GO TO EVERY YEAR BUT WE NEVER UH, TALK ABOUT?

OH, YOU DIDN'T HEAR?

WELL, MORTY! SAY HELLO TO YOUR NEW CAM--URRP!--CAMP COUNSELOR!

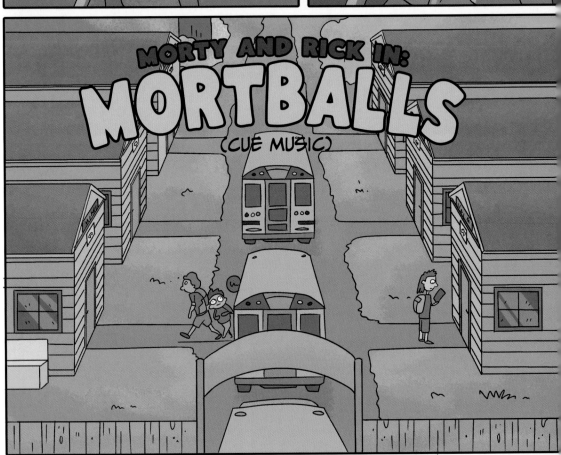

MORTY AND RICK IN:
MORTBALLS
(CUE MUSIC)

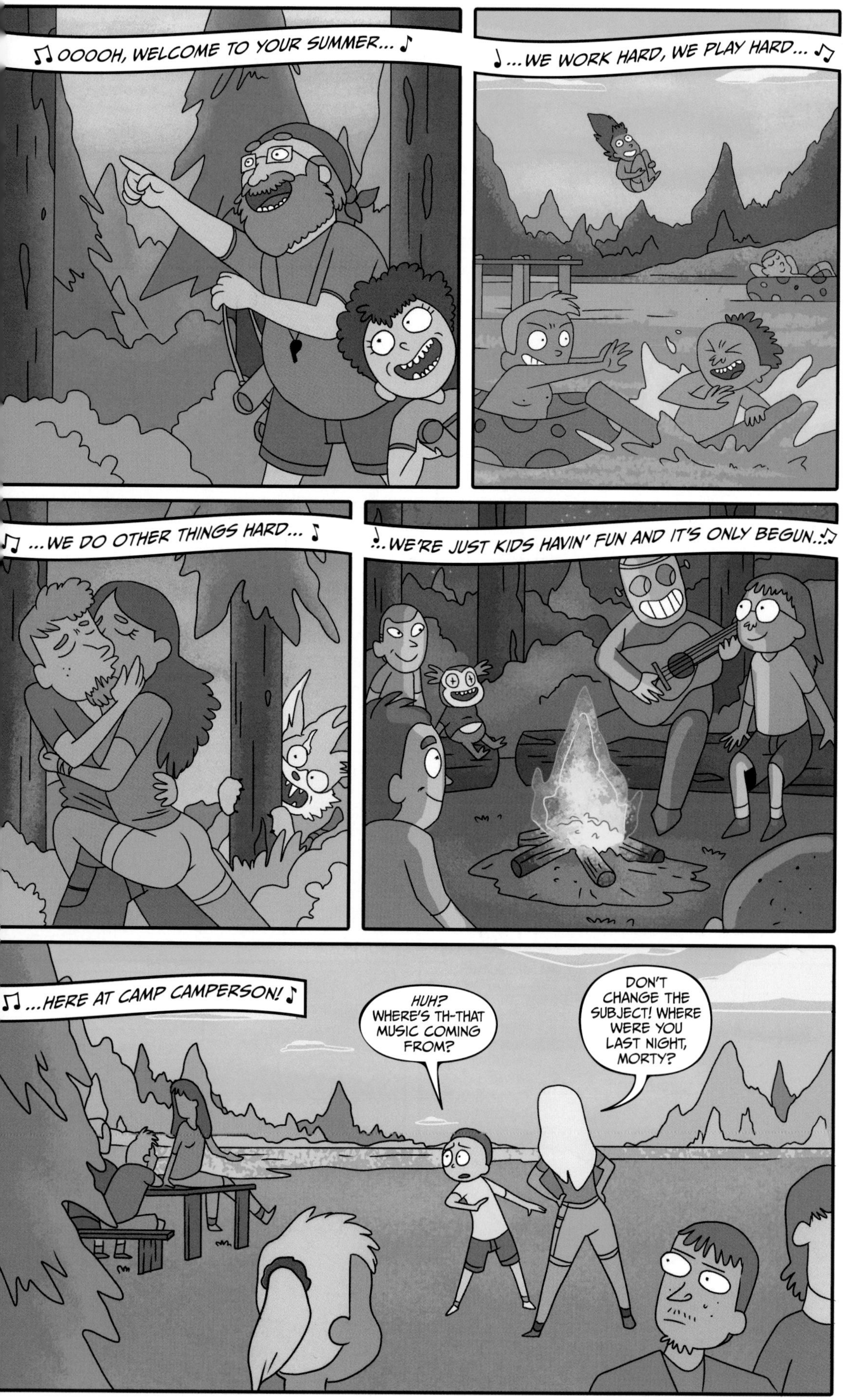
♫ OOOOH, WELCOME TO YOUR SUMMER... ♪
♪ ...WE WORK HARD, WE PLAY HARD... ♫
♫ ...WE DO OTHER THINGS HARD... ♪
♪ ...WE'RE JUST KIDS HAVIN' FUN AND IT'S ONLY BEGUN... ♫
♫ ...HERE AT CAMP CAMPERSON! ♪
HUH? WHERE'S TH-THAT MUSIC COMING FROM?
DON'T CHANGE THE SUBJECT! WHERE WERE YOU LAST NIGHT, MORTY?

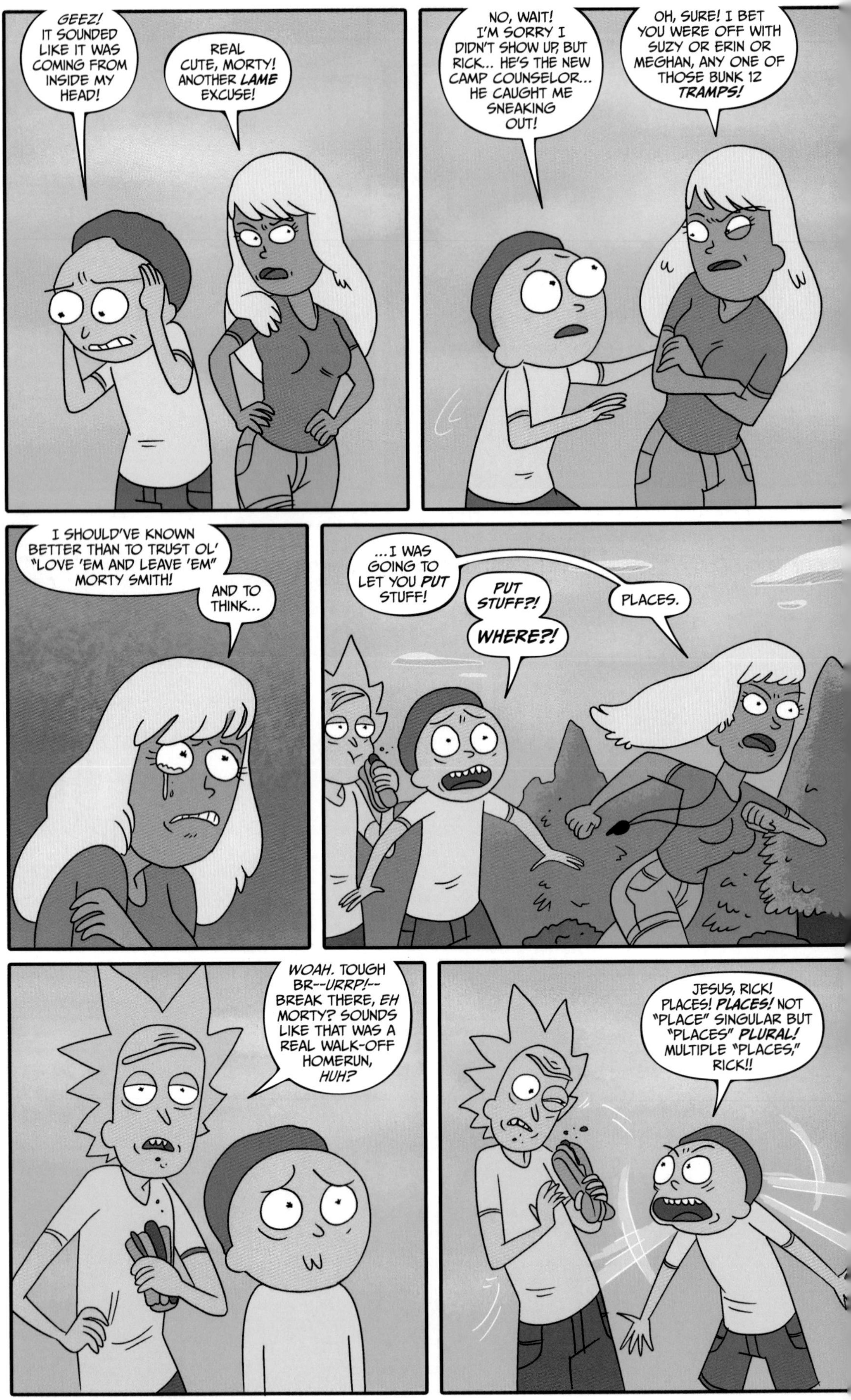
GEEZ! IT SOUNDED LIKE IT WAS COMING FROM INSIDE MY HEAD!
REAL CUTE, MORTY! ANOTHER LAME EXCUSE!
NO, WAIT! I'M SORRY I DIDN'T SHOW UP, BUT RICK... HE'S THE NEW CAMP COUNSELOR... HE CAUGHT ME SNEAKING OUT!
OH, SURE! I BET YOU WERE OFF WITH SUZY OR ERIN OR MEGHAN, ANY ONE OF THOSE BUNK 12 TRAMPS!
I SHOULD'VE KNOWN BETTER THAN TO TRUST OL' "LOVE 'EM AND LEAVE 'EM" MORTY SMITH!
AND TO THINK...
...I WAS GOING TO LET YOU PUT STUFF!
PLACES.
PUT STUFF?!
WHERE?!
WOAH. TOUGH BR--URRP!--BREAK THERE, EH MORTY? SOUNDS LIKE THAT WAS A REAL WALK-OFF HOMERUN, HUH?
JESUS, RICK! PLACES! PLACES! NOT "PLACE" SINGULAR BUT "PLACES" PLURAL! MULTIPLE "PLACES," RICK!!

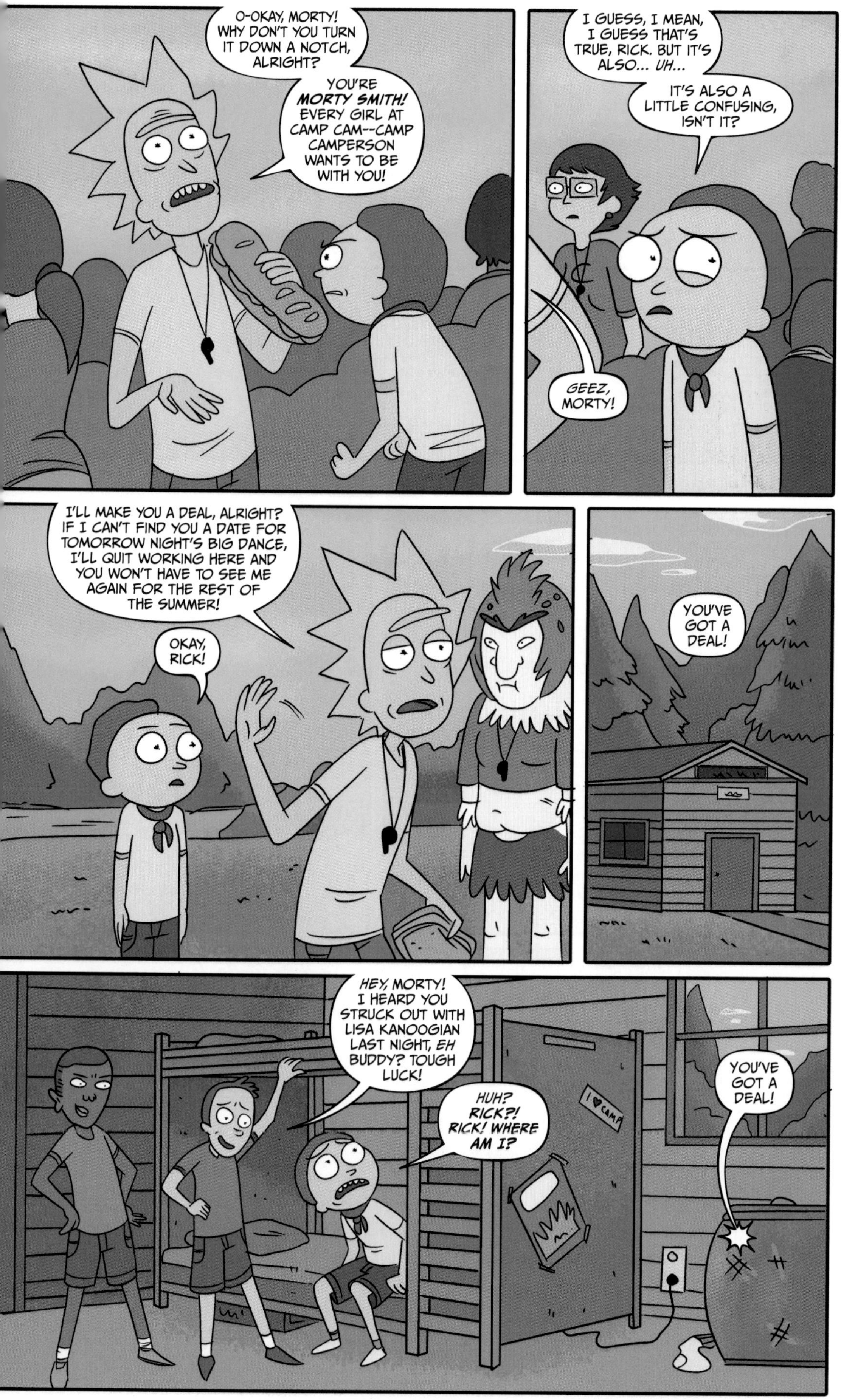
O-OKAY, MORTY! WHY DON'T YOU TURN IT DOWN A NOTCH, ALRIGHT?
YOU'RE MORTY SMITH! EVERY GIRL AT CAMP CAM--CAMP CAMPERSON WANTS TO BE WITH YOU!
I GUESS, I MEAN, I GUESS THAT'S TRUE, RICK. BUT IT'S ALSO... UH...
IT'S ALSO A LITTLE CONFUSING, ISN'T IT?
GEEZ, MORTY!
I'LL MAKE YOU A DEAL, ALRIGHT? IF I CAN'T FIND YOU A DATE FOR TOMORROW NIGHT'S BIG DANCE, I'LL QUIT WORKING HERE AND YOU WON'T HAVE TO SEE ME AGAIN FOR THE REST OF THE SUMMER!
OKAY, RICK!
YOU'VE GOT A DEAL!
HEY, MORTY! I HEARD YOU STRUCK OUT WITH LISA KANOOGIAN LAST NIGHT, EH BUDDY? TOUGH LUCK!
HUH? RICK?! RICK! WHERE AM I?
YOU'VE GOT A DEAL!
I ♥ CAMP

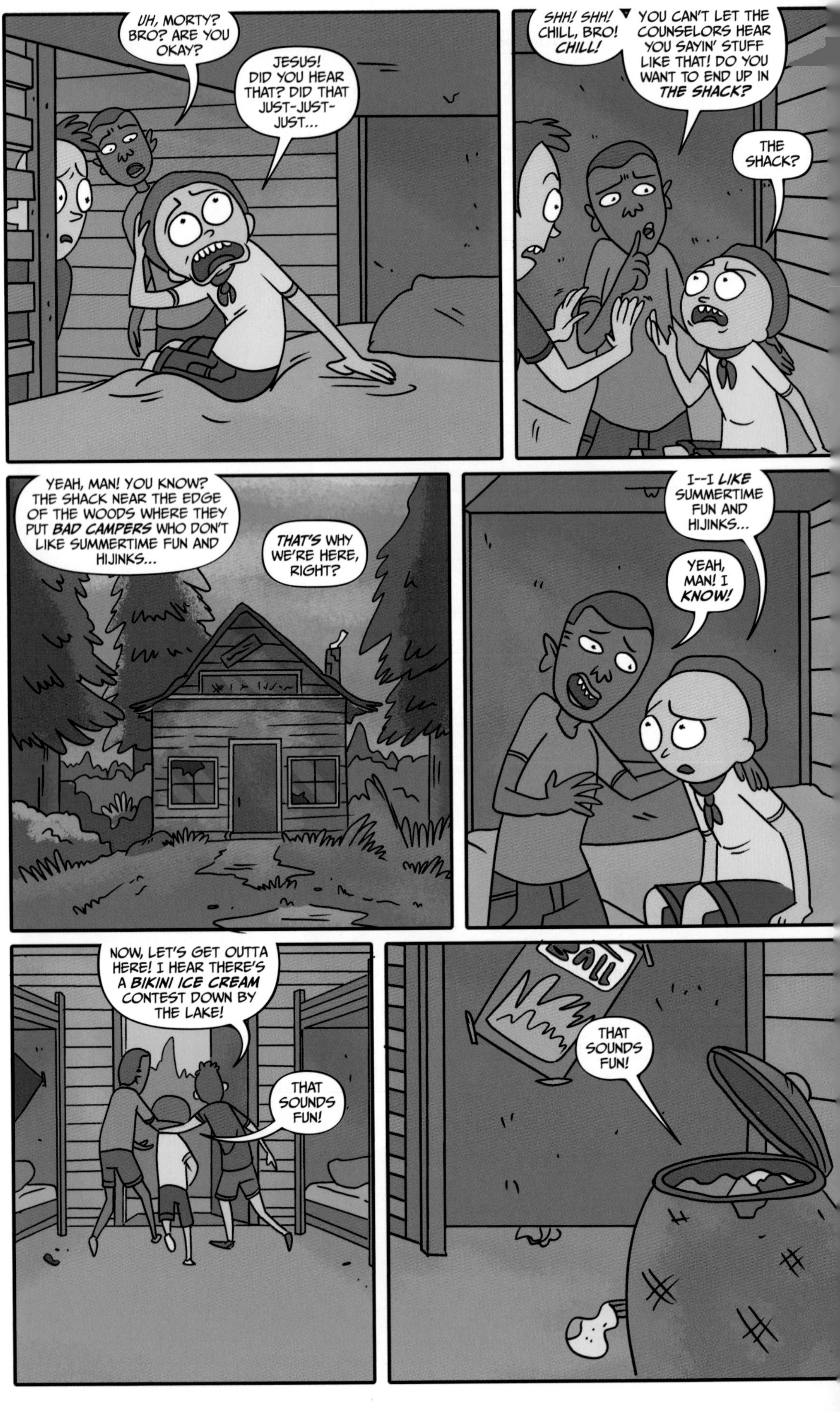
UH, MORTY? BRO? ARE YOU OKAY?
JESUS! DID YOU HEAR THAT? DID THAT JUST-JUST-JUST...
SHH! SHH! CHILL, BRO! CHILL!
YOU CAN'T LET THE COUNSELORS HEAR YOU SAYIN' STUFF LIKE THAT! DO YOU WANT TO END UP IN THE SHACK?
THE SHACK?
YEAH, MAN! YOU KNOW? THE SHACK NEAR THE EDGE OF THE WOODS WHERE THEY PUT BAD CAMPERS WHO DON'T LIKE SUMMERTIME FUN AND HIJINKS...
THAT'S WHY WE'RE HERE, RIGHT?
I--I LIKE SUMMERTIME FUN AND HIJINKS...
YEAH, MAN! I KNOW!
NOW, LET'S GET OUTTA HERE! I HEAR THERE'S A BIKINI ICE CREAM CONTEST DOWN BY THE LAKE!
THAT SOUNDS FUN!
THAT SOUNDS FUN!

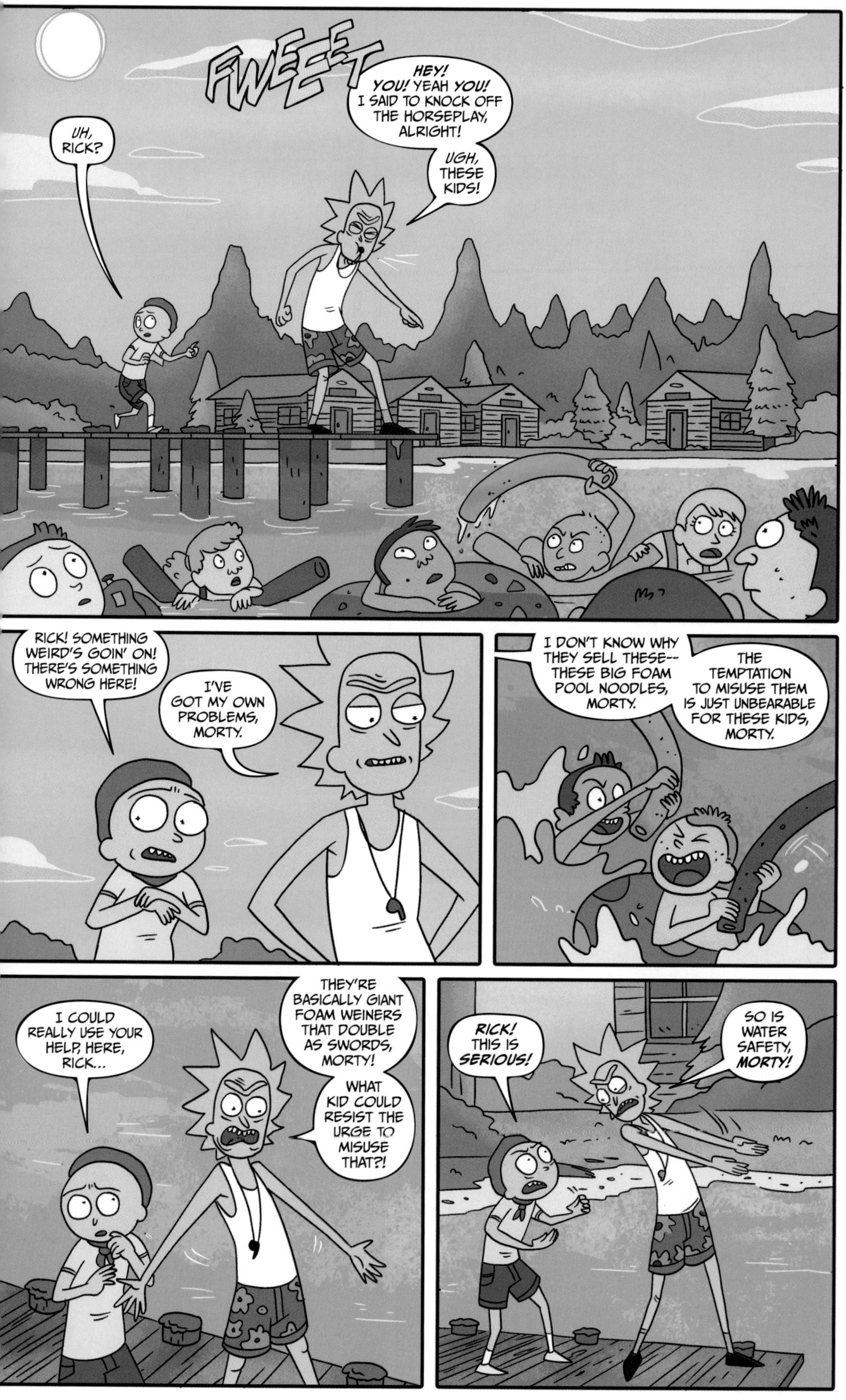
FWEEEET
UH, RICK?
HEY! YOU! YEAH YOU! I SAID TO KNOCK OFF THE HORSEPLAY, ALRIGHT!
UGH, THESE KIDS!
RICK! SOMETHING WEIRD'S GOIN' ON! THERE'S SOMETHING WRONG HERE!
I'VE GOT MY OWN PROBLEMS, MORTY.
I DON'T KNOW WHY THEY SELL THESE-- THESE BIG FOAM POOL NOODLES, MORTY.
THE TEMPTATION TO MISUSE THEM IS JUST UNBEARABLE FOR THESE KIDS, MORTY.
I COULD REALLY USE YOUR HELP, HERE, RICK...
THEY'RE BASICALLY GIANT FOAM WEINERS THAT DOUBLE AS SWORDS, MORTY!
WHAT KID COULD RESIST THE URGE TO MISUSE THAT?!
RICK! THIS IS SERIOUS!
SO IS WATER SAFETY, MORTY!

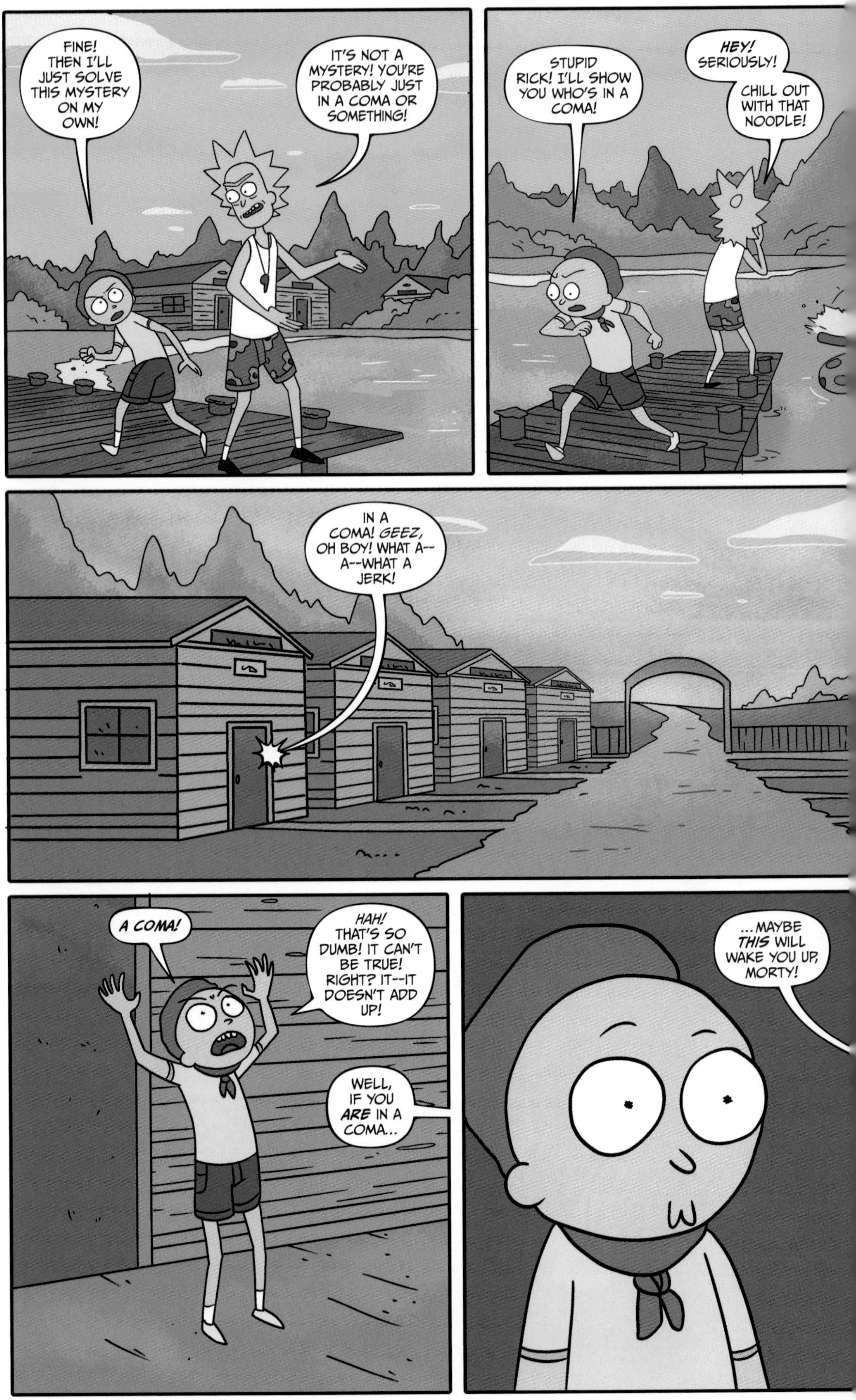
FINE! THEN I'LL JUST SOLVE THIS MYSTERY ON MY OWN!
IT'S NOT A MYSTERY! YOU'RE PROBABLY JUST IN A COMA OR SOMETHING!
STUPID RICK! I'LL SHOW YOU WHO'S IN A COMA!
HEY! SERIOUSLY!
CHILL OUT WITH THAT NOODLE!
IN A COMA! GEEZ, OH BOY! WHAT A-- A--WHAT A JERK!
A COMA!
HAH! THAT'S SO DUMB! IT CAN'T BE TRUE! RIGHT? IT--IT DOESN'T ADD UP!
WELL, IF YOU ARE IN A COMA...
...MAYBE THIS WILL WAKE YOU UP, MORTY!

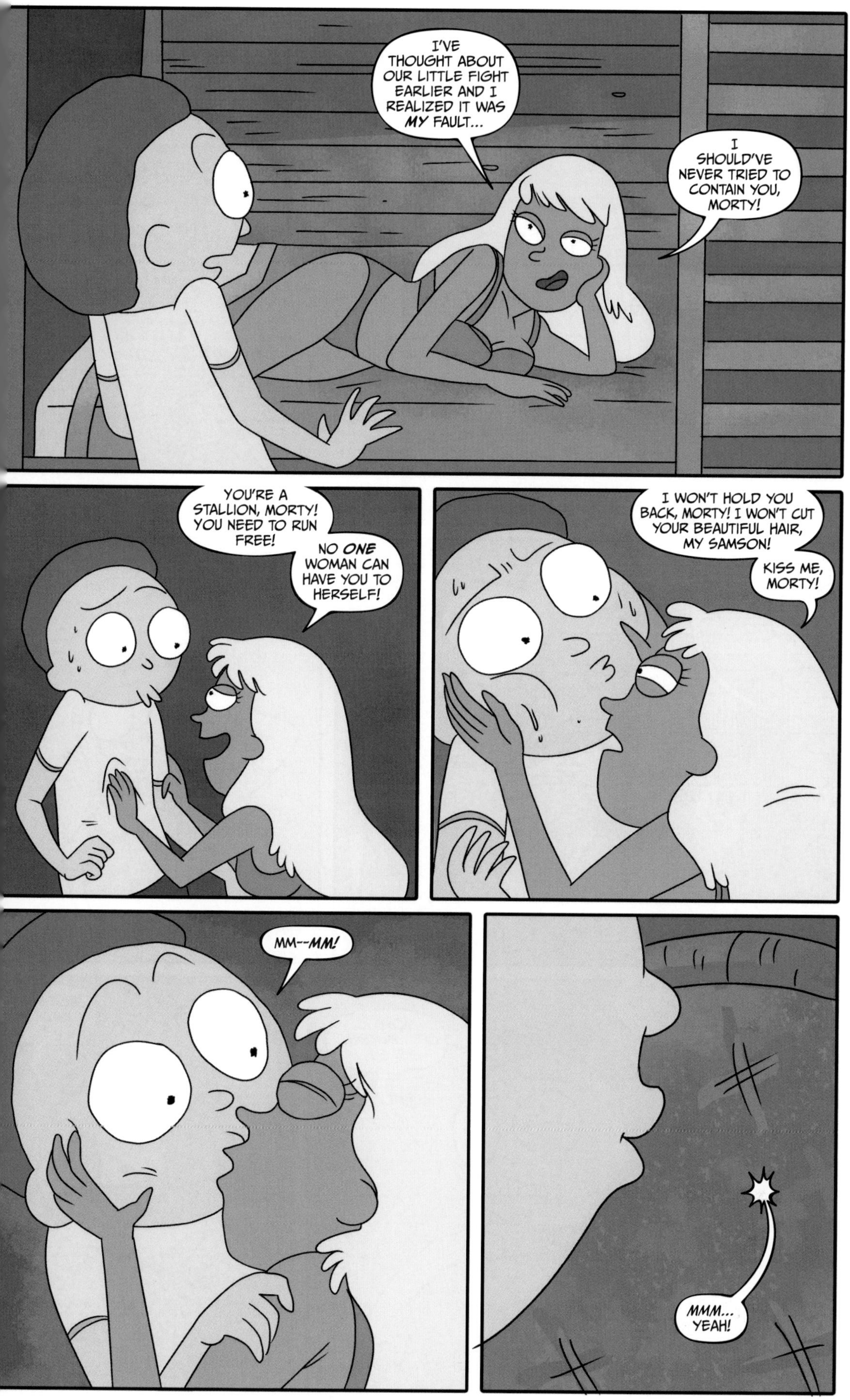
I'VE THOUGHT ABOUT OUR LITTLE FIGHT EARLIER AND I REALIZED IT WAS *MY* FAULT...
I SHOULD'VE NEVER TRIED TO CONTAIN YOU, MORTY!
YOU'RE A STALLION, MORTY! YOU NEED TO RUN FREE!
NO *ONE* WOMAN CAN HAVE YOU TO HERSELF!
I WON'T HOLD YOU BACK, MORTY! I WON'T CUT YOUR BEAUTIFUL HAIR, MY SAMSON!
KISS ME, MORTY!
MM--*MM!*
MMM... YEAH!

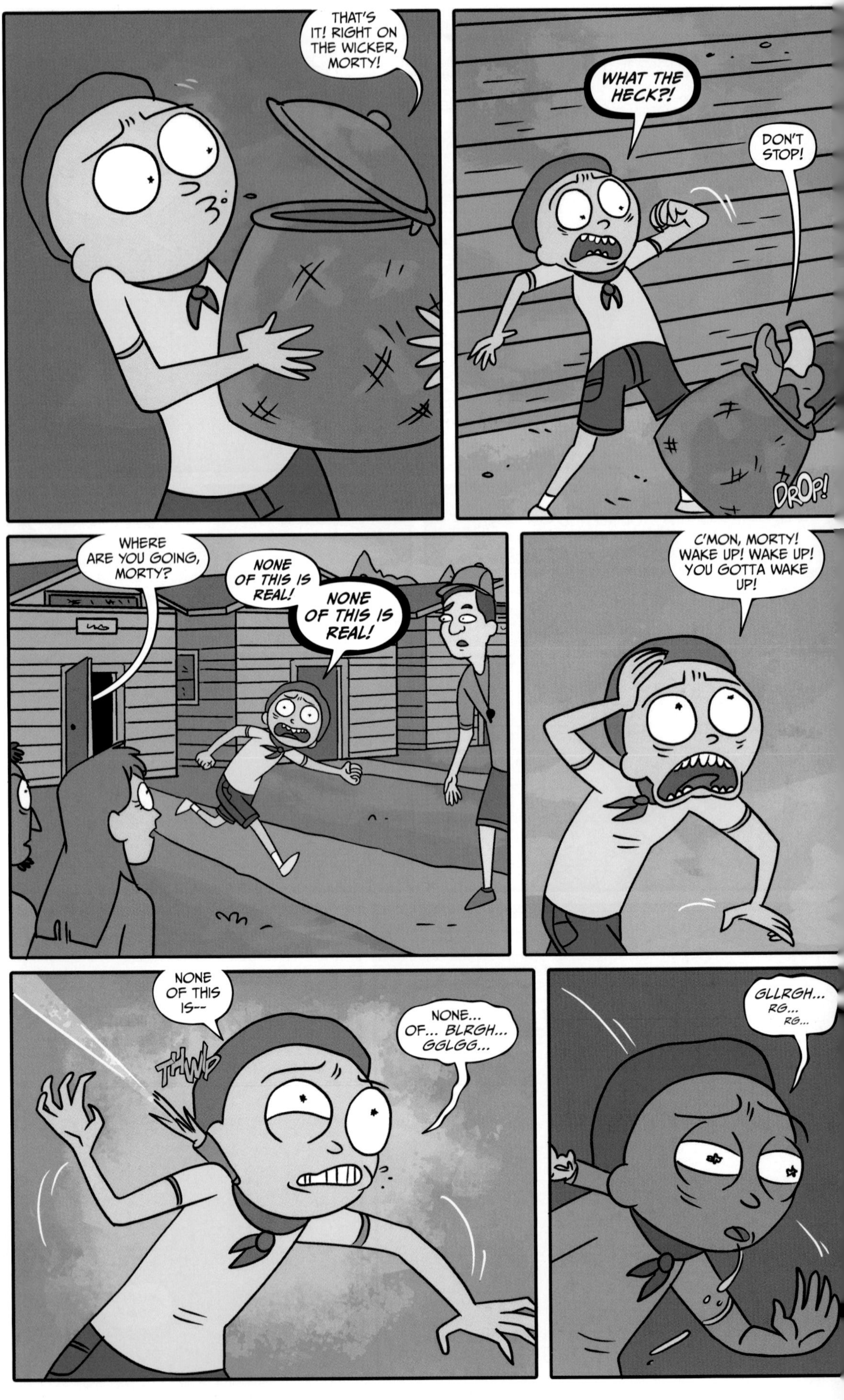
THAT'S IT! RIGHT ON THE WICKER, MORTY!
WHAT THE HECK?!
DON'T STOP!
DROP!
WHERE ARE YOU GOING, MORTY?
NONE OF THIS IS REAL!
NONE OF THIS IS REAL!
C'MON, MORTY! WAKE UP! WAKE UP! YOU GOTTA WAKE UP!
NONE OF THIS IS--
THWP
NONE... OF... BLRGH... GGLGG...
GLLRGH... RG... RG...

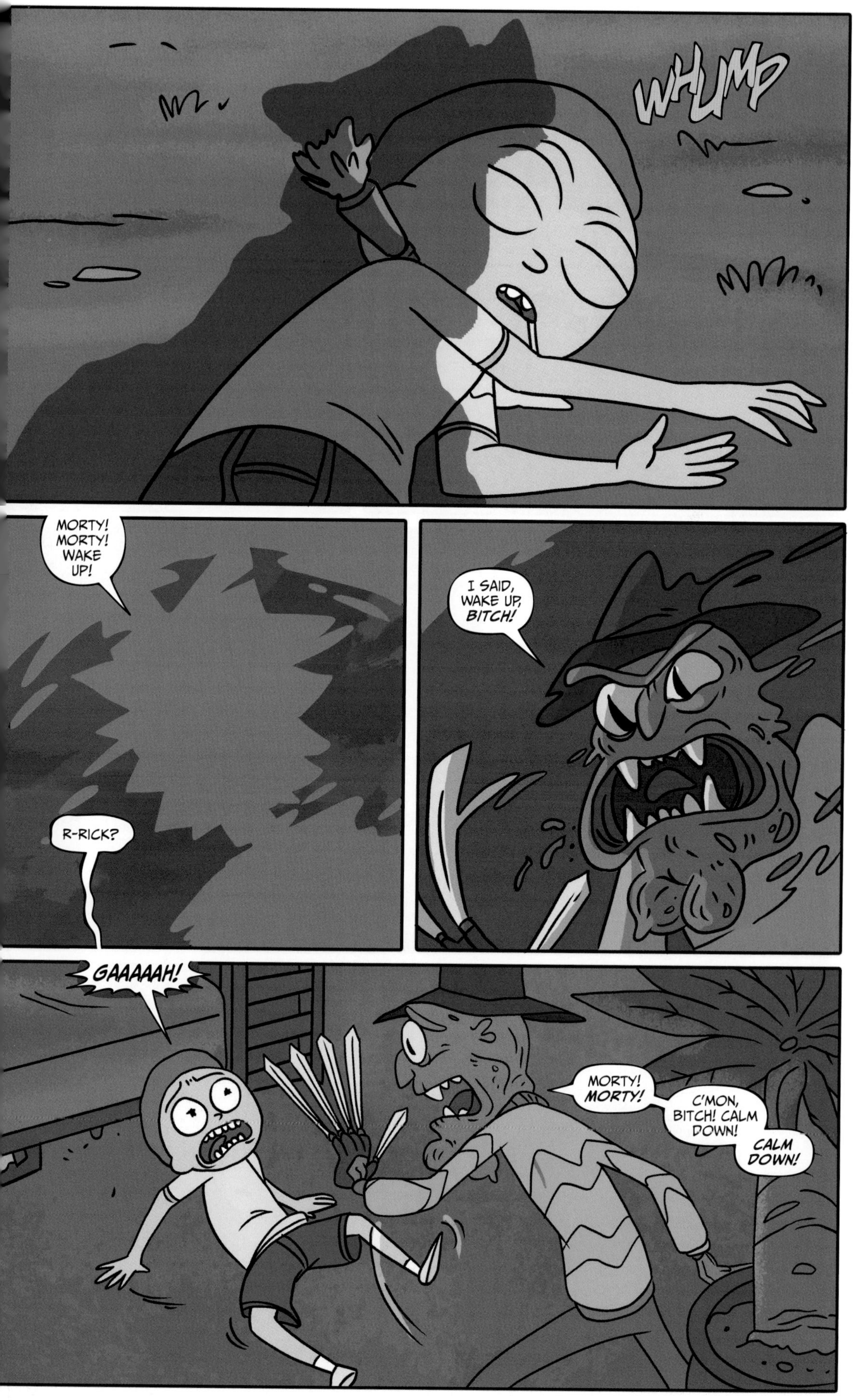
WHUMP
MORTY! MORTY! WAKE UP!
R-RICK?
I SAID, WAKE UP, BITCH!
GAAAAAH!
MORTY! MORTY!
C'MON, BITCH! CALM DOWN!
CALM DOWN!

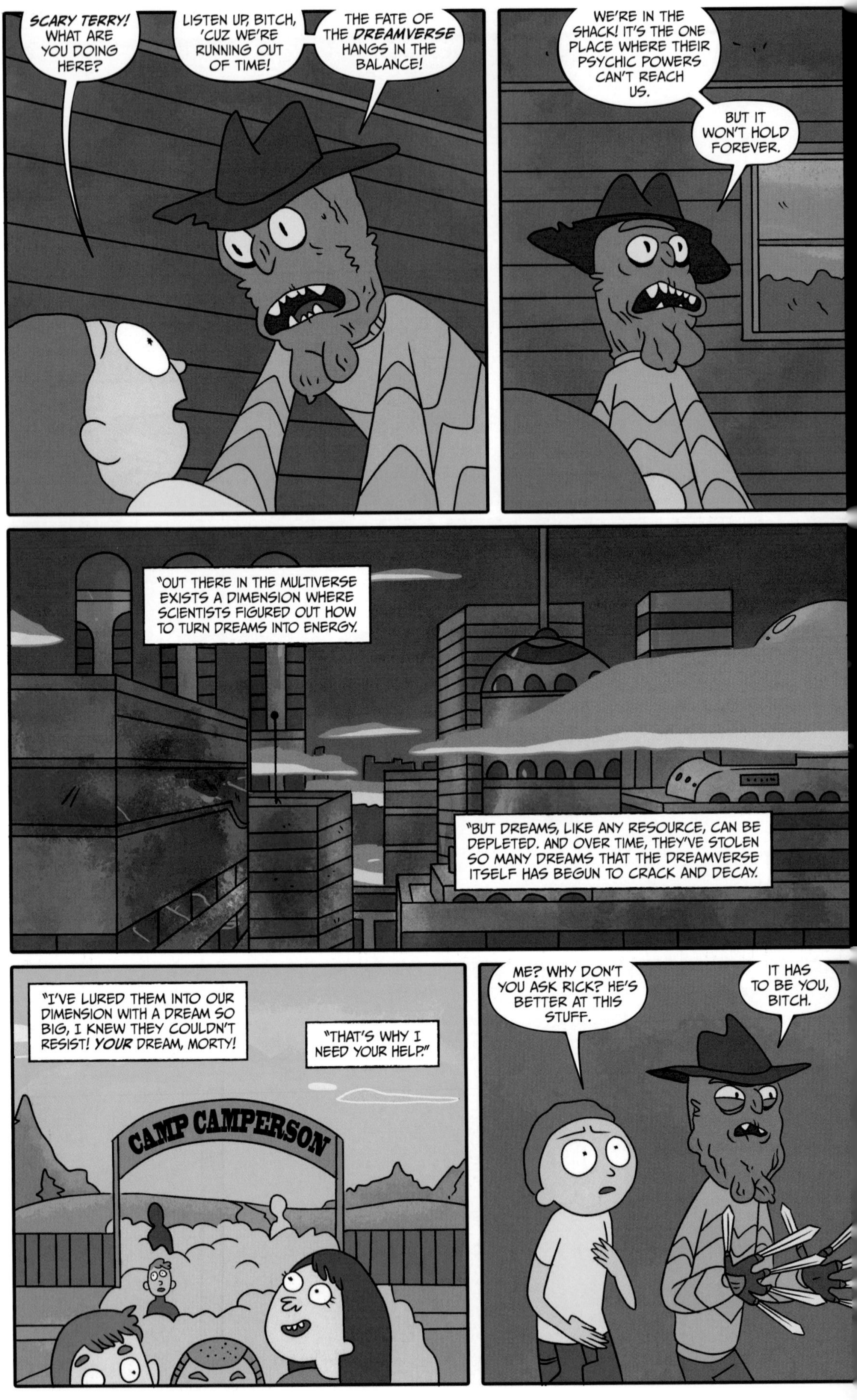
SCARY TERRY! WHAT ARE YOU DOING HERE?
LISTEN UP, BITCH, 'CUZ WE'RE RUNNING OUT OF TIME!
THE FATE OF THE DREAMVERSE HANGS IN THE BALANCE!
WE'RE IN THE SHACK! IT'S THE ONE PLACE WHERE THEIR PSYCHIC POWERS CAN'T REACH US.
BUT IT WON'T HOLD FOREVER.
"OUT THERE IN THE MULTIVERSE EXISTS A DIMENSION WHERE SCIENTISTS FIGURED OUT HOW TO TURN DREAMS INTO ENERGY.
"BUT DREAMS, LIKE ANY RESOURCE, CAN BE DEPLETED. AND OVER TIME, THEY'VE STOLEN SO MANY DREAMS THAT THE DREAMVERSE ITSELF HAS BEGUN TO CRACK AND DECAY.
"I'VE LURED THEM INTO OUR DIMENSION WITH A DREAM SO BIG, I KNEW THEY COULDN'T RESIST! YOUR DREAM, MORTY!
"THAT'S WHY I NEED YOUR HELP."
CAMP CAMPERSON
ME? WHY DON'T YOU ASK RICK? HE'S BETTER AT THIS STUFF.
IT HAS TO BE YOU, BITCH.

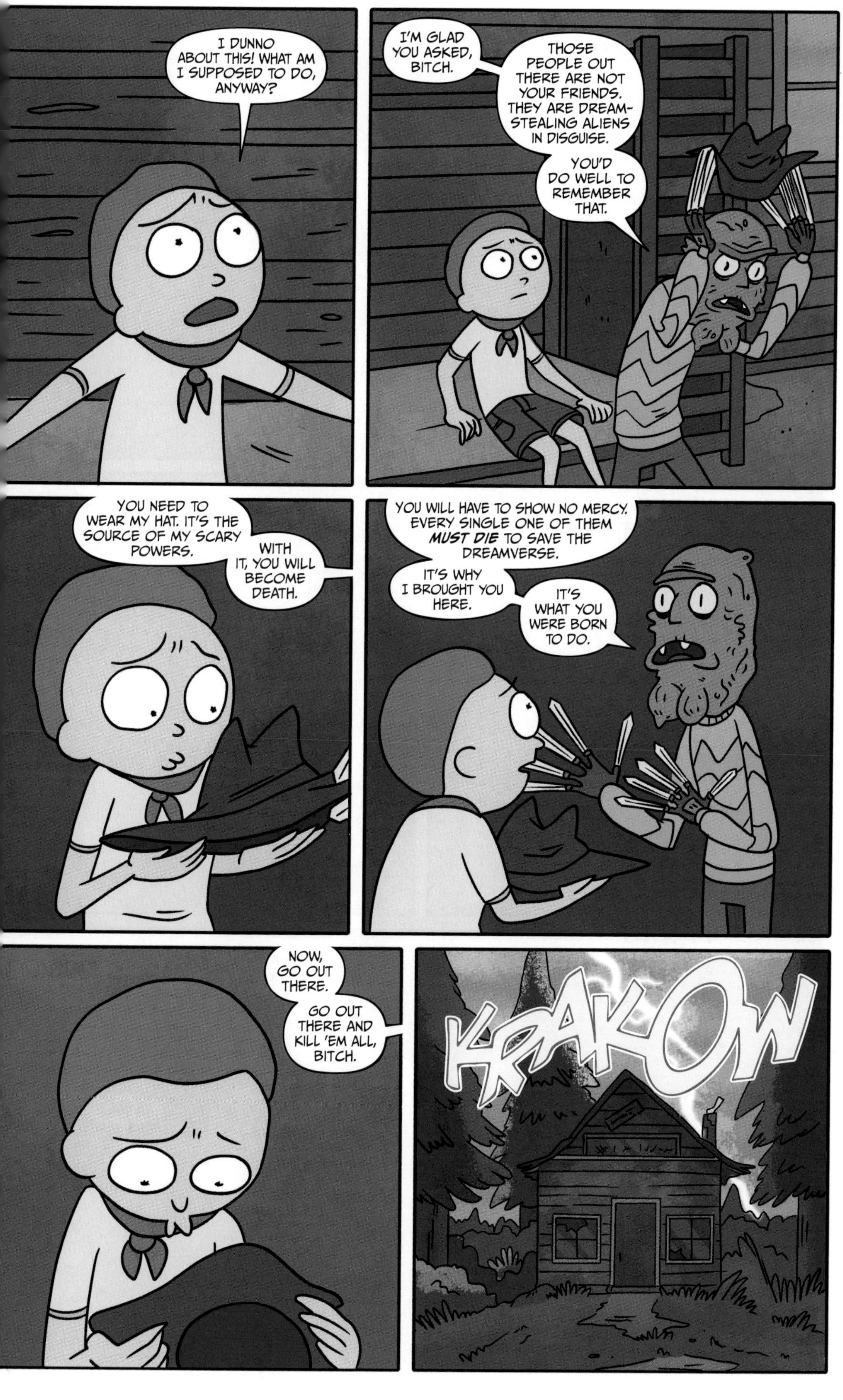
I DUNNO ABOUT THIS! WHAT AM I SUPPOSED TO DO, ANYWAY?
I'M GLAD YOU ASKED, BITCH.
THOSE PEOPLE OUT THERE ARE NOT YOUR FRIENDS. THEY ARE DREAM-STEALING ALIENS IN DISGUISE.
YOU'D DO WELL TO REMEMBER THAT.
YOU NEED TO WEAR MY HAT. IT'S THE SOURCE OF MY SCARY POWERS.
WITH IT, YOU WILL BECOME DEATH.
YOU WILL HAVE TO SHOW NO MERCY. EVERY SINGLE ONE OF THEM *MUST DIE* TO SAVE THE DREAMVERSE.
IT'S WHY I BROUGHT YOU HERE.
IT'S WHAT YOU WERE BORN TO DO.
NOW, GO OUT THERE.
GO OUT THERE AND KILL 'EM ALL, BITCH.
KRAKOW

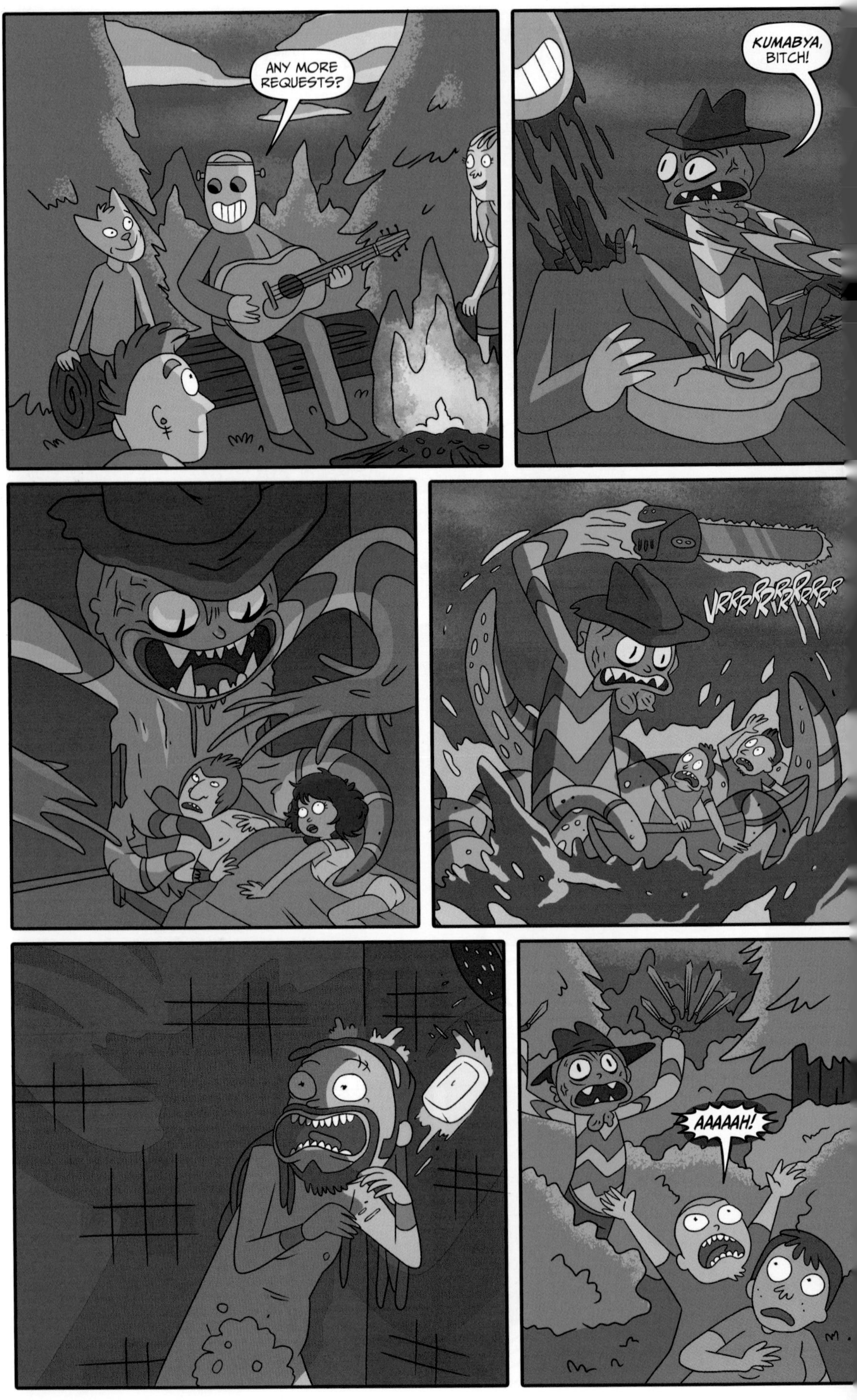
ANY MORE REQUESTS?
KUMABYA, BITCH!
VRRRRRRRRRRR
AAAAAH!

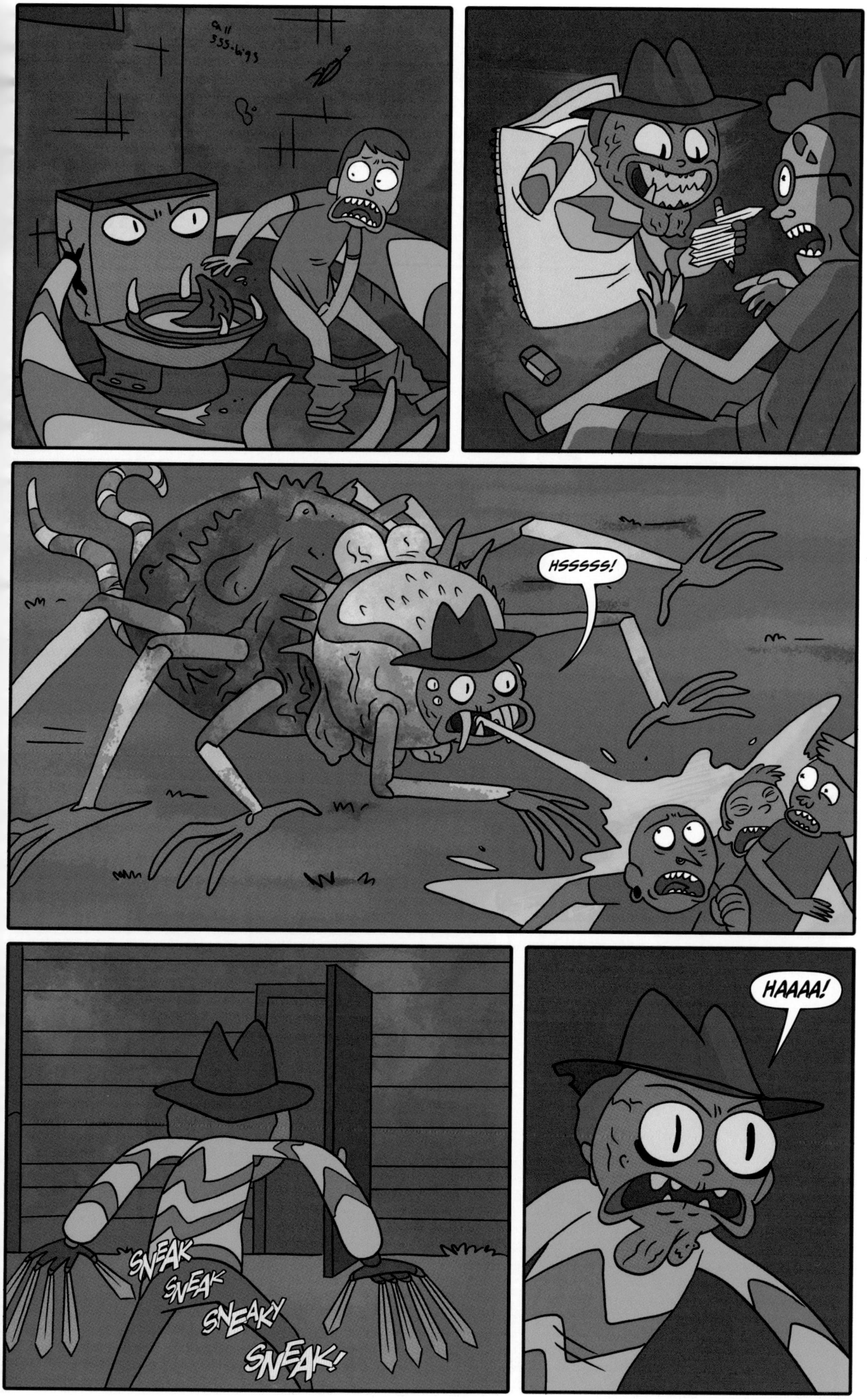
call
555-bigs
HSSSSS!
SNEAK
SNEAK
SNEAKY
SNEAK!
HAAAA!

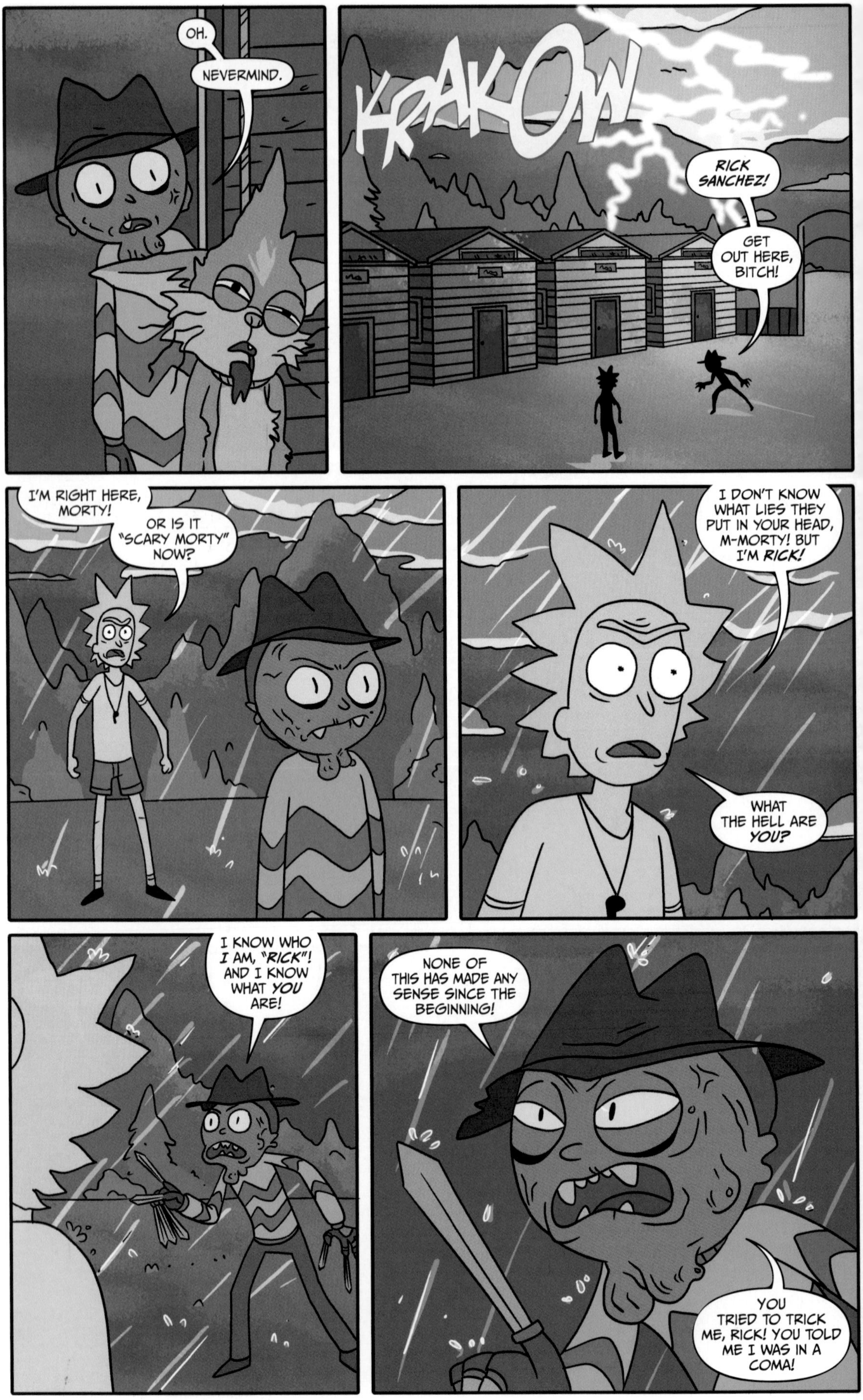
OH.
NEVERMIND.
KRAKOW
RICK SANCHEZ!
GET OUT HERE, BITCH!
I'M RIGHT HERE, MORTY!
OR IS IT "SCARY MORTY" NOW?
I DON'T KNOW WHAT LIES THEY PUT IN YOUR HEAD, M-MORTY! BUT I'M RICK!
WHAT THE HELL ARE YOU?
I KNOW WHO I AM, "RICK"! AND I KNOW WHAT YOU ARE!
NONE OF THIS HAS MADE ANY SENSE SINCE THE BEGINNING!
YOU TRIED TO TRICK ME, RICK! YOU TOLD ME I WAS IN A COMA!

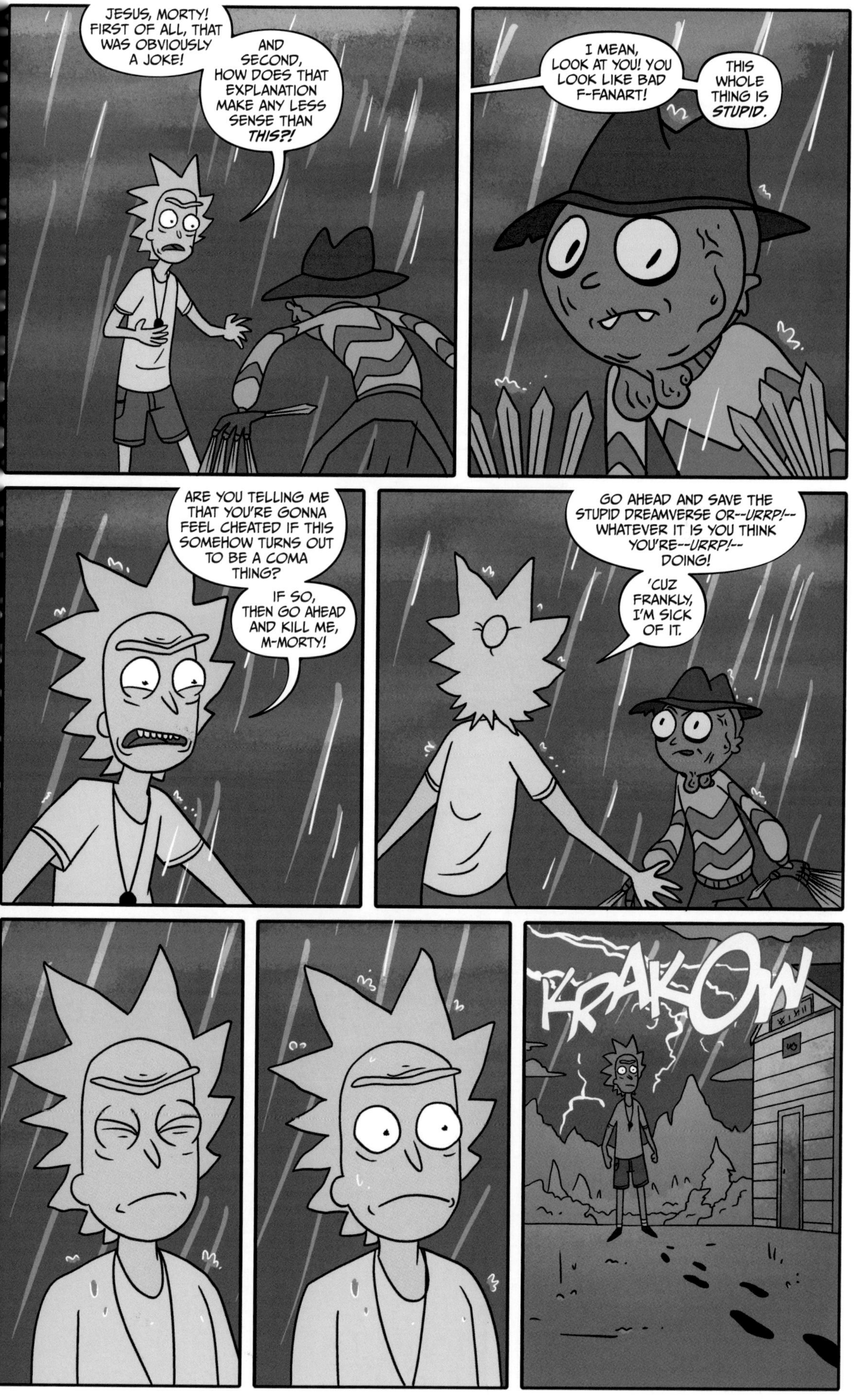
JESUS, MORTY! FIRST OF ALL, THAT WAS OBVIOUSLY A JOKE!
AND SECOND, HOW DOES THAT EXPLANATION MAKE ANY LESS SENSE THAN THIS?!
I MEAN, LOOK AT YOU! YOU LOOK LIKE BAD F-FANART!
THIS WHOLE THING IS STUPID.
ARE YOU TELLING ME THAT YOU'RE GONNA FEEL CHEATED IF THIS SOMEHOW TURNS OUT TO BE A COMA THING?
IF SO, THEN GO AHEAD AND KILL ME, M-MORTY!
GO AHEAD AND SAVE THE STUPID DREAMVERSE OR--URRP!--WHATEVER IT IS YOU THINK YOU'RE--URRP!--DOING!
'CUZ FRANKLY, I'M SICK OF IT.
KRAKOW

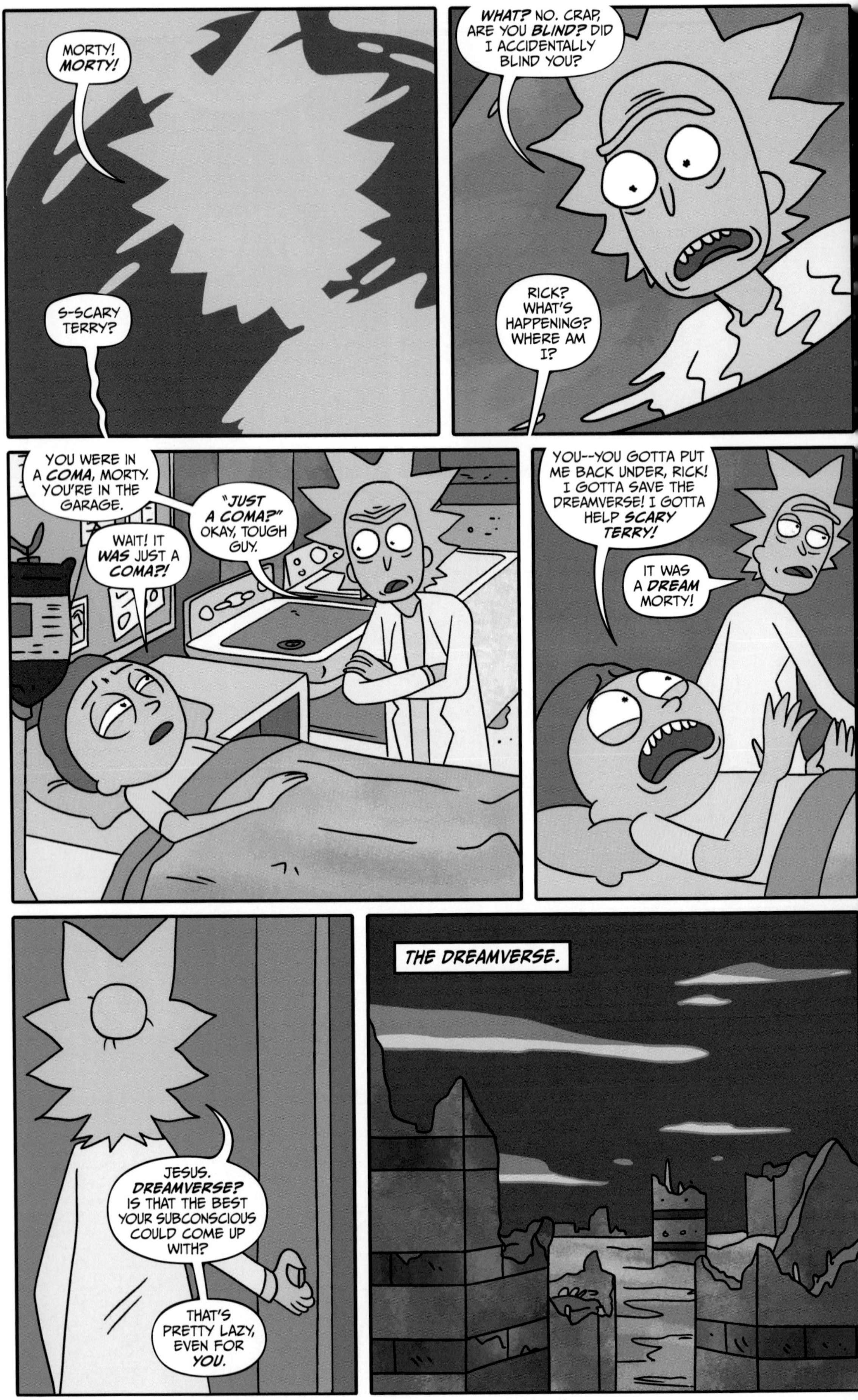
MORTY! MORTY!
S-SCARY TERRY?
WHAT? NO. CRAP, ARE YOU BLIND? DID I ACCIDENTALLY BLIND YOU?
RICK? WHAT'S HAPPENING? WHERE AM I?
YOU WERE IN A COMA, MORTY. YOU'RE IN THE GARAGE.
WAIT! IT WAS JUST A COMA?!
"JUST A COMA?" OKAY, TOUGH GUY.
YOU--YOU GOTTA PUT ME BACK UNDER, RICK! I GOTTA SAVE THE DREAMVERSE! I GOTTA HELP SCARY TERRY!
IT WAS A DREAM MORTY!
JESUS. DREAMVERSE? IS THAT THE BEST YOUR SUBCONSCIOUS COULD COME UP WITH?
THAT'S PRETTY LAZY, EVEN FOR YOU.
THE DREAMVERSE.

BONUS SHORTS

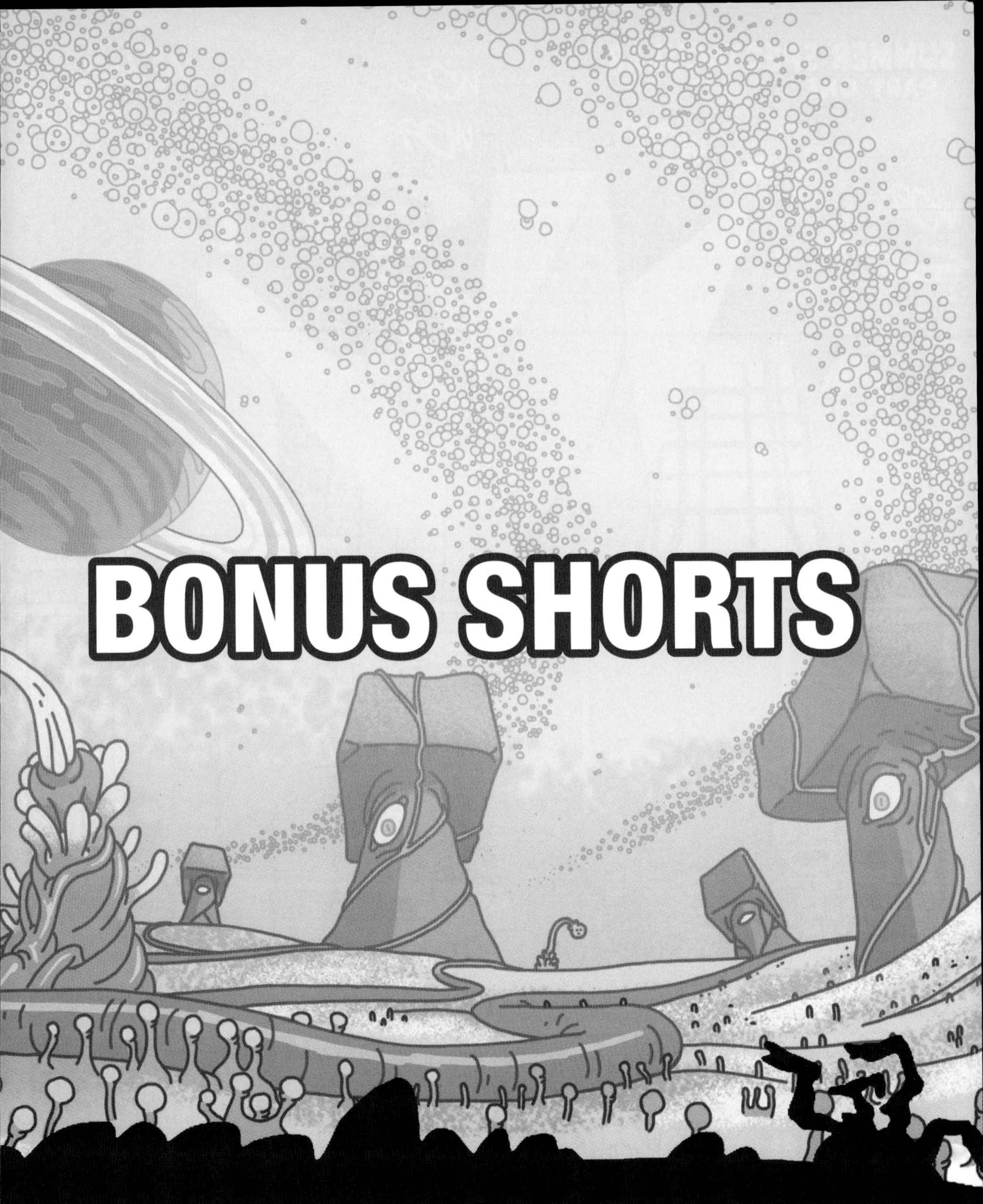

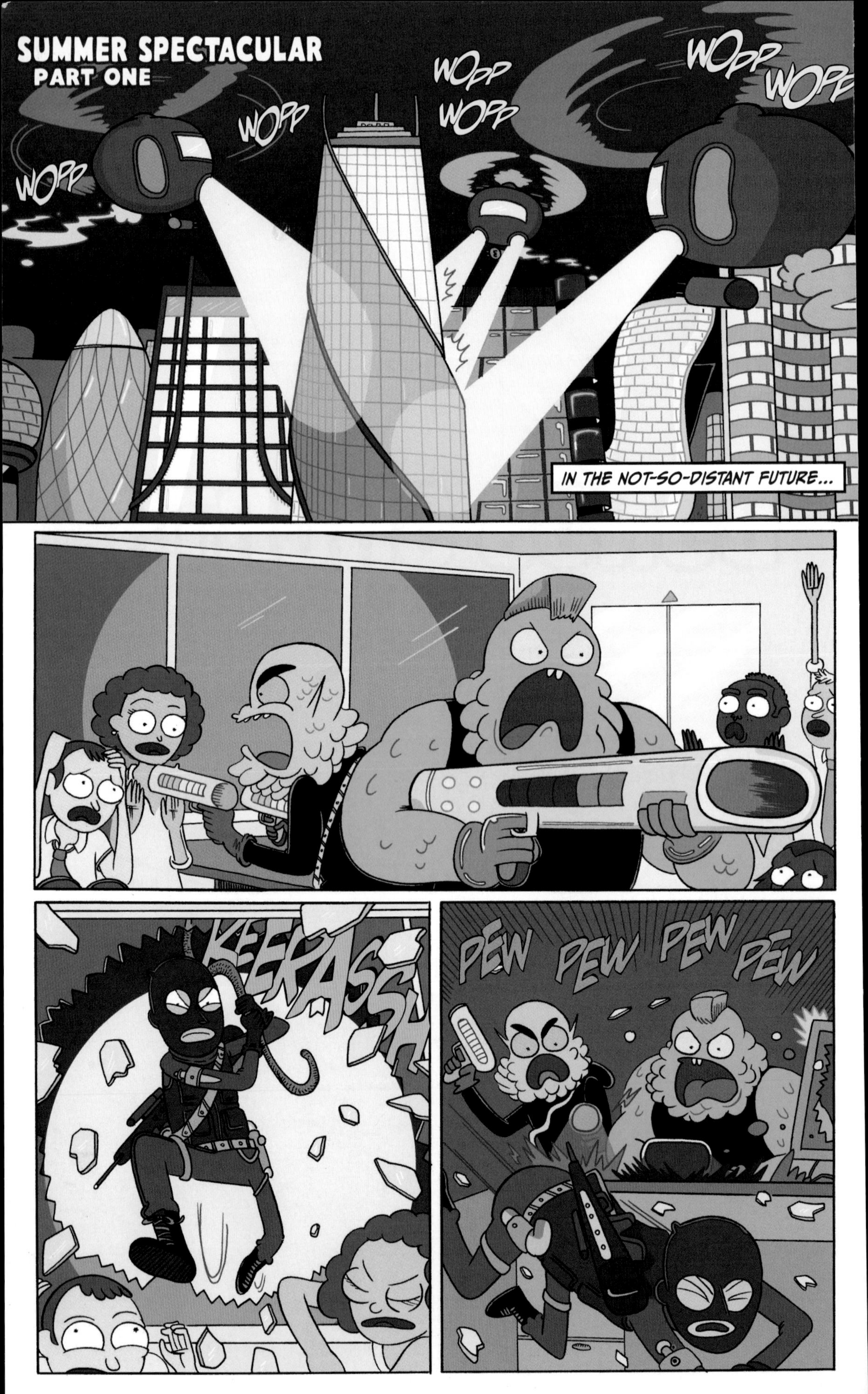
SUMMER SPECTACULAR
PART ONE
WOPP
WOPP
WOPP
WOPP
WOPP
WOPP
IN THE NOT-SO-DISTANT FUTURE...
KEERASSH
PEW PEW PEW PEW

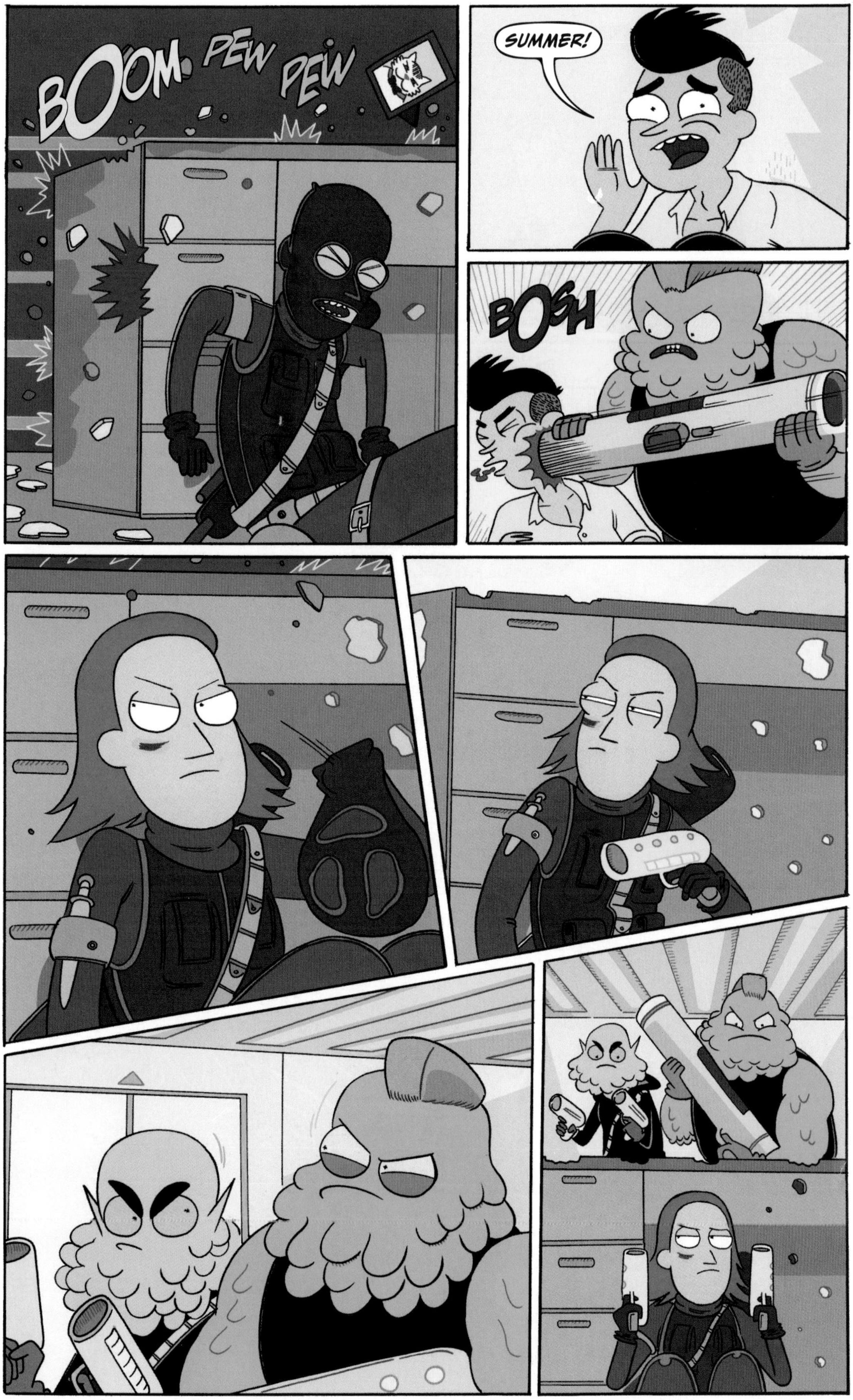
BOOM PEW PEW PEW
SUMMER!
BOSH

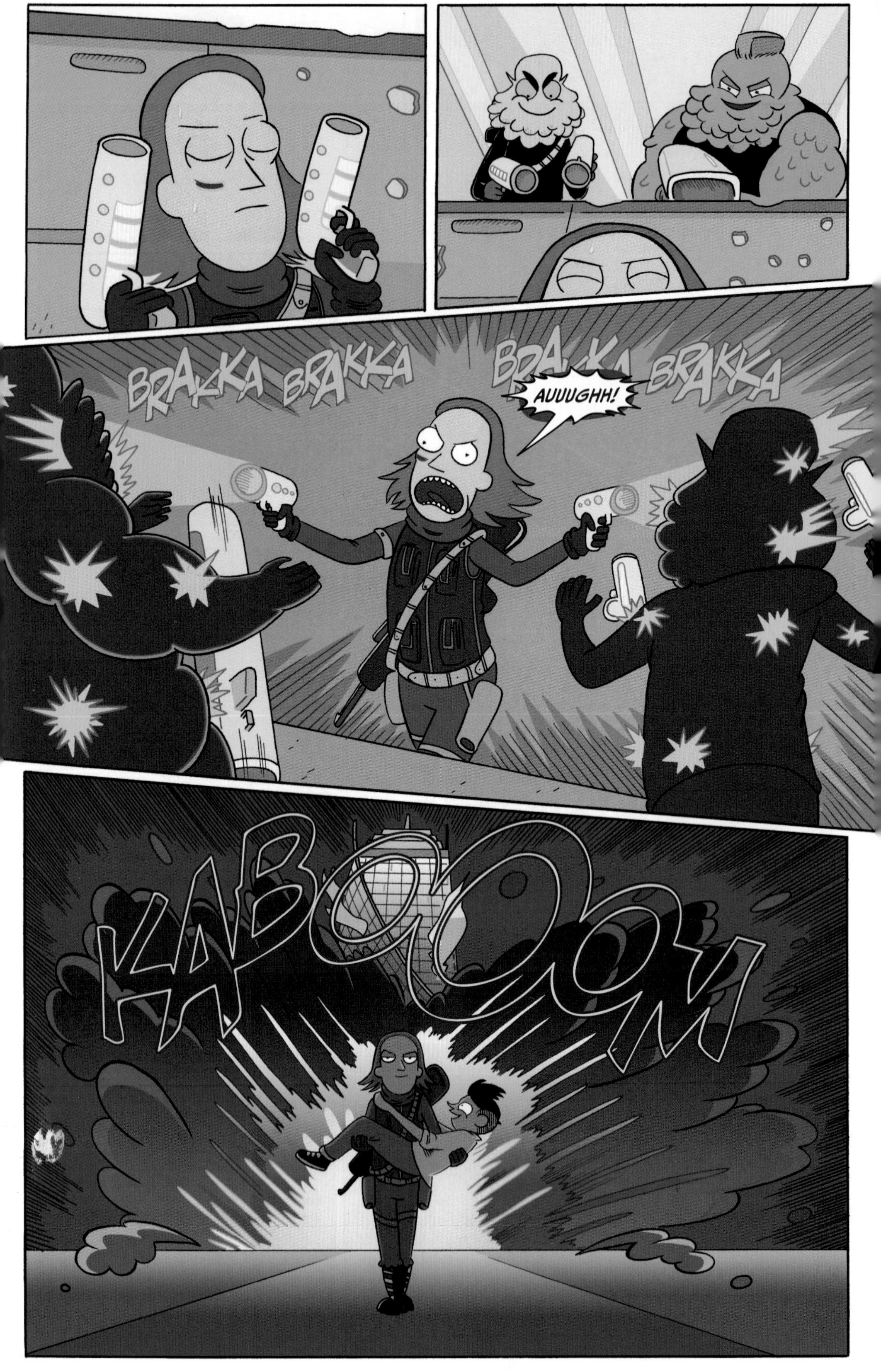
BRAKKA BRAKKA
BRAKKA BRAKKA
AUUUGHH!
KABOOOM

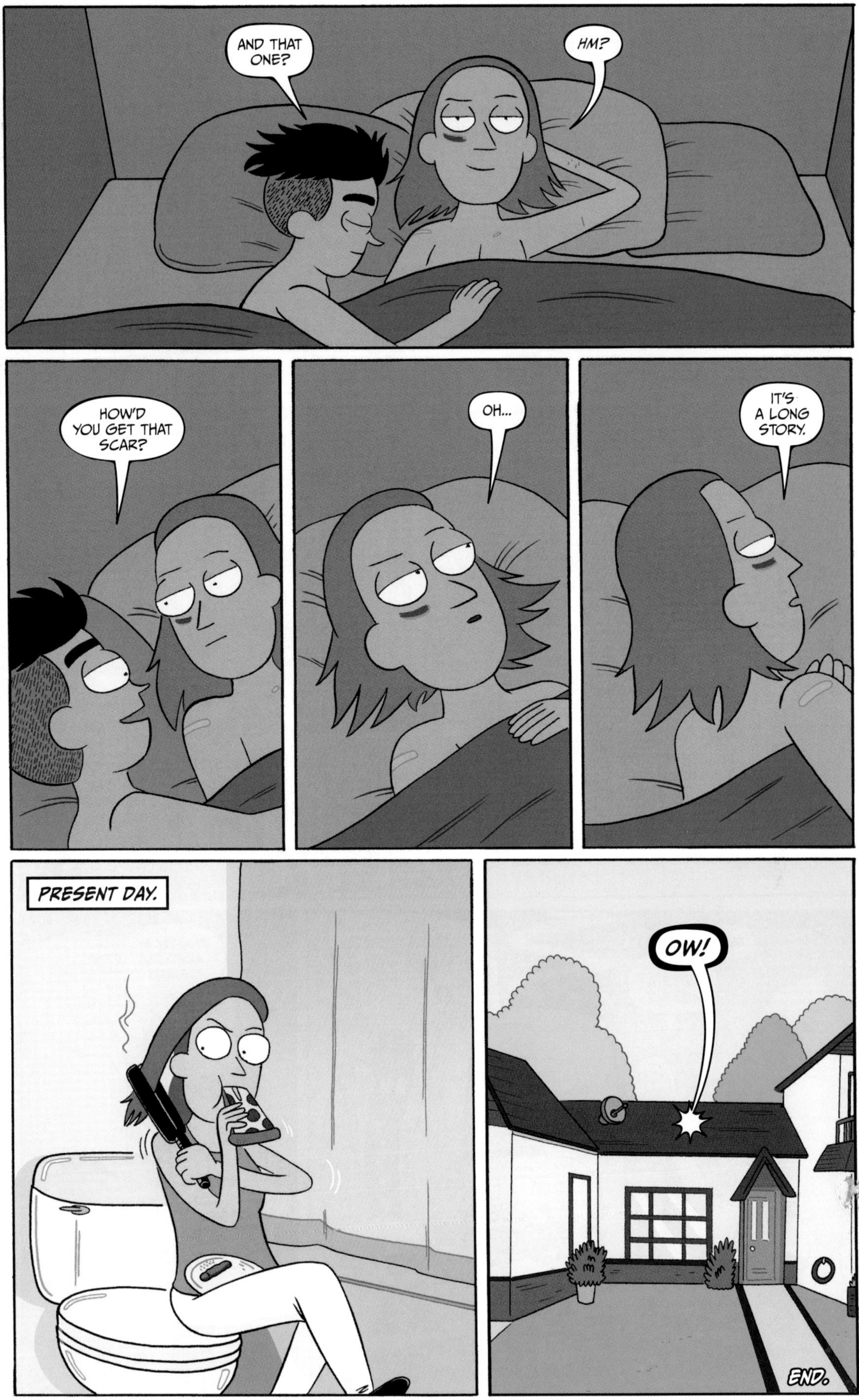
AND THAT ONE?
HM?
HOW'D YOU GET THAT SCAR?
OH...
IT'S A LONG STORY.
PRESENT DAY.
OW!
END.

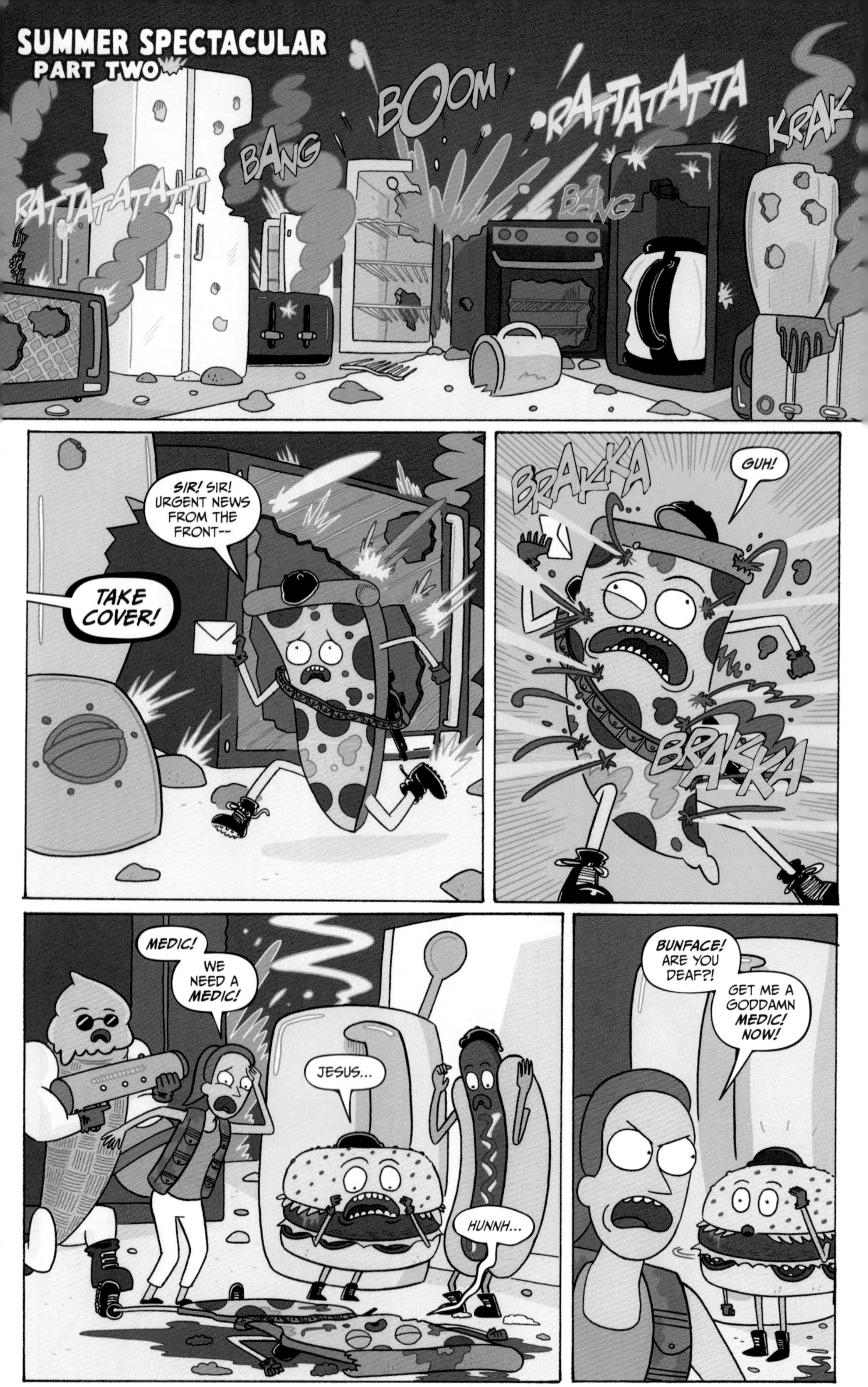

SUMMER SPECTACULAR
PART TWO
RATTATATATT
BANG
BOOM
RATTATATTA
KRAK
BANG
SIR! SIR! URGENT NEWS FROM THE FRONT--
TAKE COVER!
BRAKKA
GUH!
BRAKKA
MEDIC!
WE NEED A MEDIC!
JESUS...
HUNNH...
BUNFACE! ARE YOU DEAF?!
GET ME A GODDAMN MEDIC! NOW!

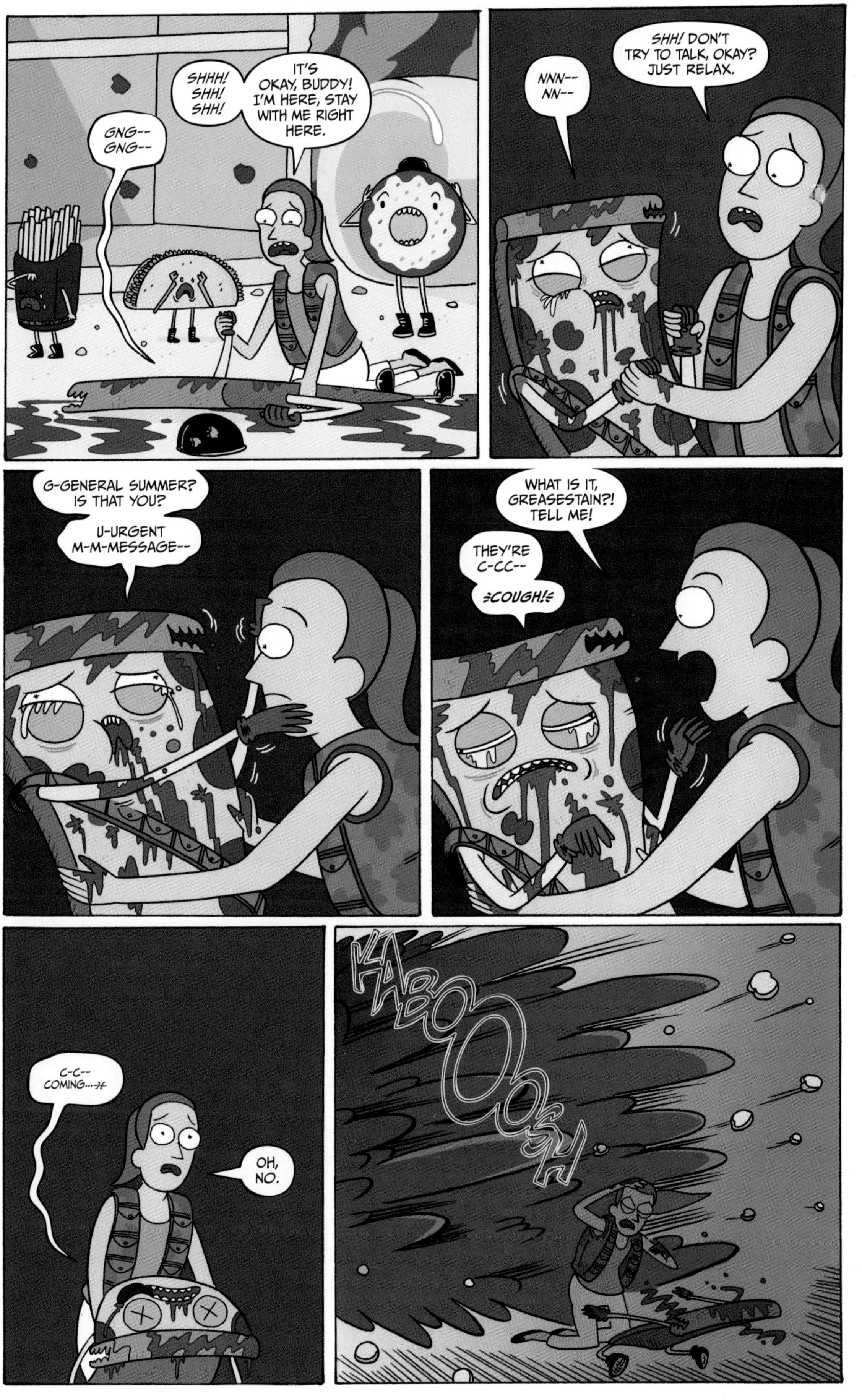
GNG--
GNG--
SHHH!
SHH!
SHH!
IT'S OKAY, BUDDY! I'M HERE, STAY WITH ME RIGHT HERE.
NNN--
NN--
SHH! DON'T TRY TO TALK, OKAY? JUST RELAX.
G-GENERAL SUMMER? IS THAT YOU?
U-URGENT M-M-MESSAGE--
WHAT IS IT, GREASESTAIN?! TELL ME!
THEY'RE C-CC--
COUGH!
C-C-- COMING...
OH, NO.
KABOOOOSH

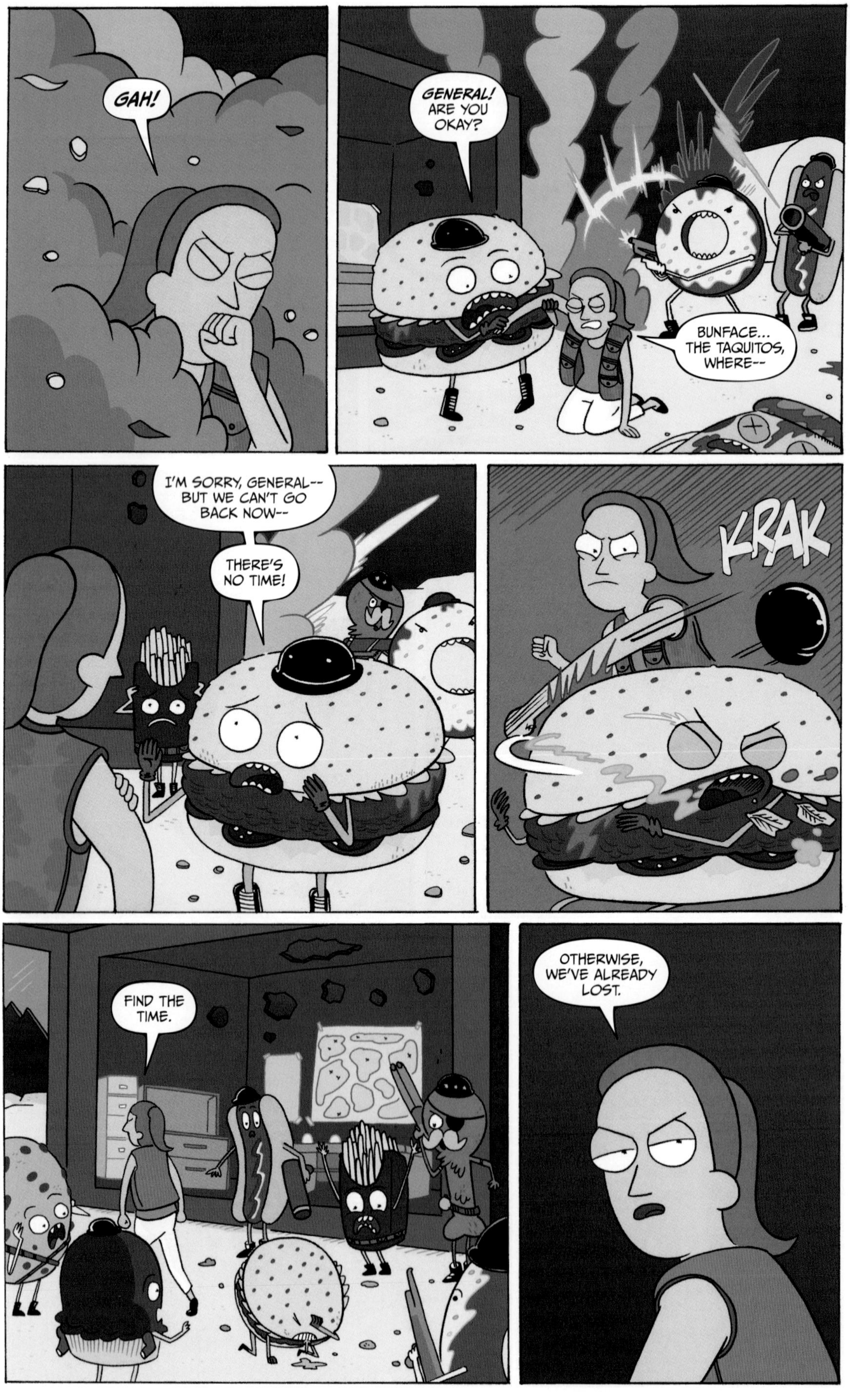
GAH!
GENERAL! ARE YOU OKAY?
BUNFACE... THE TAQUITOS, WHERE--
I'M SORRY, GENERAL-- BUT WE CAN'T GO BACK NOW--
THERE'S NO TIME!
KRAK
FIND THE TIME.
OTHERWISE, WE'VE ALREADY LOST.

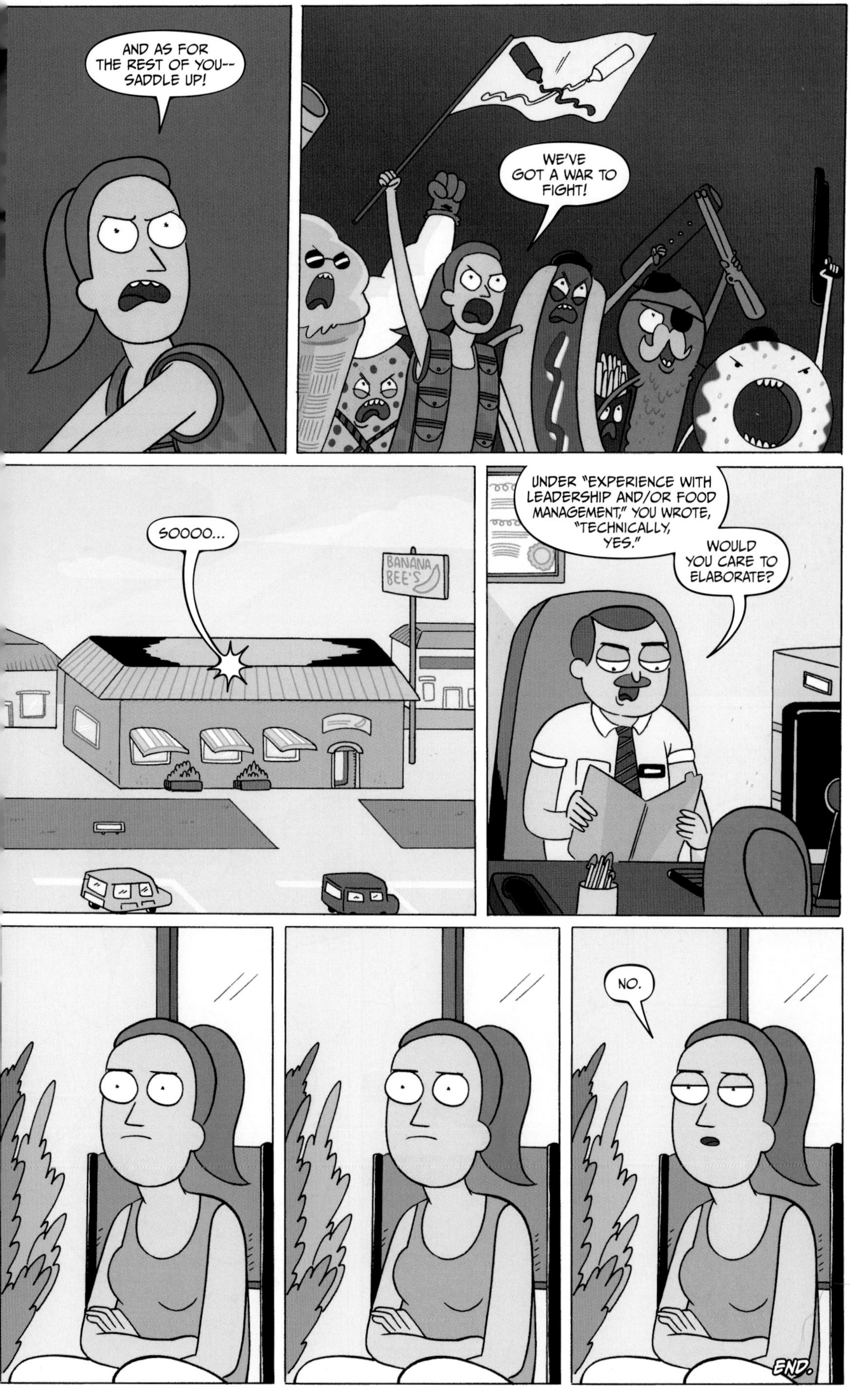
AND AS FOR THE REST OF YOU-- SADDLE UP!
WE'VE GOT A WAR TO FIGHT!
SOOOO...
BANANA BEE'S
UNDER "EXPERIENCE WITH LEADERSHIP AND/OR FOOD MANAGEMENT," YOU WROTE, "TECHNICALLY, YES."
WOULD YOU CARE TO ELABORATE?
NO.
END.

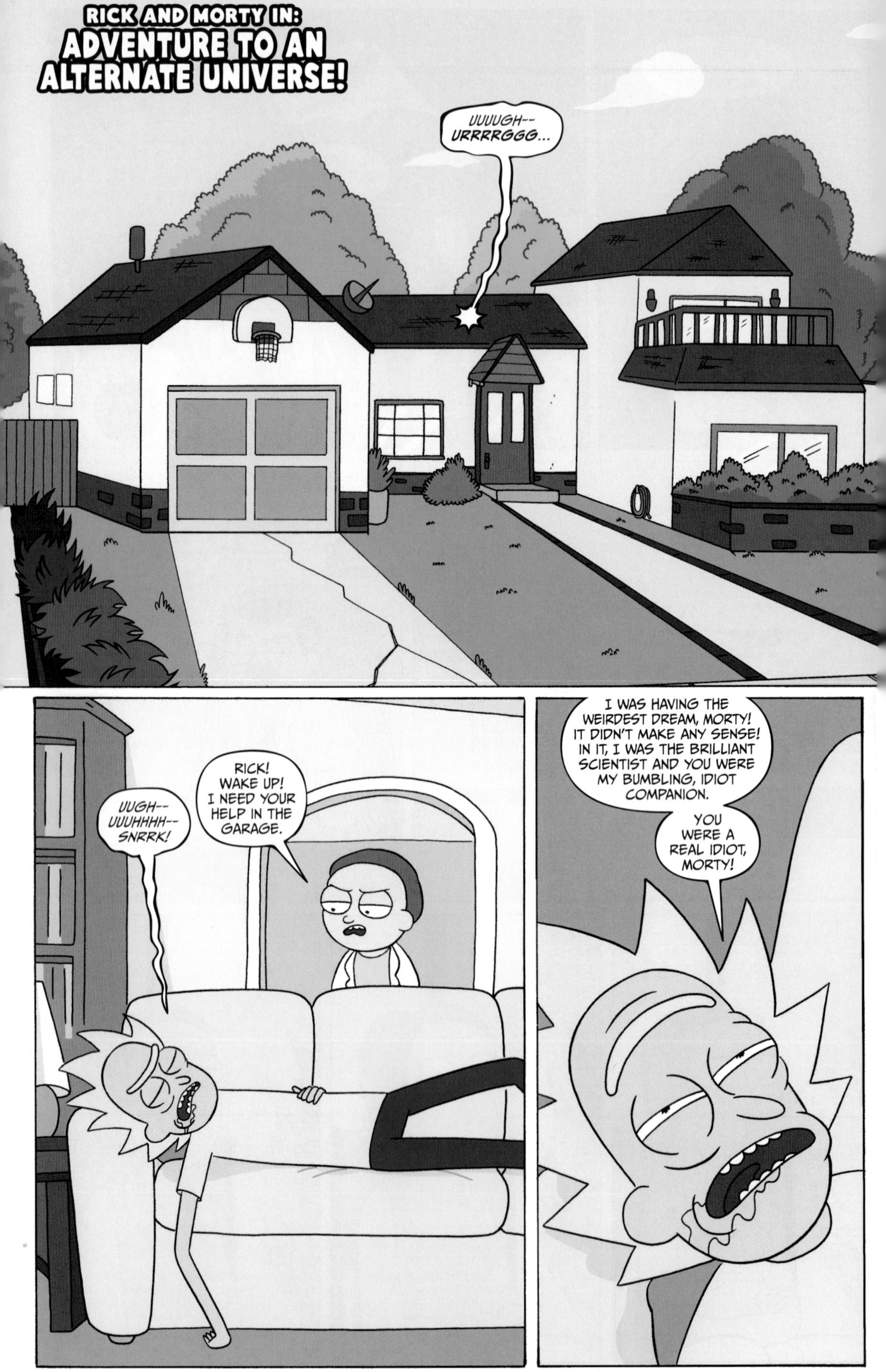
RICK AND MORTY IN:
ADVENTURE TO AN ALTERNATE UNIVERSE!
UUUUGH-- URRRRGGG...
UUGH-- UUUHHHH-- SNRRK!
RICK! WAKE UP! I NEED YOUR HELP IN THE GARAGE.
I WAS HAVING THE WEIRDEST DREAM, MORTY! IT DIDN'T MAKE ANY SENSE! IN IT, I WAS THE BRILLIANT SCIENTIST AND YOU WERE MY BUMBLING, IDIOT COMPANION.
YOU WERE A REAL IDIOT, MORTY!

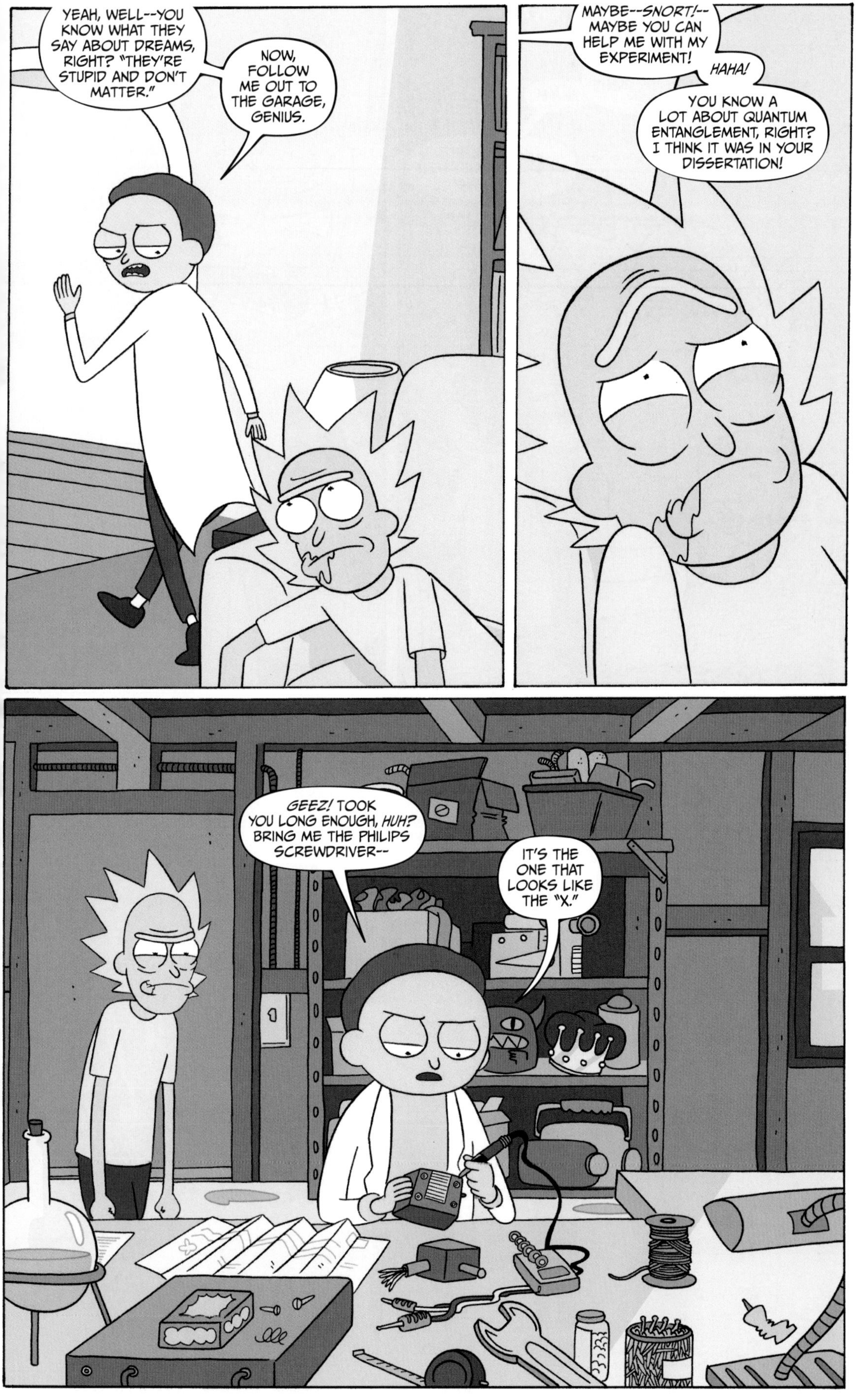
YEAH, WELL--YOU KNOW WHAT THEY SAY ABOUT DREAMS, RIGHT? "THEY'RE STUPID AND DON'T MATTER."
NOW, FOLLOW ME OUT TO THE GARAGE, GENIUS.
MAYBE--*SNORT!*--MAYBE YOU CAN HELP ME WITH MY EXPERIMENT!
HAHA!
YOU KNOW A LOT ABOUT QUANTUM ENTANGLEMENT, RIGHT? I THINK IT WAS IN YOUR DISSERTATION!
GEEZ! TOOK YOU LONG ENOUGH, *HUH?* BRING ME THE PHILIPS SCREWDRIVER--
IT'S THE ONE THAT LOOKS LIKE THE "X."

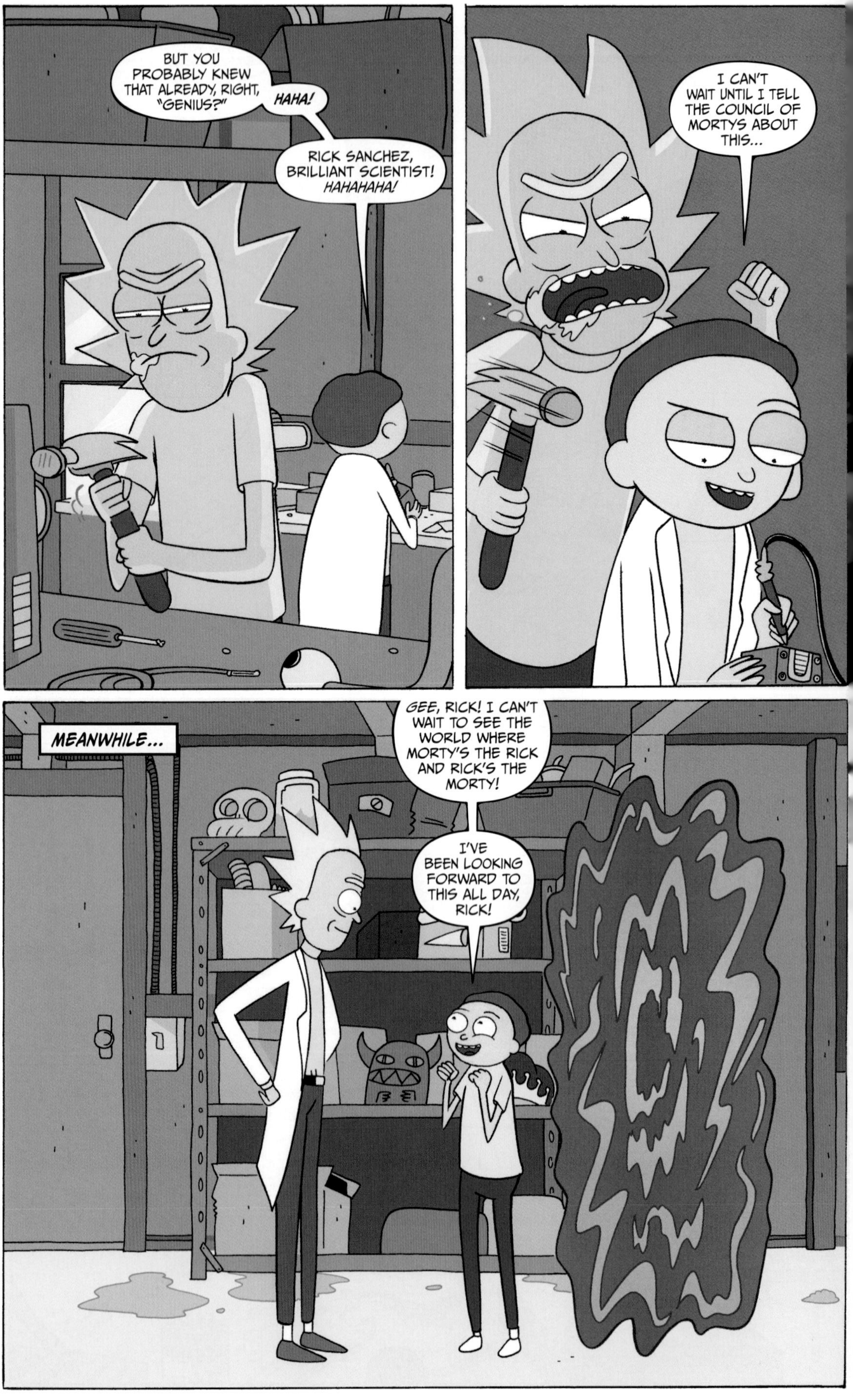
BUT YOU PROBABLY KNEW THAT ALREADY, RIGHT, "GENIUS?"
HAHA!
RICK SANCHEZ, BRILLIANT SCIENTIST! HAHAHAHA!
I CAN'T WAIT UNTIL I TELL THE COUNCIL OF MORTYS ABOUT THIS...
MEANWHILE...
GEE, RICK! I CAN'T WAIT TO SEE THE WORLD WHERE MORTY'S THE RICK AND RICK'S THE MORTY!
I'VE BEEN LOOKING FORWARD TO THIS ALL DAY, RICK!

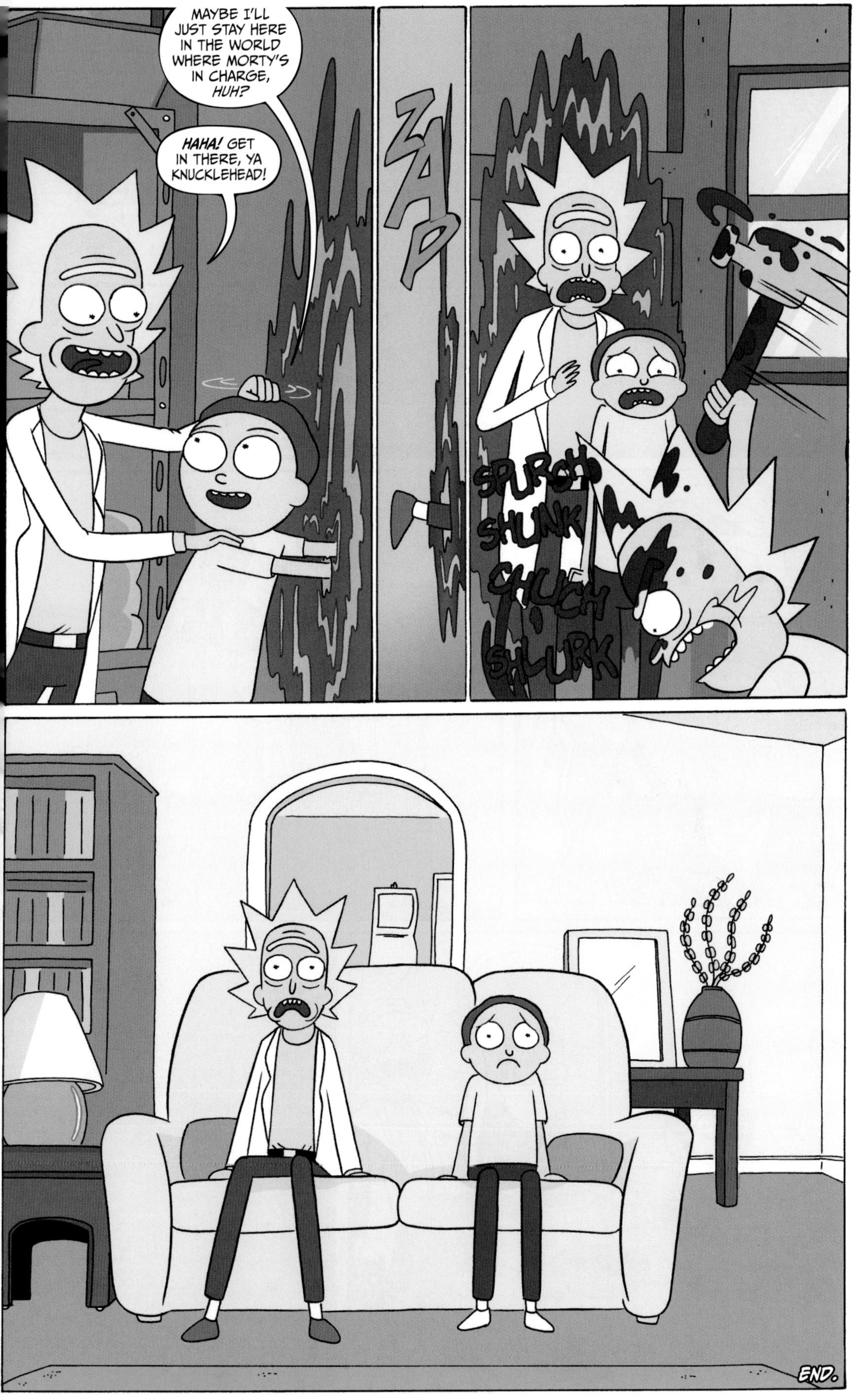
MAYBE I'LL JUST STAY HERE IN THE WORLD WHERE MORTY'S IN CHARGE, *HUH?*
HAHA! GET IN THERE, YA KNUCKLEHEAD!
ZAP
SPURCH
SHUNK
CHUCH
SHLURK
END.

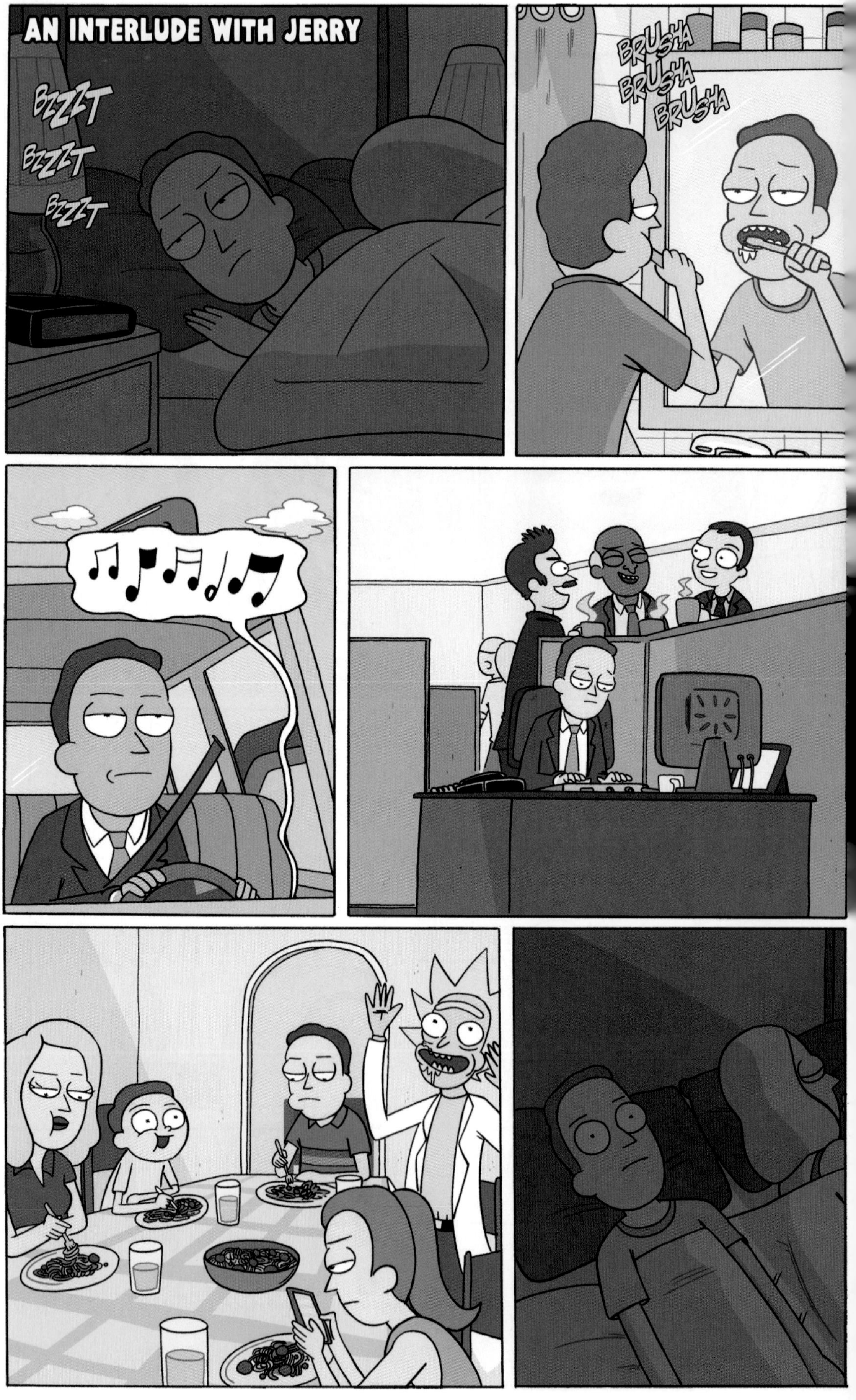
AN INTERLUDE WITH JERRY
BZZZT
BZZZT
BZZZT
BRUSHA
BRUSHA
BRUSHA

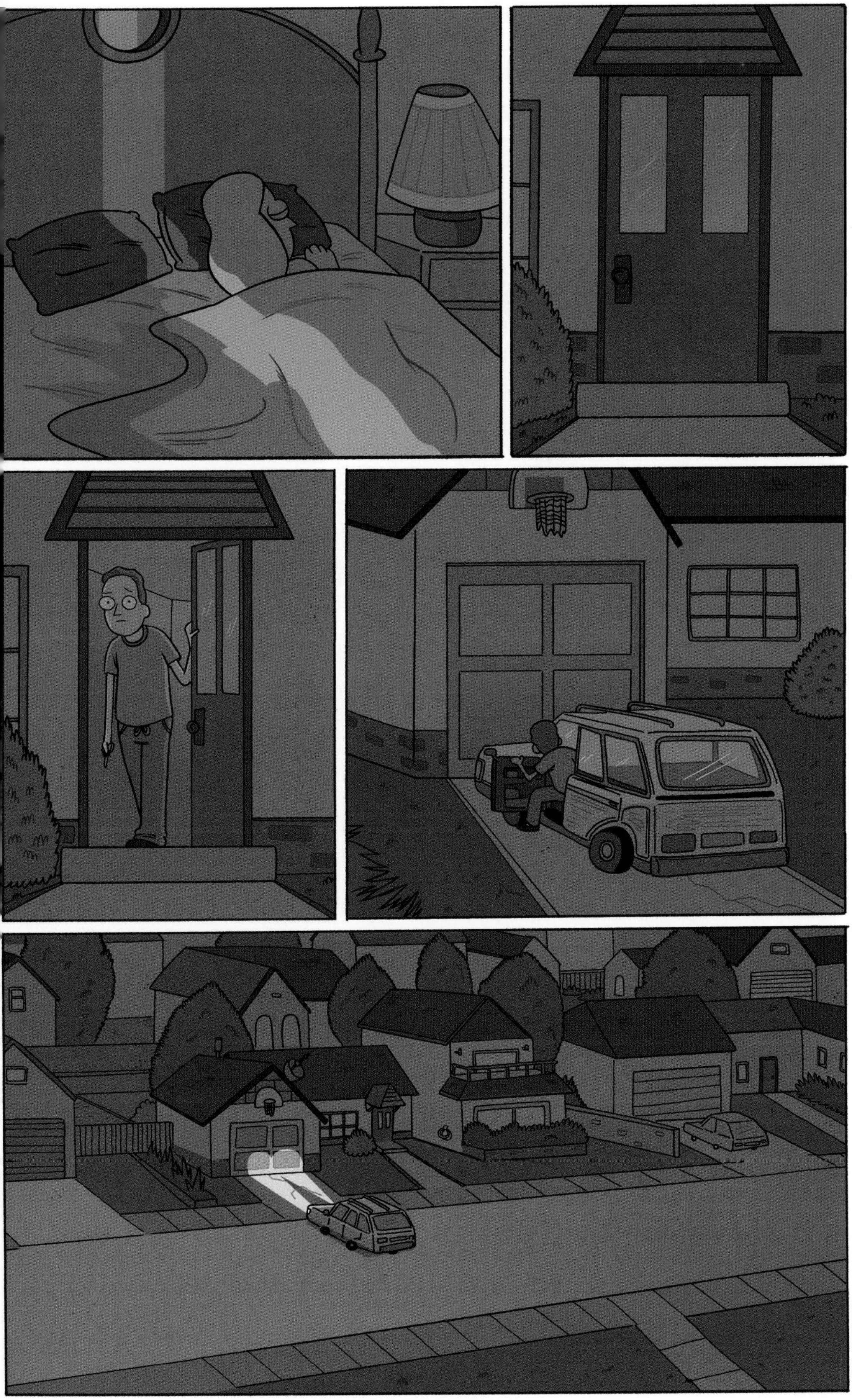

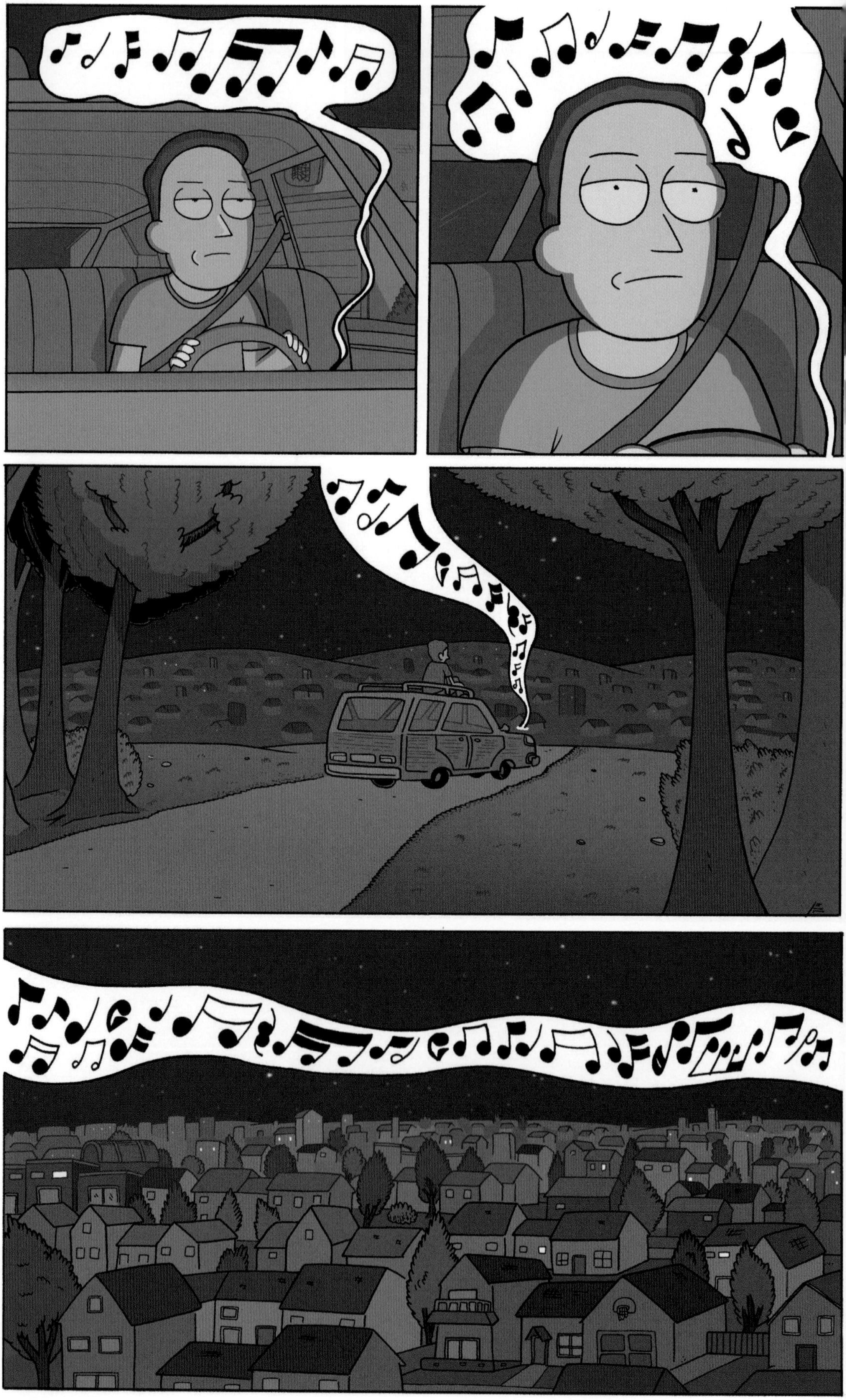

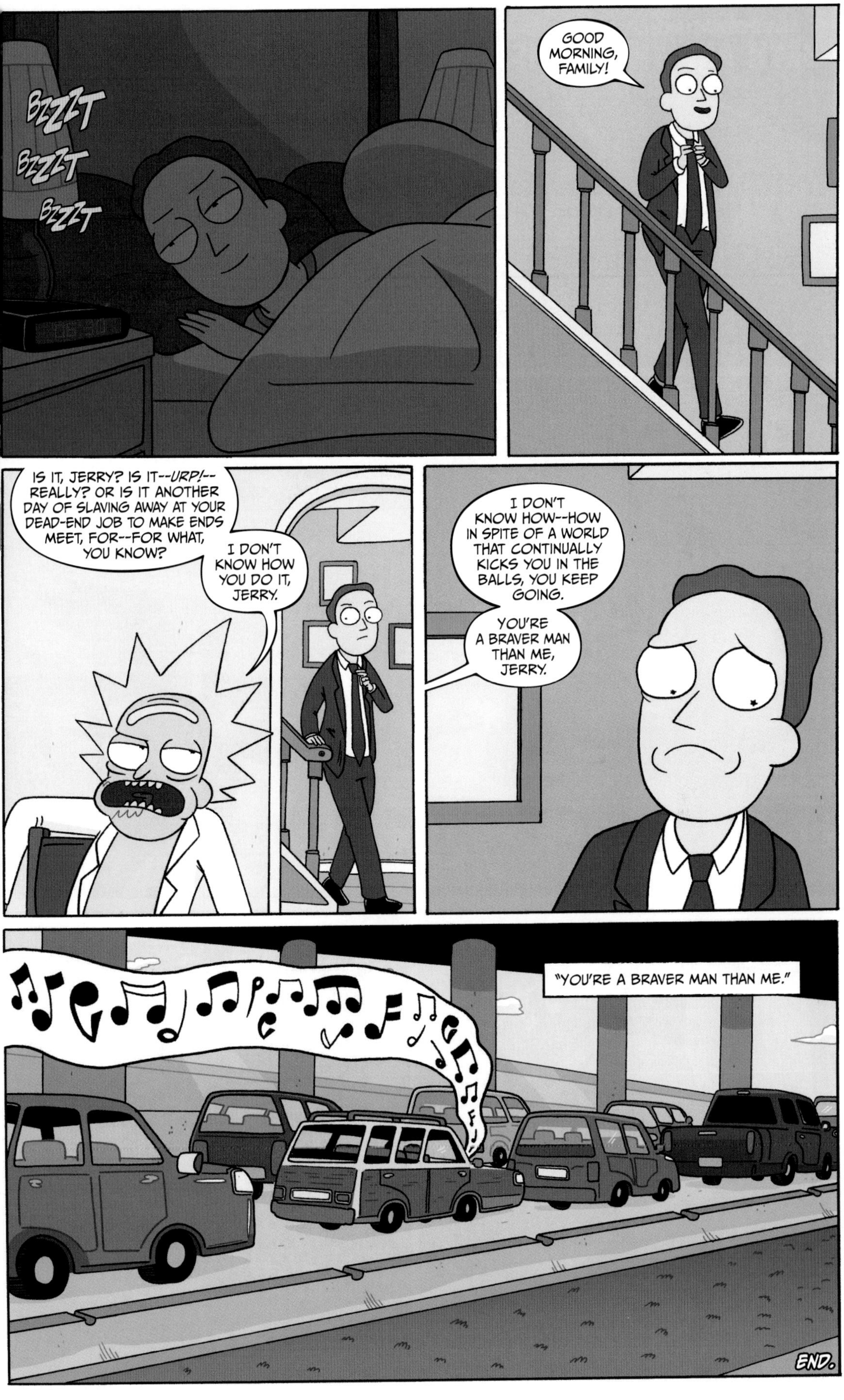
BZZZT
BZZZT
BZZZT
GOOD MORNING, FAMILY!
IS IT, JERRY? IS IT--URP!--REALLY? OR IS IT ANOTHER DAY OF SLAVING AWAY AT YOUR DEAD-END JOB TO MAKE ENDS MEET, FOR--FOR WHAT, YOU KNOW?
I DON'T KNOW HOW YOU DO IT, JERRY.
I DON'T KNOW HOW--HOW IN SPITE OF A WORLD THAT CONTINUALLY KICKS YOU IN THE BALLS, YOU KEEP GOING.
YOU'RE A BRAVER MAN THAN ME, JERRY.
"YOU'RE A BRAVER MAN THAN ME."
END.

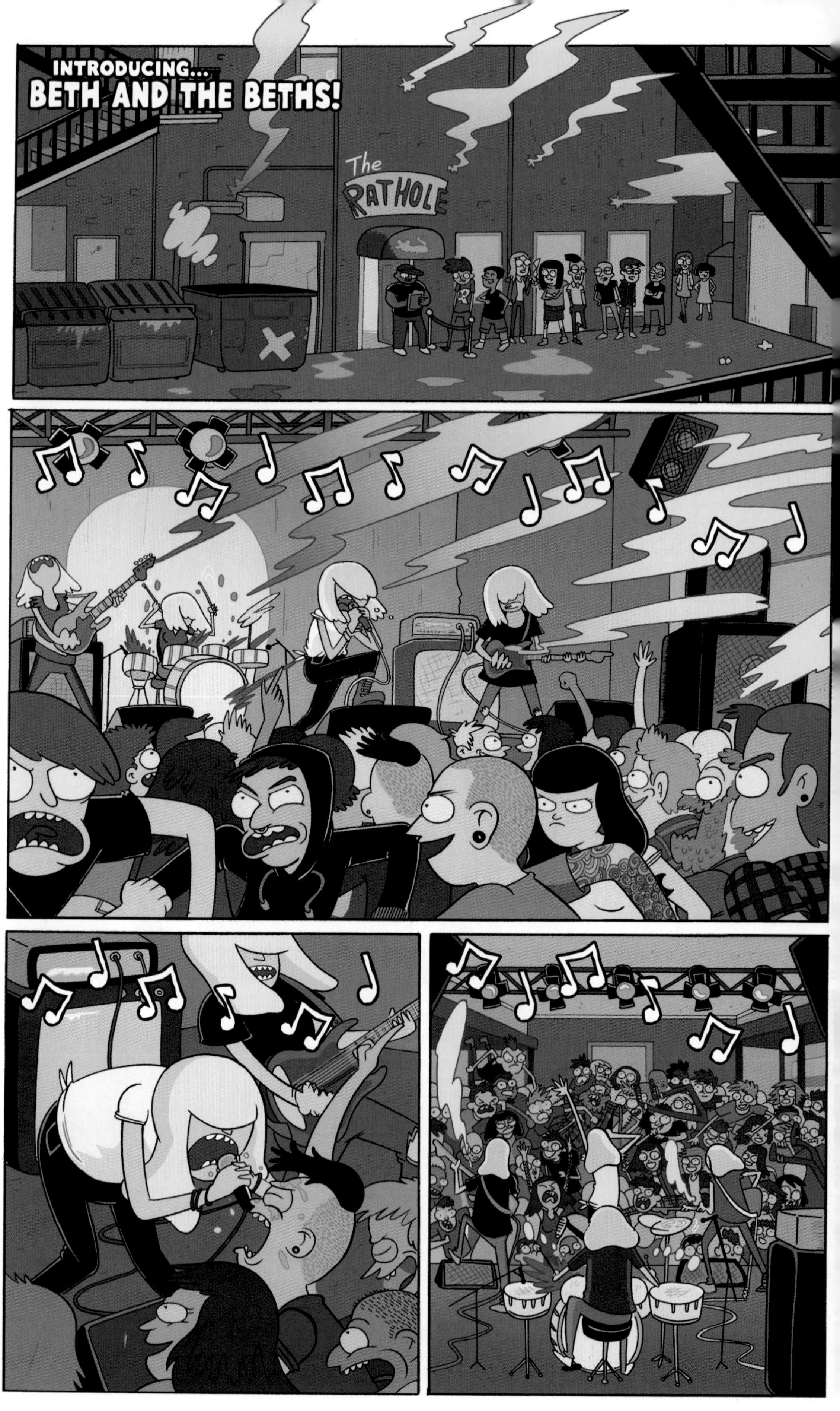
INTRODUCING...
BETH AND THE BETHS!
The RATHOLE

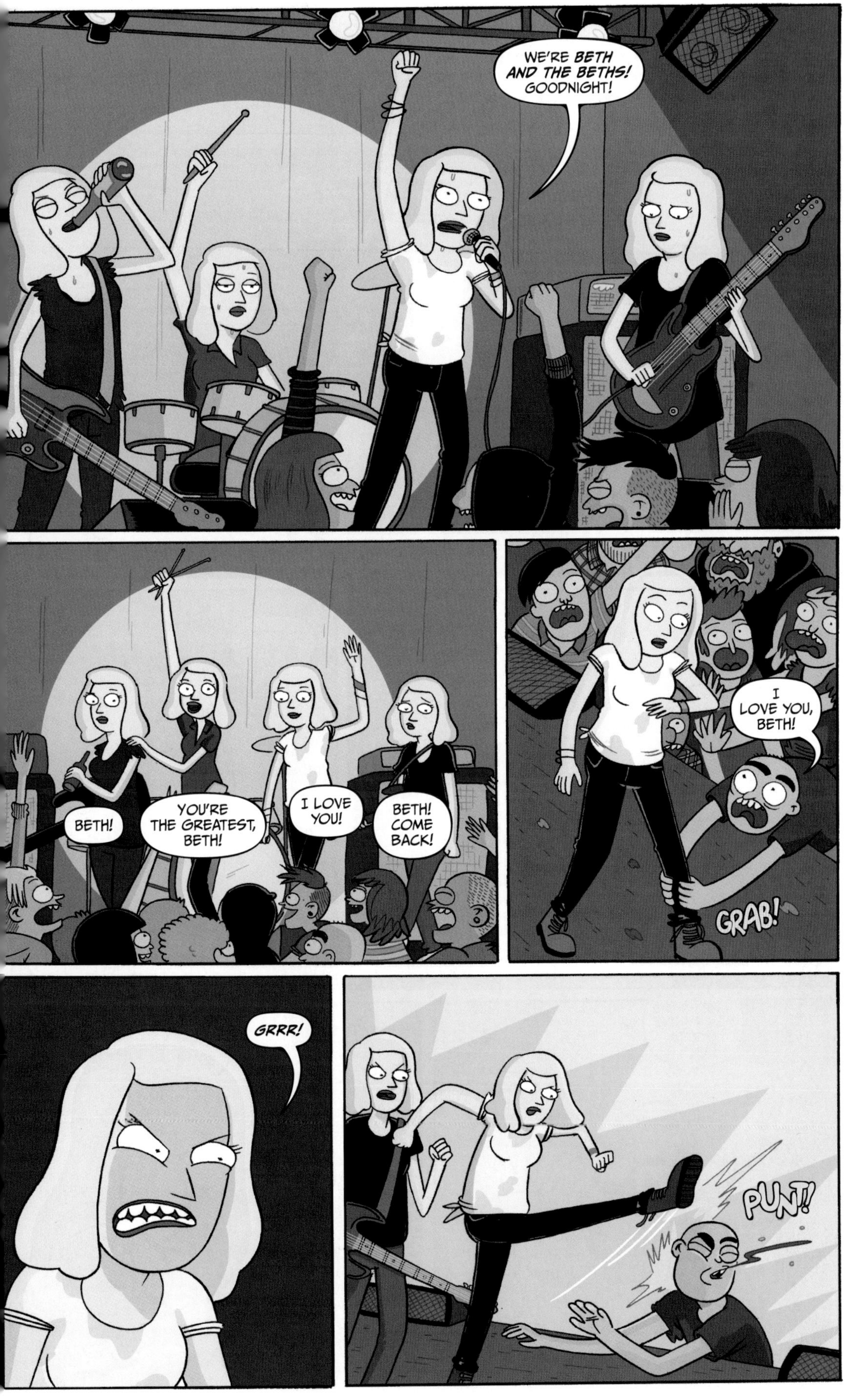
WE'RE BETH AND THE BETHS! GOODNIGHT!
BETH!
YOU'RE THE GREATEST, BETH!
I LOVE YOU!
BETH! COME BACK!
I LOVE YOU, BETH!
GRAB!
GRRR!
PUNT!

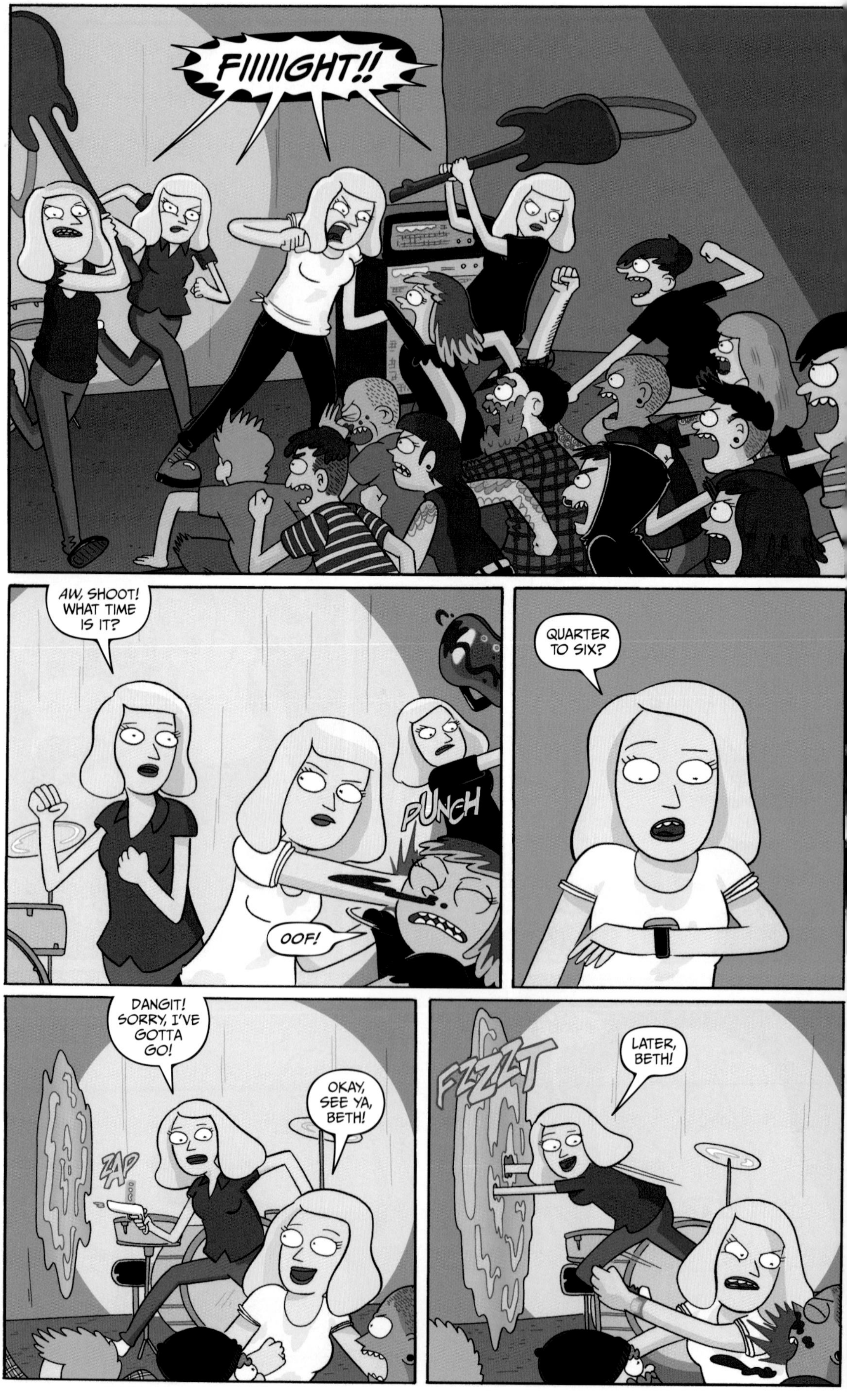
FIIIIGHT!!
AW, SHOOT! WHAT TIME IS IT?
PUNCH
OOF!
QUARTER TO SIX?
DANGIT! SORRY, I'VE GOTTA GO!
ZAP
OKAY, SEE YA, BETH!
FZZZT
LATER, BETH!

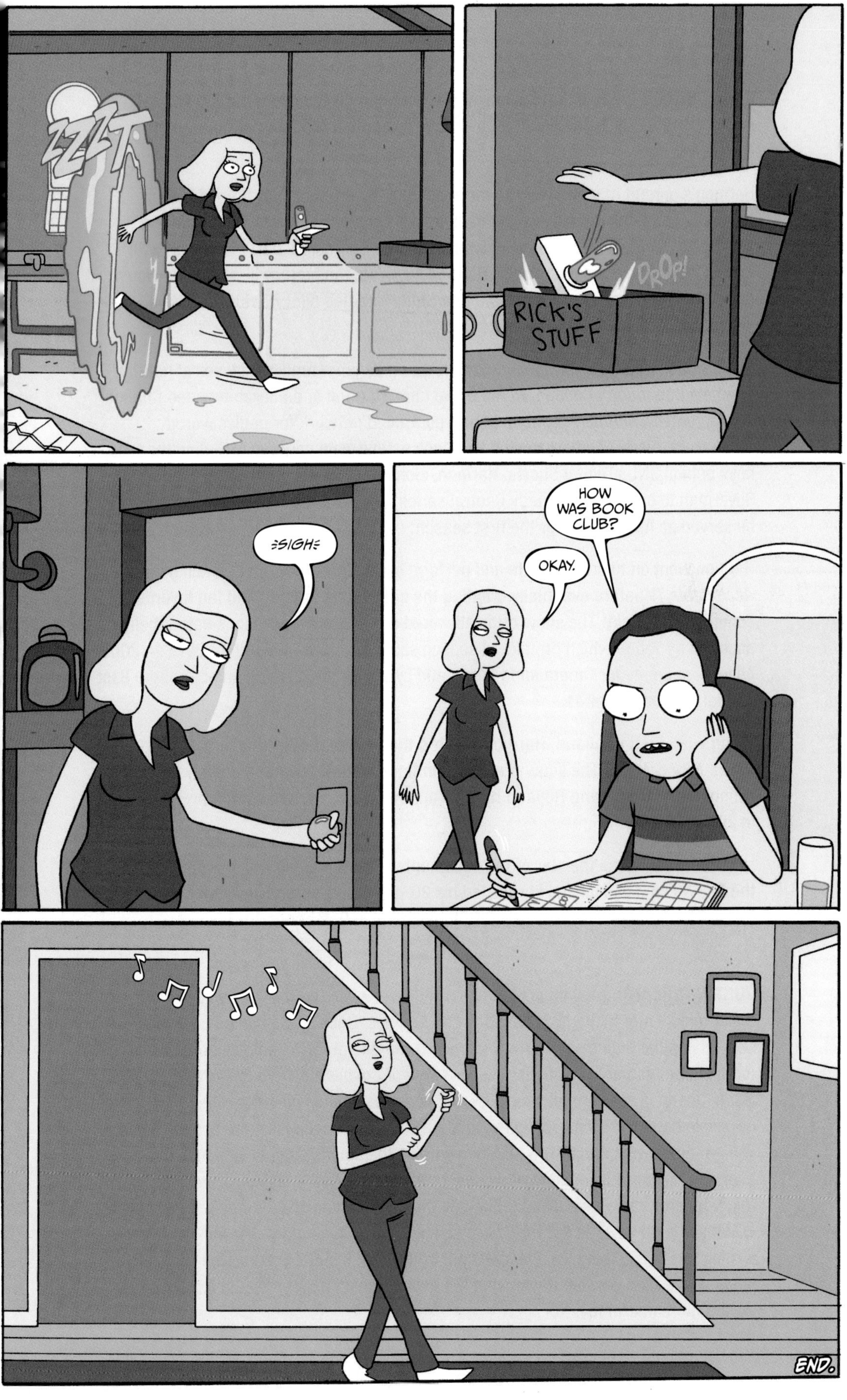
ZZZT
DROP!
RICK'S STUFF
SIGH
HOW WAS BOOK CLUB?
OKAY.
END.

DAN HARMON is the Emmy® winning creator/executive producer of the comedy series *Community* as well as the co-creator/executive producer of Adult Swim's *Rick & Morty*.

Harmon's pursuit of minimal work for maximum reward took him from stand-up to improv to sketch comedy, then finally to Los Angeles, where he began writing feature screenplays with fellow Milwaukeean Rob Schrab. As part of his deal with Robert Zemeckis at Imagemovers, Harmon co-wrote the feature film *Monster House*. Following this, Harmon co-wrote the Ben Stiller directed pilot *Heat Vision and Jack*, starring Jack Black and Owen Wilson.

Disillusioned by the legitimate industry, Harmon began attending classes at nearby Glendale Community College. At the same time, Harmon and Schrab founded Channel 101, an untelevised non-profit audience-controlled network for undiscovered filmmakers, many of whom used it to launch mainstream careers, including the boys behind SNL's Digital Shorts. Harmon, along with Schrab, partnered with Sarah Silverman to create her Comedy Central series, *The Sarah Silverman Program*, where he served as head writer for the first season.

Harmon went on to create, write and perform in the short-lived VH1 sketch series *Acceptable TV* before eventually creating the critically acclaimed and fan favorite comedy *Community*. The show originally aired on NBC for five seasons before being acquired by Yahoo which premiered season six of the show in March of 2015. In 2009 he won an Emmy for Outstanding Music and Lyrics for the opening number of the 81st Annual Academy Awards.

Along with Justin Roiland, Harmon created the breakout Adult Swim animated series *Rick & Morty*. The show premiered in December of 2013 and quickly became a ratings hit. Harmon and Roiland have wrapped up season two, which premiered in 2015.

In 2014 Harmon was the star of the documentary *Harmontown* which premiered at the SXSW Film Festival and chronicled his 20-city stand-up/podcast tour of the same name. The documentary was released theatrically in October of 2014.

——

JUSTIN ROILAND grew up in Manteca, California where he did the basic stuff children do. Later in life he traveled to Los Angeles. Once settled in, he created several popular online shorts for Channel101. Some notable examples of his work (both animated and live action) include *House of Cosbys* and *Two Girls One Cup: The Show*. Justin is afraid of his mortality and hopes the things he creates will make lots of people happy. Then maybe when modern civilization collapses into chaos, people will remember him and they'll help him survive the bloodshed and violence. Global economic collapse is looming. It's going to be horrible, and honestly, a swift death might be preferable than living in the hell that awaits mankind. Justin also really hates writing about himself in the third person. I hate this. That's right. It's me. I've been writing this whole thing. Hi. The cat's out of the bag. It's just you and me now. There never was a third person. If you want to know anything about me, just ask. Sorry this wasn't more informative.

ZAC GORMAN is an Eisner Award-wanting cartoonist and writer from Detroit, Michigan, best known for his work on beating Super Mario Bros. 2 without the use of a Game Genie. Outside comics, he frequently works in television animation, doing storyboards and character designs for several hit shows with highly financially lucrative target demographics.

—

CJ CANNON is primarily a "stripper" and self-taught artist living in Nashville, Tennessee. When they're not working on comics, outside riding their bike, or drumming, they're almost always in the house drawing gross fanart and fandom smut for similarly gross people. CJ has: two cats, three hermit crabs, a hamster, an eldritch abomination, a pacman frog, and a leopard gecko.

—

RYAN HILL has colored some comics so far. Many of these include *Stumptown, Judge Dredd Mega City 2, Age of Reptiles, Terrible Lizard, Sixth Gun: Valley of Death, Avatar The Last Airbender*, and *EGO*. The pizza guy who delivers his lunch every "ZA & Wing Wednesday" is rumored to have once said, "Not bad, man" in regard to the work.

—

MARC ELLERBY is a comics illustrator living in Essex, UK. He has worked on such titles as *Doctor Who, Regular Show*, and *The Amazing World of Gumball*. His own comics (which you should totally check out!) are *Chloe Noonan: Monster Hunter*, and *Ellerbisms*. You can read some comics if you like at marcellerby.com.

—

CHRIS CRANK has worked on several recent Oni Press books like *The Sixth Gun, Brides of Helheim, Terrible Lizard*, and others. Or maybe you've seen his letters in *Revival, Hack/Slash, God Hates Astronauts*, or *Dark Engine* from Image. Or perhaps you've read *Lady Killer* or *Sundowners* from Dark Horse. Heck, you might even be reading the award winning *Battlepug* at battlepug.com right now!

—

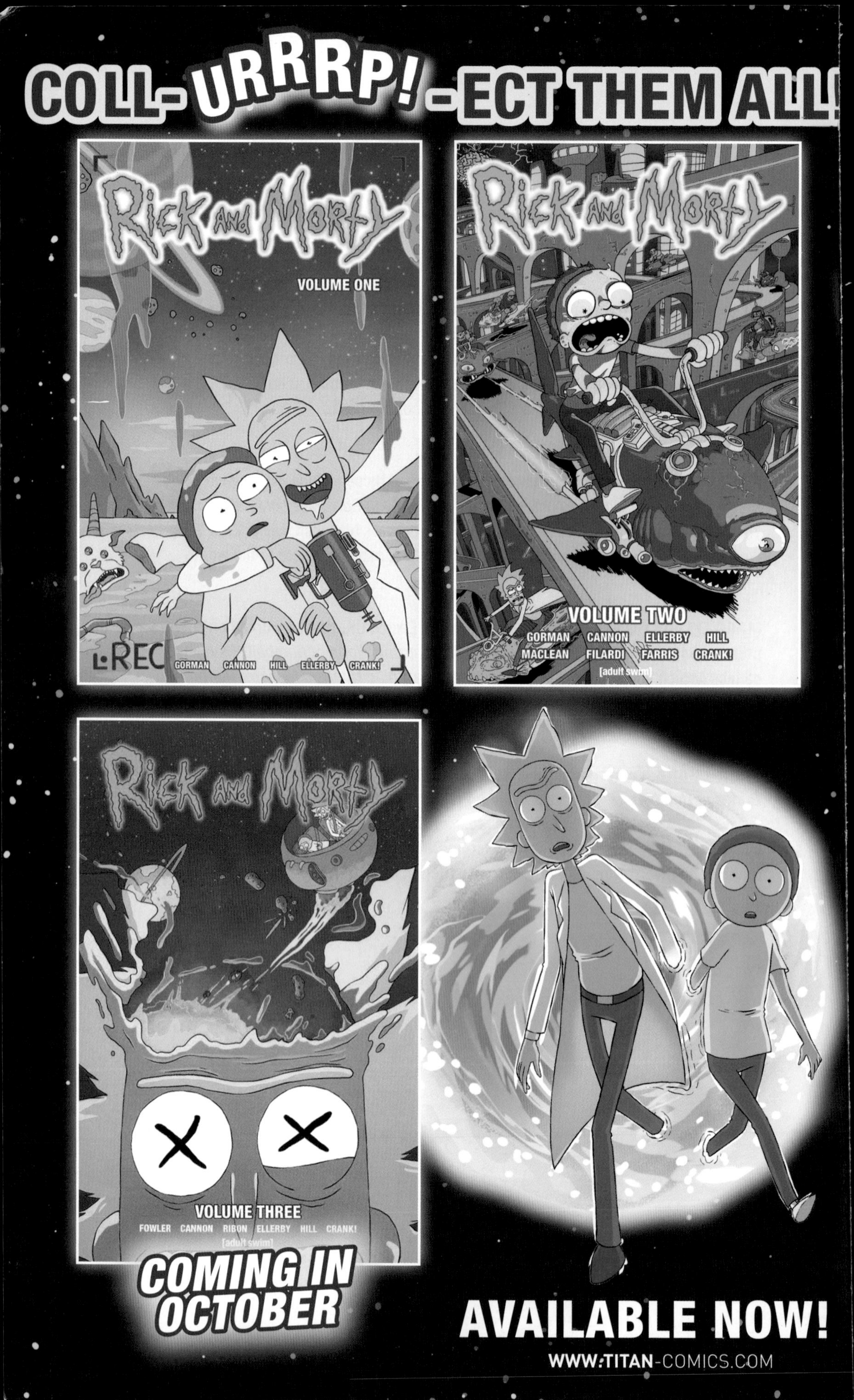
COLL-URRRP!-ECT THEM ALL!
RICK AND MORTY
VOLUME ONE
REC
GORMAN CANNON HILL ELLERBY CRANK!
RICK AND MORTY
VOLUME TWO
GORMAN CANNON ELLERBY HILL
MACLEAN FILARDI FARRIS CRANK!
[adult swim]
RICK AND MORTY
VOLUME THREE
FOWLER CANNON RIBON ELLERBY HILL CRANK!
[adult swim]
COMING IN OCTOBER
AVAILABLE NOW!
WWW.TITAN-COMICS.COM